# APPLIED
## BEHAVIOR ANALYSIS
## FOR **EVERYONE**

Edited by
Robert C. Pennington, PhD, BCBA-D

Principles and Practices Explained
by Applied Researchers Who Use Them

6448 Vista Dr.
Shawnee, KS 66218
www.aapcpublishing.com

Publisher's Cataloging-In-Publication

| | |
|---|---|
| Names: | Pennington, Robert C., editor. |
| Title: | Applied behavior analysis for everyone : principles and practices explained by applied researchers who use them / edited by Robert C. Pennington. |
| Description: | Shawnee, KS : AAPC Publishing, [2019] |
| Identifiers: | ISBN: 9781942197454 |
| Subjects: | LCSH: Behaviorism (Psychology) \| Human behavior. \| Behavior analysts--Methodology. \| Behavioral assessment. \| Behavioral assessment of children. \| Behavior modification. \| Behavior therapy--Methodology. \| Behavioral assessment--Study and teaching. \| Behavior modification--Study and teaching. \| Children with autism spectrum disorders--Treatment. \| Autistic children--Treatment. |
| Classification: | LCC: BF199 .P46 2019 \| DDC: 158/.9--dc23 |

Printed in the United States of America.

# *Acknowledgements*

*To my wonderful shapers*

*Jim, Pat, Rebecca, Dwight, Myron, Duncan, Susan,
Belva, John, Don, & Miso*

*In Paying It Forward,
I will donate all proceeds from the first 2
years of this book to support graduate students
attendance at behavior analystic conferences.*

# TABLE OF CONTENTS

# INTRODUCING APPLIED
# BEHAVIOR ANALYSIS

*Robert C. Pennington*

## KEY TERMS:

- Applied behavior analysis
- Behavior Analyst Certification Board
- Board certified behavior analyst
- Determinism
- Empiricism
- Evidence-based practice
- Experimental analysis of behavior
- Experimentation
- Philosophic doubt

- Parsimony
- Registered behavioral technician
- Generality
- Behavioral
- Analytic
- Effective
- Applied
- Technological
- Conceptually systematic

Changing behavior is no simple endeavor. Each year many of us make resolutions to establish new habits, break old ones, and do better overall. Unfortunately, many of these well-intended plans are thwarted due to unseen forces. For practitioners, whose job involves changing the behavior of others, it seems even more complex. We try our best to lead our "horses" to water, but repeatedly fail to get them to drink.

This book is about demystifying those "unseen forces" that stand in our way as we attempt to improve our lives and the lives of others. Its overall premise is that we can do better, and that there is a science of human behavior that can guide us in our personal lives and in our charge to do right by others. Within the following pages, the reader will be introduced to the field of applied behavior analysis (ABA) and its well-established collection of principles and practices that have been used to change behavior. Further, these principles and practices will be explained by applied researchers, in their own voice, with rich experiences in observing the power of ABA in real world contexts.

# ▶▶ *Defining Applied Behavior Analysis*

Though applied behavior analysis is many things to many people (e.g., therapy, profession, treatment for problem behavior), it is most accurately described as a branch of behavior analysis in which procedures derived from behavioral principles are systematically applied to improve socially significant outcomes (Baer, Wolf, & Risley, 1968; Cooper, Heron, & Heward, 2007). The field of ABA is rooted in the concepts and principles developed by researchers in a second branch of behavior analysis called the *experimental analysis of behavior* (EAB).

Psychologists applying EAB departed from their colleagues' focus on internal mental states as the cause of behavior and directed their efforts to establishing relations between behavior and observable changes in the environment. Most notably, B. F. Skinner and his colleagues conducted extensive laboratory experiments with animals in which they demonstrated predictable patterns of behavior in response to environmental changes. In 1938, Skinner published his findings in the Behavior of Organisms, which helped to firmly establish EAB as its own field of study (Cooper et al., 2007).

Researchers in EAB sought to bring the study of behavior into closer alignment with that of the natural sciences (e.g., physics, biology), and their work adhered to several key scientific attitudes (Cooper et al., 2007; Mayer, Sulzer-Azaroff, & Wallace, 2014). These attitudes are presented in Table 1.1.

## Table 1.1
*Scientific Attitudes*

| ATTITUDE | DEFINITION |
|---|---|
| Determinism | All events, including human behavior, are determined by causes external to the will |
| Empiricism | All knowledge is derived from the objective observation of phenomena |
| Experimentation | Causal relations are derived from the comparison of some objective measure of a phenomenon under at least two different conditions |
| Philosophic doubt | Continuous questioning of what is considered fact |
| Parsimony | Considering simple explanations prior to more complex and abstract ones |

As early as 1949, researchers began to apply the principles established in EAB to changing human behavior (Green, 2001). In many instances, these early pioneers used behavioral techniques to improve outcomes for persons with disabilities (Ferster & DeMyer, 1961; Ferster, Wolf, Risley, & Mees, 1964; Fuller, 1949). Then, in 1968, Don Baer, Montrose Wolf, and Todd Risley committed ABA to its own distinct field of study in their seminal paper, "Some Current Dimensions of Applied Behavior Analysis." The paper, published in the first issue of the flagship *Journal of Applied Behavior Analysis*, outlined seven key dimensions to which the practice of ABA must adhere.

First, the practice must be *applied*, in that it addresses changes in behavior that are important to the individual whose behavior is targeted for change. For example, Touchette (1971) introduced the first demonstration of the time-delay prompting procedure, wherein he taught three boys with developmental disabilities to select a particular colored lever in a laboratory setting. Though this work was critical in demonstrating the effectiveness of the procedure, it cannot be considered ABA, as the task offered little benefit to the learner. In contrast, Schuster, Gast, Wolery, and Guiltinan (1988) used time delay to teach food preparation skills to adolescents with intellectual disability. This investigation demonstrated the applied dimension of ABA, as the participants acquired skills that increased their independent functioning in natural settings.

Second, the practice must be *behavioral* in that it focuses on observable changes in behavior rather than on what is said about a behavior. These changes in behavior are observed through close inspection of continuous data. For example, if a general education teacher reports that a child is "hyper," a special education teacher might determine that the general education teacher means that the child is frequently out of his seat. They can then develop a recording system to measure daily occurrences of out-of-seat behavior in order to evaluate the effectiveness of the intervention that will be put in place.

Third, the practice must be *analytic*: that is, it must focus on a clear demonstration of the relation between particular aspects of the environment and changes in behavior. In lay terms, one seeks to understand exactly why a behavior changed and often uses a particular experimental design to show that the intervention, and not some other variable (e.g., change in medication, other interventions), was responsible for the improvement.

Fourth, ABA is *technological*, as all procedures are thoroughly described with such detail that they can be implemented by others with limited training in behavior analysis. These descriptions can help to facilitate adherence to intervention steps across diverse teams of interventionists.

Fifth, ABA is *conceptually systematic* in that procedures are derived and conceptually linked to established principles of behavior analysis. This critical linkage helps practitioners to avoid untested and potentially harmful interventions by selecting practices that are built upon previous bodies of high quality research.

Sixth, ABA is *effective*, as practitioners are expected to seek improvements that have "practical value" (Baer, Wolf, & Risley, 1968 p. 96). For example, a program designed to expand a child's acceptance of new foods may increase the number of foods accepted, but may not be effective, if it does not interrupt a dangerous decline in calorie consumption.

Finally, ABA possesses *generality*, in that improvements are expected to persist over time and across contexts. For example, a teacher presented new words in multiple fonts and contexts during reading instruction, resulting in the child's ability to read the new words in untrained settings. Continually assessing and programming for generality must not be overlooked within instruction to ensure that individuals are not taught to perform "in a box," but within the complex natural world.

Though the dimensions of ABA were crafted almost half a century ago, they remain relevant today. Any student of ABA must commit them to memory, but, more importantly must consider them in daily practice. Adherence to these tenets helps practitioners design interventions to produce behavior change that is personally relevant to the individuals with whom they are working.

## ▶▶ *The Behavior Analytic Practitioner*

Though ABA has received a great deal of attention for its use in the area of autism spectrum disorder (ASD), practitioners across many fields, including education, speech therapy, medicine, management, and mental health, have applied its principles and procedures to change behavior. Furthermore, behavioral procedures have been implemented by a range of individuals, including professionals, parents, siblings of individuals with disabilities, and persons targeting their own behavior for change.

Practitioners of ABA come from a range of backgrounds. For example, some special education teachers or therapists may have received extensive training in ABA, so their practice reflects a close adherence to behavior analytic principles. Others may adopt a few behavior analytic procedures for use in their practice. For example, many speech-language pathologists use the Picture Exchange Communication System (Bondy & Frost, 2011) and incidental teaching procedures with clients, though they may offer a different perspective on why they are effective. Similarly, occupational therapists may use task analysis to assess a client's functioning on a particular task or behavioral feeding techniques without knowledge of the behavioral concepts of stimulus control and stimulus pairing.

The use of most behavior analytic techniques by a range of professionals is appropriate and encouraged, especially in light of their potency as interventions. It is important to acknowledge that the application of these procedures by practitioners with a firm grounding in behavior analytic principles is desirable. For example, the application of time-out procedures can be rendered ineffective – even dangerous – if the implementer does not understand the environmental conditions that make it most effective. Similarly, the delivery of intensive one-to-one instruction (e.g., discrete trial) without an understanding of the basic principles of prompt fading or generalization may impede an instructor's ability to respond to a student's lack of progress in the real world. Since it is unlikely that all practitioners who use behavior analytic techniques will have been trained in behavior analysis, it is recommended that they seek consultation from behavioral practitioners prior to and during implementation of these techniques whenever possible.

Some practitioners seek certification in behavior analysis. These individuals attend specialized training programs in behavior analysis and meet requirements for certification (i.e., qualified master's degree, coursework, supervision, exam) through the Behavior Analysis Certification Board (BACB). These board-certified behavior analysts (BCBAs) work in a range of settings (e.g., schools, homes, clinics) and are typically responsible for the design, implementation, and evaluation of behavioral treatment programs.

The BCBA, as a behavioral practitioner, is unique in two significant ways. First, a BCBA must demonstrate specific competencies in ABA that have been identified as necessary by a board of experts in the field. This suggests that a BCBA has a firm understanding of behavioral principles and techniques. Second, the behavior analyst must adhere to behavior analytic practice through compliance with a professional and ethical code of conduct (www.bacb.com/ethics-code); some states require that BCBAs also obtain licensure before practicing within the community. Violations of this code can result in the loss of licensure and certification. This additional compliance mechanism serves to help ensure that BCBAs practice ethically and in service of the client.

Often BCBAs are employed to supervise other behavioral practitioners (e.g., therapists, paraprofessionals, technicians). For example, one BCBA may supervise several therapists working with different children and families in their homes. In this context, the BCBA designs and monitors programming and also is accountable for the actions of the supervisee. Recently, the BACB established a special credential for a paraprofessional that works under the close supervision of a BCBA. To obtain this certification as a registered behavioral technician (RBT), a paraprofessional must obtain 40 hours of training and pass an RBT competency exam.

## ▶▶ *Making a Difference through ABA*

Though aspirations of "saving the world" are most often made with tongue in cheek, practitioners in the field of ABA have great cause for optimism towards making a positive difference in the lives of others. First, applications of ABA are supported by more than half a century of rigorous experimental research. In many cases, procedures have been evaluated repeatedly, resulting in refinement and a deeper understanding of the conditions under which the procedure is most effective. For example, Beavers, Iwata, and Lerman (2013) summarized the findings of 435 studies that used functional analysis (an assessment procedure for determining the purpose a problem behavior serves for an individual) and identified a range of effective procedural variations designed to address differences among consumers and intervention settings while reducing the potential harm to those being assessed.

Many behavior analytic procedures have accumulated sufficient research support to be deemed an evidence-based practice (Horner, Carr, Halle, McGee, Odom, & Wolery, 2005). Defining evidence-based practice (EBP) is critical, as it serves as a guidepost for practitioners in selecting interventions that are most likely to be effective. This EBP movement parallels the expectations for professionals in medicine to use the safest and most effective treatments to avoid doing harm to their patients. Many behavioral EBPs have been widely adopted in schools and clinical settings. For example, the National Autism Center (NAC), the National Professional Development Center on Autism Spectrum Disorders (NPDC) and the Centers for Medicare and Medicaid Services (CMS) have identified EBPs for working with children with ASD, many of which are derived from the field of behavior analysis (Table 1.2).

## Table 1.2
*Examples of Behavior Analytic Evidence-Based Practices*

| | |
|---|---|
| Differential Reinforcement of Alternative Behavior | Response Interruption/Redirection |
| Functional (Behavior) Assessment | Self-Management Strategies |
| Functional Communication Training | Time Delay |
| Picture Exchange Communication Systems | Extinction |
| Pivotal Response Training | Discrete Trial Training |

Furthermore, ABA has the potential to have a broad impact on the world at large and has been used to tackle a range of difficult problems. For example, researchers have used behavior analysis to teach pouched rats to locate landmines hidden in residential areas (Poling et al., 2010), young children to avoid to avoid firearms (Miltenberger et al., 2005) and evade abduction (Gast, Collins, Wolery, & Jones, 1993), adults with disabilities to use fire safety skills (Mechling, Gast, & Gustafson, 2009), children with ASD to tell socially appropriate lies (Bergstrom, Najdowski, Alvarado, & Tarbox, 2016), and athletes to improve performance (Harding, Wacker, Berg, Rick, & Lee, 2004). Many people use ABA in their daily interactions as they provide positive feedback to their child, reward themselves for maintaining a specific caloric intake, or withhold a payment to a contractor for a job poorly executed. The fact is that ABA is already loosely woven into the social fabric of modern society.

Despite the obvious workings of behavior analysis within our daily lives, some people are resistant to the use of ABA in educational and therapeutic settings. Some may have been introduced to behaviorism as an outdated and obsolete philosophy within an introduction to psychology course, whereas others may find the idea of directly influencing the behaviors of others uncomfortable.

A resistance to ABA often results from a general lack of understanding of how it works. Prominent leaders in the field of behavior analysis have suggested that ABA practitioners and researchers have not been effective in explaining what they do (Friman, 2014). Behavior analysts often pride themselves on their use of technically accurate language, and as a result may not seize the opportunity to share behavior analysis using terms and examples familiar to the people with whom they interact.

The purpose of this book is to present behavior analysis more simply and clearly. Specifically, the intent is to provide an opportunity for behavior analytic researchers to explain, in their own words and from their own perspective, concepts and practices critical to a basic understanding of ABA using language that is easily understood by a wide range of readers. This book is not intended to be an exhaustive compendium of ABA, as many great books are readily available (see Table 1.3), but a threshold towards behavior analytic practice. We hope you enjoy it.

## Table 1.3
*Important Textbooks in Applied Behavior Analysis*

| TITLE | AUTHOR |
|---|---|
| *Applied Behavior Analysis* | Cooper, Heron, & Heward (2007) |
| *Behavior Analysis for Lasting Change* | Mayer, Sulzer-Azaroff, & Wallace (2014) |
| *Handbook of Applied Behavior Analysis* | Fisher, Piazza, & Roane (2011) |
| *Applied Behavior Analysis for Teachers* | Alberto & Troutman (2013) |
| *Principles of Behavior* | Malott & Shane (2015) |
| *Concepts and Principles of Behavior Analysis* | Michael (2004) |

# References

Alberto, P. A., & Troutman, A. C. (2012). *Applied behavior analysis for teachers*. Upper Saddle Creek, NJ: Pearson.

Baer, D. M., Wolf, M. M., & Risley, T. R. (1968). Some current dimensions of applied behavior analysis. *Journal of Applied Behavior Analysis, 1*, 91-97.

Beavers, G. A., Iwata, B. A., & Lerman, D. C. (2013). Thirty years of research on the functional analysis of problem behavior. *Journal of Applied Behavior Analysis, 46*, 1-21.

Bergstrom, R., Najdowski, A. C., Alvarado, M., & Tarbox, J. (2016). Teaching children with autism to tell socially appropriate lies. *Journal of Applied Behavior Analysis, 49*, 405-410.

Bondy, A., & Frost, L. (2011). *A picture's worth*: PECS *and other visual communication strategies in autism. Woodbine House.*

Cooper, J. O., Heron, T. E., & Heward, W. L. (2007). *Applied behavior analysis*. Upper Saddle Creek, NJ: Pearson.

Ferster, C. B., & DeMyer, M. K. (1961). Increased performances of an autistic child with prochlorperizine administration. *Journal of the Experimental Analysis of Behavior, 4*, 84.

Fisher, W. W., Piazza, C. C., & Roane, H. S. (Eds.). (2011). *Handbook of applied behavior analysis*. New York, NY: Guilford Press.

Friman, P. C. (2014). Publishing in journals outside the box: attaining mainstream prominence requires demonstrations of mainstream relevance. *The Behavior Analyst, 37*(2), 73-76.

Gast, D. L., Collins, B. C., Wolery, M., Jones, R. (1993). Teaching preschool children with disabilities to respond to the lures of strangers. *Exceptional Children, 59*, 301-311.

Green, G. (2001). Behavior analytic instruction in learners with autism: Advances in stimulus control technology. *Focus on Autism and Other Developmental Disabilities, 16*, 72-85.

Harding, J. W., Wacker, D. P., Berg, W. K., Rick, G., & Lee, J. F. (2004). Promoting response variability and stimulus generalization in martial arts training. *Journal of Applied Behavior Analysis, 37*, 185-195

Horner, R. H., Carr, E. G., Halle, J., McGee, G., Odom, S., & Wolery, M. (2005). The use of single-subject research to identify evidence-based practice in special education. *Exceptional Children, 71*, 165-179.

Malott, R., & Shane, J. T. (2015). *Principles of behavior*. New York, NY: Psychology Press.

Mayer, G. R., Sulzer-Azaroff, B., & Wallace, M. (2014). *Behavior analysis for lasting change*. Cornwall, NY: Sloan Publishing.

Mechling, L. C., Gast, D. L., & Gustafson, M. R. (2009). Use of video modeling to teach extinguishing of cooking related fires to individuals with moderate intellectual disabilities. *Education and Training in Developmental Disabilities, 44*, 67-79.

Michael, J. L. (1993). *Concepts and principles of behavior analysis*. Kalamazoo, MI: Association for Behavior Analysis International.

Miltenberger, R. G., Gatheridge, B. J., Satterlund, M., Egemo-Helm, K. R., Johnson, B. M., Jostad, C., Kelso P., & Flessner, C. A. (2005). Teaching safety skills to children to prevent gun play: An evaluation of in situ training. *Journal of Applied Behavior Analysis, 38*, 395-39

Poling, A., Weetjens, B. J., Cox, C., Beyene, N. W., & Sully, A. (2010). Using giant African pouched rats (Cricetomys gambianus) to detect landmines. The *Psychological Record, 60*, 715-728.

Schuster, J. W., Gast, D. L., Wolery, M., & Guiltinan, S. (1988). The effectiveness of a constant time-delay procedure to teach chained responses to adolescents with mental retardation. *Journal of Applied Behavior Analysis, 21*, 169-178.

Touchette, P. E. (1971). Transfer of stimulus control: Measuring the moment of transfer. *Journal of the Experimental Analysis of Behavior, 15*, 347-354.

# WHY BEHAVIOR "HAPPENS"

*Robert C. Pennington*

## KEY TERMS:

- Behavior
- Explanatory fiction
- Circular reasoning
- Respondent behavior
- Habituation
- Respondent conditioning
- Unconditioned stimulus

- Conditioned stimulus
- Neutral stimulus
- Conditioned response
- Respondent extinction
- Operant behavior
- Negative reinforcement
- Positive punishment

- Negative punishment
- Discriminative stimulus
- Motivating operation
- Establishing operation
- Abolishing operation
- Positive Reinforcement

## ▶▶ *What Is Behavior?*

On the path to understanding why behavior happens, we must start by determining what constitutes behavior. Simply put, *behavior* can be described as the things that people do (Scott, 2017). More precisely, behaviors must be observable and thus, verifiable. That is, multiple individuals must be able to agree on whether or not a behavior has occurred.

Consider the common verb *read*. Most people have an idea of what *reading* looks like, but may not be able to agree on when a person is actually reading. Some might consider that a passenger looking at a book on the subway is reading, whereas another might suggest that the same person is just looking at the pictures in the book or thinking about something else. Further, to verify that somebody is reading, some require the person to speak the written words aloud, and others expect the person to be able to do so with some level of fluency. A proficient reader will engage in a range of behaviors (e.g., looking, pronouncing, answering comprehension questions), and each of these may be of interest to an observer.

When identifying a target behavior for observation or intervention, we must carefully consider its relevance to the issue at hand and whether it can be measured (e.g., counted or timed). If a behavior cannot be accurately measured, then the effectiveness of an intervention or teaching procedure cannot be determined; in that case, what's the point? Measurement is a cardinal feature of behavior analytic practice and will be covered in detail in Chapter 3. Table 2.1 provides several non-examples of behaviors that may be difficult to verify, as well as some helpful alternatives.

## Table 2.1
*Behaviors That Are Difficult to Verify*

| NON-EXAMPLE OF BEHAVIOR | ALTERNATIVE (SPECIFIC BEHAVIOR) |
|---|---|
| Read | State, say aloud, answer, point to correct word |
| Attend or Listen | Orient toward speaker, look at speaker, answer a comprehension question |
| Identify | Point to (item/object), touch the (item/object) say the (item/object) |
| Calculate | Write the answer, enter the correct equation into a calculator |
| Act Aggressively | Kick, hit, scratch, pinch |
| Disrupt | Speak while others are talking, throwing objects |

## ▶▶ *Problems in Defining People by Their Behavior*

In contrast to the popular notion that we are defined by our actions, it is important to not label people by patterns of problematic behavior. Teachers and therapists often refer to children by the behavior they have emitted (e.g., biter, runner, scratcher) or by how their behavior is viewed by others (e.g., aggressive, disrespectful, manipulative). In addition to the lack of dignity in such usage, these descriptors fail to bring the interventionist closer to a solution, as it appears to suggest that a characteristic of the learner is the source of the problem behavior. These terms, when used to explain the reason a person engages in a behavior, are referred to as *explanatory fictions* (Skinner, 1974) and can envelop the interventionist in a distracting cycle of *circular reasoning*.

Consider the complaint by a teacher that a particular student is disrespectful. A behavior consultant asks the teacher to describe what the student's disrespect looks like and receives the answer that the student engages in "talking back," or verbal protest. The consultant then asks, "Why do you think the student 'talks back?," to which the teacher responds, "Because he is disrespectful." This circular reasoning can be applied to many descriptions of behavior and their sources (e.g., aggressive, noncompliant) used in everyday conversations.

The template in Figure 2.1 illustrates how behaviors and their sources can be misinterpreted in a circuitous argument.

## ▶▶ *Two Types of Behavior*

From a behavior analytic perspective, there are two broad classes of behavior. The first, *respondent behavior*, involves responses that are a part of a reflex (i.e., an involuntary response) and require no prior learning to occur. Such responses are a part of our genetic "wiring" and a result of centuries of natural selection. Examples of common respondent behaviors include blinking, salivation, and kicking when one's funny bone is tapped. The second class of behavior, *operant behavior*, occurs because of a prior learning history or exposure to consequences. These learned behaviors are acquired throughout one's lifetime and can take a variety of forms. The table below provides some basic differences in respondent and operant behavior.

## Table 2.2
*Basic Differences in Respondent and Operant Behavior*

| RESPONDENT BEHAVIOR | OPERANT BEHAVIOR |
| --- | --- |
| Genetic endowment | Learned across the lifetime |
| Elicited by environmental stimuli | Maintained by consequences |
| Form of response predetermined by genes | Range of forms determined by environment |
| *Examples:* | *Examples:* |
| A tickle in the throat elicits coughing | Coughing to get someone's attention |
| Hearing a dog bark elicits elevated heart rate | Opening a refrigerator to access food |
| Touching a hot stove elicits rapid removal of a hand | Pushing a button to access an elevator |

## ▶▶ *Respondent Behavior*

Blinking in response to a foreign object in your eye or a sudden increase in heart rate in the presence of an assailant are both examples of respondent behavior. These responses play a critical role in preserving our existence. At one point, the latter example helped us avoid becoming food for saber-toothed tigers, whereas now it is more likely to alert us to extra creepy people on dating websites. People are quite aware of their respondent behaviors, but commonly talk about them as emotional responses (e.g., fear, surprise, anxiety). These emotional responses can be viewed as descriptions of our perceptions of respondent behaviors (e.g., increased heart rate, galvanic skin responses, adrenaline secretion).

Respondent behavior is a relation between a response and the stimulus (i.e., event or object) that immediately precedes it (S-R) (Keller & Schoenfeld, 1950). When describing this relation, it is said that an antecedent stimulus (e.g., gunshot) elicits a respondent behavior (e.g., startle). The more intense the stimulus, the quicker and stronger the response it elicits. Consider the lighting of fireworks on the 4th of July: whereas an unexpected pow from a small firecracker may elicit a mild and delayed wash of discomfort over an individual (i.e., increased blood flow), a loud *boom* from a large firecracker may elicit that same person's immediate scramble for cover. Understanding this relation may help interventionists as they plan for situations when an individual might be exposed to an aversive stimulus within their environment (e.g., fire alarm, visit to the doctor's office).

Sometimes a stimulus fails to elicit a response or produces a weakened response. This may be due to an important concept referred to as *habituation*. Habituation occurs when the response decreases in magnitude after repeated presentations of an eliciting stimulus (Pierce & Cheney, 2013). For example, when somebody starts using contact lenses, they typically squint and their eyes fill with tears, but after several days, the response weakens and the user is able to comfortably apply the contact lens.

Habituation has many practical applications. For example, parents may notice that the overuse of a loud reprimand gradually produces less of an effect on their child's behavior. Furthermore, an interventionist may find that gradual and repeated exposure to a stimulus (e.g., a brother's pet tarantula) helps reduce a client's fear of that stimulus. Finally, it is important to note that after a sustained absence of the stimulus, the respondent behavior may recover. For example, if the individual mentioned above decided to take a month's break from wearing contact lenses, the reintroduction would probably elicit the responses of squinting and tearing up again.

## ▶▶ *Respondent Conditioning*

Though we are wired from birth to emit respondent behavior in the presence of certain stimuli, we may find ourselves engaging in these behaviors in the presence of stimuli that are not genetically predetermined. For example, a boy who was given ice cream while receiving chemotherapy finds that ice cream elicits a gagging response following chemotherapy. Similarly, a coworker, recently admonished by his boss, finds that the scheduling of a second meeting with the boss elicits a panic attack.

This phenomenon is a result of what is referred to *as classical or respondent conditioning* (Pavlov, 1960). The reader may recall the story of Ivan Pavlov, who paired a bell with food to condition a dog to salivate upon the ringing of the bell. This process occurs when a *neutral stimulus* (NS) is presented just before an *unconditioned stimulus* (US) to elicit an *unconditioned response* (UR). After repeated presentations, the neutral stimulus becomes a *conditioned stimulus* as it begins to elicit the respondent behavior, which has now become a *conditioned response* (CR). Terms related to respondent conditioning are summarized in Table 2.3,

## Table 2.3
*Respondent Conditioning Terminology*

| TYPE OF STIMULUS/ RESPONSE | DEFINITION OF STIMULUS/RESPONSE |
|---|---|
| Neutral Stimulus | Stimulus that does not elicit a respondent behavior |
| Unconditioned Stimulus | Stimulus that elicits a respondent behavior without prior conditioning |
| Unconditioned Response | Respondent behavior elicited by an unconditioned stimulus |
| Conditioned Stimulus | Stimulus that elicits a respondent behavior due to pairing with an unconditioned stimulus |
| Conditioned Response | A respondent behavior elicited by a conditioned stimulus |

Consider a boy who regularly visits a pet store and is enamored with a beautiful colored cockatiel. Each time the boy approaches the cockatiel (NS), he is pecked (US), which elicits an increased heart rate (UR). After some time, the sight of the cockatiel alone (CS) increases the pounding in the boy's chest (CR). The same process may be used to condition neutral stimuli to elicit responses associated with pleasure. For example, the presentation of a particular therapist, teacher, or family member prior to the presentation of delicious treats may elicit pleasurable feelings in a child that person approaches. This pairing procedure is a key component in instructional delivery, especially for individuals who do not find social interaction pleasurable.

It is important to note that these effects may not be permanent. In a process referred to as *respondent extinction* (Cooper, Heron, & Heward, 2007; Pierce & Cheney, 2013), the repeated presentation of a conditioned stimulus (e.g., the cockatiel) in the absence of the unconditioned stimulus (e.g., the bite) will result in a gradual decrease in the respondent behavior (e.g., change in heart rate). Similarly, the once preferred teacher may lose a student's favor after the presentation of multiple instructional settings without the delivery of preferred toys or edibles.

An understanding of respondent behavior is critical to working with individuals of all ages. Unfortunately, our attention to respondent behavior sometimes gets lost in clinical and educational settings. For example, focus on operant behavior has increased in schools due to the federally mandated application of functional behavior assessment (IDEA, 2004), but attention to the role of respondent behavior in schools is often overlooked. Knowing the principles associated with respondent behavior can help interventionists design environments that facilitate learning and promote emotional regulation through the careful management of eliciting stimuli. (e.g., negative adult feedback, the presentation of novel experiences or difficult tasks, the presence of a bully).

## ▶▶ *Operant Behavior*

Much of what we do is a result of our personal history of consequences. Consider a boy who bumps his elbow on a table and begins to cry to his mother. It might seem that the bump elicited his crying behavior, but this limited analysis does not take fully into account the variables most relevant to the boy's crying. For instance, it is important to consider why the boy cried instead of cursing or whistling. It is probable that his crying behavior had a prior history of gaining his mother's attention.

*Operant behaviors* are those that occur because of a history of consequences. These consequences are comprised of two broad categories: (a) access to preferred stimuli (e.g., attention, tangible items, sensory feedback), and (b) avoidance of unpleasant or aversive stimuli (Skinner, 1953). We continuously engage in behaviors because of the effect those behaviors have had previously on our lives. Sometimes we are aware of the contingencies at work, as we "choose" to talk to an attractive person or change gears on our bicycle to decrease the difficulty of an uphill ride, but sometimes we are completely unaware of responses selected by our environment. For example, somebody may sit a certain way on the couch to avoid an uncomfortable seam in the upholstery or may use exaggerated facial expressions because they have resulted in increased attention by a communicative partner. Whether we know it or not, we behave for the promise of a desirable outcome.

## ▶▶ *Four Critical Relations*

One of B. F. Skinner's greatest contributions to our understanding of human behavior was the introduction of the *three-term contingency*. In the three-term contingency, sometimes referred to as antecedent-behavior-consequence (ABC) or represented in the notation S -R- S, Skinner (1953) suggested that in the presence of an antecedent stimulus, a response will occur, contingent on access to or escape from a stimulus. This relation between response and consequence is referred to as *reinforcement*. Technically, reinforcement is observed when a response, followed immediately and contingently by a stimulus, is strengthened in the future. That is, the response occurs more often, for longer periods of time, or with more intensity.

*Positive reinforcement* involves the contingent presentation of a stimulus. For example, when a homeowner hands out high-quality candy on Halloween, he may notice several repeat visits from the same trick-or-treater, or when a child who earns stickers for picking his clothes up from the bedroom floor continues to keep his room tidy.

*Negative reinforcement* involves the contingent and immediate removal of a stimulus. For instance, when a trip to a noisy grocery store is cut short by a child's tantrum, the parents observe that the child tantrums upon the announcement of a subsequent trip to the grocery store. Similarly, a teenager completes his homework independently during the week because in the past it has resulted in the removal of weekend chores.

# Table 2.4

*Examples of Positive and Negative Reinforcement*

| POSITIVE REINFORCEMENT | NEGATIVE REINFORCEMENT |
|---|---|
| Jermaine swings because in the past it has produced a pleasant breeze on his face | Mike wears a seatbelt because in the past he has avoided the obnoxious seatbelt alarm |
| Shu Chen uses a fireman's carry because it has previously resulted in her opponent's pin to the wrestling mat | Alice walks down Miller Street to avoid the inappropriate comments by workers on Barnes and Wilson Streets |
| Bobby keeps working to solve the equation, because in the past his persistence has resulted in the correct answer | Manuel hums to drown out the aversive pop song playing on the neighbors' radio |

Reinforcement contingencies are central to an understanding of human behavior and help to explain learning, socio-communication, and challenging behavior. In essence, we emit a range of responses at particular times because of the availability of reinforcers within the environment. For example, a child disrupts a classroom during a difficult lesson because past disruption has resulted in her being sent to the principal's office. The child's teacher may perceive this dismissal to be an appropriate response if she fails to acknowledge the environment's role in the occurrence of problem behavior. But a closer look may reveal aversive conditions that warrant the child's attempt to escape, including the delivery of complex instructional demands with low rates of teacher praise and feedback, and the close proximity of peers that frequently snicker in response to the child's errors. Further, this closer analysis may help the teacher to address the problem behavior by improving the instructional environment instead of strengthening the child's strategy for escape.

Reinforcement contingencies are essential to, but not solely responsible for, how we behave. Another set of relations, punishment contingencies, also serve to direct our actions and form our repertoires. *Punishment* is observed when a response, followed immediately and contingently by a stimulus, is weakened or occurs less frequently in the future (Cooper et al., 2007). Like reinforcement, punishment contingencies can be either negative or positive.

*Positive punishment* is observed when an aversive stimulus is presented contingent on the occurrence of a behavior and, as a result, some characteristic of the behavior is weakened in the future. For example, one day a child decides to jump into a neighbor's pool, starts to sink, and takes water into his lungs. Fortunately, he is quickly rescued by a nearby swimmer, but avoids the pool on future visits to the neighbor's house.

*Negative punishment* involves the removal of a preferred stimulus contingent on a behavior that also results in a weakening in the future occurrence of that behavior. For example, an angry football fan throws his beer can at the television set following what he deemed was a bad play. The television sputters and goes black; he is consequently unable to watch the rest of the game. After purchasing a new television set, he refrains from lobbing projectiles towards his flat screen.

These two examples reflect the ubiquitous nature of *punishment*. Though we often relegate the word punishment to describing a set of practices (e.g., spankings, fines, imprisonment), in ABA, punishment describes a relation between a stimulus and its effect on future behavior. From this view, punishment is not defined by a person's actions, but by the effect of those actions; a spanking may not be punishment unless it results in a future decrease in behavior. On the other hand, a poorly delivered kiss may be punishment if it results in a reduction of phone calls to the clumsy admirer.

**The role of the antecedent**. So far, we have described the role of consequences in the occurrence of behavior, but it is important to note that contingencies of reinforcement do not occur in a vacuum. Each time a behavior is reinforced, particular environmental stimuli or conditions are present that also may contribute to the occurrence of a behavior. For example, a request for ice cream is more likely to occur under important relevant conditions such as an unseasonably hot day, one's presence at an ice cream shop, or an empty stomach.

These critical antecedent stimuli can increase the probability that a response will occur in two general ways. First, the antecedent can serve to signal the availability of reinforcers for a particular response. This signaling antecedent is referred to as a *discriminative stimulus* ($S^D$), and plays a critical role in learning. The discriminative stimulus comes to control a response because it has been present when the response was reinforced in the past (Micheal, 1982). For example, when a child sees a picture of a train, says, "Choo-choo," and afterwards receives adult attention, the child learns that saying, "Choo-choo," when a picture of a train is present results in access to a reinforcer.

Teachers and therapists carefully design educational programs around the concept of *stimulus* control. That is, they present an antecedent stimulus (e.g., 2+2), wait for or prompt a response (e.g., *four*), and immediately deliver a reinforcer (e.g., praise). After repeated presentations or trials, a target response comes under control of the instructional stimulus – in other words, it is learned.

## Table 2.5
*Examples of S$^D$ - Behavior Relations*

| ANTECEDENT (S$^D$) | BEHAVIOR | CONSEQUENCE (REINFORCER) |
|---|---|---|
| Triangle depicted on card | Individual says, "Triangle" | Teacher praise |
| Greeting from a colleague | Position for a handshake | Receipt of handshake |
| Lines on a highway | Driving within lines | Avoidance of a crash |
| Sight of dirty hands | Washing of hands | Clean hands |

The second way in which antecedents affect the likelihood of a behavior occurring is by strengthening or weakening the value of reinforcers (Micheal, 1982). Consider a young man who, when short of spending money, decides to comb the neighborhood to obtain lawn mowing jobs. After three weeks of mowing lawns, he scratches off a $5,000-dollar lottery ticket, resulting in the immediate evaporation of his entrepreneurial spirit and lawn mowing efforts. This temporary abundance of money probably weakened the value of the small amounts of money he had previously received for difficult work.

From this example, it is clear to see how changes in one's circumstances or environment can have a powerful – but, most likely, temporary – effect on behavior. These changes or conditions, referred to as *motivating operations* (MO), are described as environmental variables that (a) alter the current frequency of behavior previously reinforced by that particular reinforcer (Micheal, 2004). In general, there are two types of MOs: establishing operations (EO) and abolishing operations (AO).

Establishing operations have an establishing effect on the value of reinforcers, resulting in an evocative effect on behavior. For example, a walk through the desert may have an establishing effect on water as the reinforcer and an evocative effect on the behavior of drinking from a muddy puddle.

Abolishing operations serve to abolish stimuli as reinforcers, resulting in an abative effect on behavior. For example, turning up the thermostat may abolish warmth as a reinforcer and abate all warmth-seeking behaviors (e.g., searching for a blanket, huddling next to the family dog).

Finally, it is important to note that some MOs are effective as a part of our genetic endowment. These *unconditioned motivating operations* (UMOs) are likely to affect the behavior of most individuals and include conditions such as food/water deprivation, sleep deprivation, oxygen deprivation, and the presence of pain, heat, or cold. Other MOs are conditioned across an individual's lifetime (*conditioned motivating operation* [CMO]), Michael, 2007). For example, the request for a specific employee to come into the boss's office has regularly preceded the delivery of a series of unpleasant questionings by the boss. This request may serve to strengthen the value of avoiding or delaying a visit to the office. Therefore, the nervous employee might take a sudden trip down to the mail room. The CMO of the boss's request is only effective because of the employee's prior experiences.

Understanding the roles of and differences between the $S^D$ and MOs is essential to understanding behavior and programming for behavior change. Several authors have published papers that may be helpful in deepening one's understanding of these two concepts (see Langthorne & McGill, 2009; Laraway, Snycerski, Micheal, & Poling, 2003; Michael, 1993). In general, the SD signals that a response will result in a desired outcome and acquires this characteristic as a result of a history of consequences. The MO does not indicate that reinforcement is available but increases or decreases a reinforcer value at a particular time. Table 2.6 depicts several examples of the SD and MO to help clarify the difference.

## Table 2.6
*Examples of MO-S<sup>D</sup>-Behavior Relations*

| MO | S<sup>D</sup> | BEHAVIOR | CONSEQUENCE |
|---|---|---|---|
| Child misses breakfast (food deprivation) | Mother approaches (signals availability) | Child asks for cookie | Mother presents cookie |
| Light switch broken in dark room (light deprivation) | Light behind curtain (signals availability) | Man opens curtains | Room illuminated |
| Student working alone in a study carrel (attention deprivation) | Peer walks by (signals availability) | Student makes a farting sound | Peer laughs |

## ▶▶ *Summary: Putting It All Together*

Framing behavior in the context of its relation to antecedents and consequences improves our understanding of why people do the things they do, but it does not take away from the complexity and uniqueness of each person. From birth, we are exposed to both striking and subtle differences in the environments that shape distinct qualities in us that are loved (or disliked) by the people around us. Our diversity directly mirrors the constantly changing world in which we live. If not careful, the practitioner with only a cursory understanding of behavior analysis may overlook the complex nature of the environments in which a behavior occurs, and as a result may fail to intervene in ways that produce meaningful behavior change.

A teacher may view a teenager's disruption as a cry for attention yet fail to acknowledge his struggles in learning the content or recognize his desire for specific features of attention. Further, the teacher may arrange an environment that produces positive change, but is so dissimilar to the natural world that the student fails to make improvements outside of the classroom. Though the principles described in this chapter are powerful, their application to each individual requires thoughtful and careful analysis, and in some cases, carefully designed procedures that will be described in later chapters.

# *References*

Cooper, J. O., Heron, T. E., & Howard, W. L. (2007). *Applied behavior analysis.* Upper Saddle Creek, NJ: Pearson.

Individuals with Disabilities Education Act, 20 U.S.C. § 1400 (2004).

Keller, F. S., & Schoenfeld, W. N. (1950). *Principles of psychology: A systematic text in the science of behavior.* New York, NY: Appleton-Century-Crofts Inc.

Langthorne, P., & McGill, P. (2009). A tutorial on the concept of the motivating operation and its importance to application. Behavior Analysis in Practice, 2, 22-31.

Laraway, S., Snycerski, S., Michael, J., & Poling, A. (2003). Motivating operations and terms to describe them: Some further refinements. *Journal of Applied Behavior Analysis,* 36, 407-414.

Michael, J. (1982). Distinguishing between discriminative and motivational functions of stimuli. *Journal of the Experimental Analysis of Behavior,* 37, 149-155.

Michael, J. (1993). Establishing operations. *The Behavior Analyst,* 16, 191-206.
Pavlov, I. P. (1960). Conditioned reflexes: *An investigation of the physiological activity of the cerebral cortex* (G. V. Anrep, trans.). New York, NY: Dover.

Pierce, W. D., & Cheney, C. D. (2013). *Behavior analysis and learning.* New York, NY: Psychology Press.

Scott, T. (2017). *Teaching behavior: Managing classroom through effective instruction.* Thousand Oaks, CA: Corwin

Skinner, B. F. (1953). *Science and human behavior.* New York, NY: The MacMillan Company.

Skinner, B. F. (1974). *About behaviorism. New York,* NY: Vintage.

# COLLECTING, DISPLAYING, AND ANALYZING DATA

*Charles L. Wood & Kerry W. Kisinger*

## KEY TERMS:

- Operational definition
- Count
- Frequency (Rate)
- Duration
- Latency
- Magnitude
- Topography

- Anecdotal recording
- Permanent product re-cording
- Event recording
- Duration recording
- Whole-interval recording
- Partial-interval recording

- Momentary time sampling
- PLA-Check
- Level
- Trend
- Stability
- Variability

## ▶▶ *Why Target, Measure, and Analyze Behavior?*

Targeting, measuring, and analyzing behavior are essential parts of ABA by assisting interventionists (e.g., teachers, therapists) in determining which behavior(s) to observe, whether an intervention is effective, and when to make changes to an intervention or introduce new targets. Consider that when a doctor prescribes medicine to reduce a patient's blood pressure, he must measure the patient's heart rate to ensure the drug is effective and to assess whether there have been any harmful effects. Teachers, therapists, and behavior analysts also address important responses, and they, too, must collect data on the progress of individuals under their care. This chapter describes how interventionists can identify target behaviors for intervention, collect data on those targets, display their data on graphs or charts, and analyze their data.

## ▶▶ *Selecting and Defining Behaviors for Intervention*

When people talk about behavior in schools and other contexts, they are often referring to challenging or unconventional behavior, but it is important to note that behaviors can be targeted for reduction (e.g., off-task behavior, shouting out) or for an increase (e.g., asking for help with a difficult task). Several factors are important to consider when targeting a behavior to change.

First, it is desirable for the target behavior to produce reinforcement for the individual in the natural environment long after the intervention has ended (Ayllon & Azrin, 1968). For example, teaching a child to ask for items using the American Sign Language (ASL) sign for "more" might be effective in an environment where teachers know the child's preferences, but not in the community where there are countless potential reinforcers and communicative partners. Therefore, one might decide to target a communication response where a child presents easily discernible pictures of specific items to a communicative partner.

Second, the target behavior must be age-appropriate and socially acceptable. For example, you would not teach an adult to use the word *potty* to request access to the bathroom.

Third, when targeting problem behavior, it is important to determine whether the behavior is actually a problem. For instance, a residential care staff may request that a behavior analyst targets a resident's protesting behavior (i.e., complaining), but the behavior analyst quickly learns that the protesting behavior is appropriate for the client and just annoying to the staff.

Finally, if a problem behavior (e.g., hitting, screaming) is targeted for reduction, an appropriate, functionally equivalent behavior must be taught as a replacement. For example, if a young man pushes others to get their attention, it is best to teach him other ways to get the attention of those around him.

It is important to develop an *operational definition* of the target behavior. An operationally defined target behavior is one that is observable, measureable, and clear (Hawkins & Dotson, 1975). A behavior that is observable and measurable is one that can be seen, agreed upon by others, and counted or timed. An operational definition is clear when it is unambiguous and boundaries are set for what the behavior is and what it is not (O'Neill, McDonnell, Billingsley, & Jenson, 2011). Table 3.1 lists examples and non-examples of operational definitions.

## Table 3.1
*Operational Definitions*

| TARGET BEHAVIOR | OPERATIONAL DEFINITION | NON-EXAMPLE |
|---|---|---|
| Raise hand to ask for help | James quietly extends arm and hand above his head and waits to be called on. | James moves hand to get teacher's attention. |
| Tantrum | Carla falls to the floor and bangs her fists loudly on the floor. | Carla pitches a fit and is out of control. |
| Out-of-seat | Ben removes his bottom from the chair for more than three seconds, sits on his feet, leans on two legs of the chair, or leaves his desk area. | Ben gets up during class. |

## ▶▶ *Dimensions of Behavior*

Determining the dimension of the target behavior can help you select the most appropriate method of data collection. Cooper, Heron, and Heward (2007) described several dimensions (i.e., features that can be measured) of behavior, including *count, frequency (rate), duration, latency, magnitude, and topography*. Table 3.2 provides a definition and examples for these common behavioral dimensions used in analyzing specific behavioral responses.

## Table 3.2
*Behavioral Dimensions*

| DIMENSION | DEFINITION | EXAMPLE |
|---|---|---|
| Count | The number of times a response occurred (a tally) | 1. Number of times Zavier raised his hand quietly during math class<br>2. Number of pictures Hannah accurately identified |
| Frequency/Rate | The number of times (also called rate) the response occurred during a specific period of time (count per time) | Number of words Taku read per minute |
| Duration | The amount of time the response occurred (reported as seconds, minutes, days, etc.) | Amount of time Dani was out of her seat during the school assembly. Amount of time Terrell stayed in the playground area with his peers. |
| Latency | The amount of time that elapses between a stimulus (e.g., a direction) and when the response begins (reported as seconds, minutes, etc.) | Amount of time that passed before Kate started putting her belongings in her backpack when the teacher said, "Time to get ready for the bus." Amount of time that passed after Clara's teacher said, "What is the first sound in the word mop?" and when Clara said, "Mmm." |
| Magnitude | The force or strength of the response (often counted as meeting a criterion such as frequency of produced noise at a certain decibel level) | Thomas turned the container lid hard enough for it to open. Shantrice spoke too quietly for others to hear her. |
| Topography | The form or shape of the response (i.e., how it looks) | Kenneth makes a fist when striking his head. Trevor walks on his toes. |

## ▶▶ *Collecting Data*

After developing a sound operational definition of a target behavior and then selecting the behavioral dimension most relevant to the situation (e.g., the behavior happens too often or not long enough), one must determine an appropriate method for collecting data on that dimension of behavior. Several methods may be used to collect data. Some are easy to use, and others can be challenging and time intensive.

**Anecdotal recording.** *Anecdotal recording* involves taking detailed, written notes of the observed behavior during a specific time. Typically, anecdotal notes are used to capture the antecedents (what happened immediately before a behavior occurred), the behavior, and the consequences (what happened immediately after a behavior occurred). Referred to as ABC recording, this type of anecdotal recording is often used in functional behavior assessment to help determine the function of the problem behavior (see Chapter 6).

**Permanent product recording**. *Permanent product recording* is used to collect data on behavior that can be reviewed at a later time. That is, the behavior produces a product, such as the number of correct answers written on a math quiz, the number of correctly formed letters on a handwriting sheet, or the number of toys put away in a toy bin. Permanent product recording also can be used for data collection on audio- or video-recorded behavior (e.g., making tally marks for self-injurious behavior while watching a video of a student completing a difficult task).

**Event recording**. *Event recording* may be used to capture the count or frequency of behavior. It involves simply counting the occurrence of the target behavior during an observation period. The observer can use tally marks with paper and pencil, move coins from one pocket to another, or use technology such as a smartphone or tablet to mark the occurrence of a target behavior. Multi-counter apps for smartphones allow practitioners to track multiple behaviors or behaviors across different students by simply tapping the screen for each occurrence of the target behavior. Total count or frequency can then be plotted on a graph or chart for that observation. Frequency (i.e., rate) data can provide meaningful day-to-day comparisons when intervention periods change across sessions. For instance, Thomas may have talked out five times during a 10-minute period on the first day of data collection, and 10 times in a 20-minute period the next day. It may seem that Thomas talked out more the next day, but the frequency would be the same as the first.

*Figure* **3.1** provides examples of forms used for event recording.

| Observer: Nelson |
| Student: J |
| Date: September 16, 2017 |
| Target Behavior: Shouts out in class |
| Observation Time: 9:00 – 9:30 AM, Reading Group |

| 9:00 – 9:30 | / / / / / / / |
|---|---|
| Total: | 7 |

Date: 4/12/18     Observer: Baker     Student: B.
Activity: Free time with peers
Target Behavior: Grabs toys from peers
Time: 2:00 – 2:40

| 1̸ | 2̸ | 3̸ | 4̸ | 5̸ | 6̸ | 7̸ | 8̸ | 9̸ | 10 |
|---|---|---|---|---|---|---|---|---|---|
| 11 | 12 | 13 | 14 | 15 | 16 | 17 | 18 | 19 | 20 |
| 21 | 22 | 23 | 24 | 25 | 26 | 27 | 28 | 29 | 30 |

Total: 9

*Figure 3.1. Example event-recording forms*

**Duration recording.** *Duration recording* is used to capture the amount of time that an individual engages in the target behavior. For example, a teacher might want to determine how long her seventh-grade student, Lyle, is out of his seat during a 50-minute social studies class. She could use a timer, stopwatch, smartphone, or tablet to record the duration of out-of-seat behavior. In this case, duration recording would be preferred over event recording. For instance, using event recording, an observer could note, "He was out of his seat only one time during class." But with duration recording, another observer might note, "Yes, he was out of his seat one time, but that one occurrence lasted 16 minutes." That is, duration data allow observers to present the total amount of time spent engaged in a behavior or present the average duration per occurrence (DPO). Figure 3.2 shows an example of a form that may be used to collect data on total duration and DPO.

| Observer: Preslar | Occurrence | Duration |
|---|---|---|
| Student: L | 1 | 0:16 |
| Date: January 22, 2018 | 2 | 1:15 |
| Target Behavior: Out of seat | 3 | 2:44 |
| Observation Time: 1:00 – 1:50 PM, Soc. St. | 4 | 0:37 |
| | 5 | |
| | Total | 4:52 |

*Figure 3.2. Example data collection sheet for duration recording*

**Interval recording**. *Interval recording* allows an observer to sample occurrences of a target behavior during an observation. First, the observer determines the total observation time (e.g., 20 minutes). Next, the observer divides the observation into shorter, equal intervals (e.g., 15 seconds) and records the presence or absence of the target behavior for each interval. For example, a 20-minute observation comprised of 15 second intervals would result in 80 intervals (4 intervals per minute x 20). After recording the total number of intervals in which the target behavior occurred, scores can be plotted on a graph or chart.

There are two general types of interval recording: *whole-interval recording and partial-interval recording*. Observers can use whole-interval recording for interventions designed to increase appropriate behavior. In this case, the target behavior must occur during the entire interval (i.e., *whole* interval) for an occurrence to be counted. It is important to note that whole interval recording is most appropriate for behaviors that are longer in duration (e.g., staying in the seat, oriented towards instructional materials), because behaviors with short durations (commenting, spitting) may not last an entire interval. Because interventions that target appropriate behavior often aim to have the behavior occur with longer durations, whole interval recording may provide a good test of the intervention's strength.

Partial interval recording can be used to evaluate behaviors that are short in duration and may occur too often to easily count accurately. In this case, the target behavior only has to occur once at any time (i.e., *part* of the interval) during an interval for an occurrence to be counted. Some frequently occurring problem behavior may be more difficult to reduce; therefore, partial-interval recording provides a more conservative measure of an intervention's effectiveness. In other words, an intervention must be strong enough to decrease more occurrences of the behavior, even those that only occur in *parts* of the intervals.

Interval recording typically involves using a data collection sheet on which intervals are arranged as a table. Figure 3.3 shows an example data sheet used for interval recording. Data collectors can use a timer or audio-recorded prompts to signal times to observe and record. To make data collection easier, observers can use interval timer apps on smartphones or tablets to set recurring signals that cue (e.g., a vibration or change in screen color) the appropriate time to record the target behavior before automatically resetting for the next interval.

Session data are reported as percent of intervals and calculated by counting the number of intervals in which the target behavior occurred and dividing by the total number of intervals used during the observation (e.g., 12 intervals marked for the occurrence of tantrums out of 50 intervals equals 24% for that session).

Observer: MacKaye
Student: I
Date: 5/2/17
Session: 4

Partial-Interval Data Collection: 2S second observation; 5 second record. Circle off task if student is off task at any time during the 25 second interval.

| Minute | 0 - 25 Seconds | | | | 30 - 55 Seconds | | | |
|--------|-----|------|-----|------|-----|------|-----|------|
| 1 | off | task | on | ~~task~~ | (off | task) | on | ~~taks~~ |
| 2 | (off | task) | on | task | off | taks | on | ~~task~~ |
| 3 | off | task | on | ~~task~~ | off | task | on | ~~task~~ |
| 4 | (off | task) | on | task | (off | task) | on | task |
| 5 | off | task | on | ~~task~~ | off | task | on | ~~task~~ |
| 6 | (off | task) | on | ~~task~~ | off | task | on | ~~task~~ |
| 7 | off | task | on | task | off | task | on | ~~task~~ |
| 8 | off | task | on | ~~task~~ | off | task | on | ~~task~~ |
| 9 | off | task | on | ~~task~~ | off | task | on | ~~task~~ |
| 10 | off | task | on | ~~task~~ | off | task | on | ~~task~~ |
| 11 | off | task | on | ~~task~~ | off | task | on | ~~task~~ |
| 12 | off | task | on | ~~task~~ | off | task | on | ~~task~~ |
| 13 | off | task | on | ~~task~~ | off | task | on | ~~task~~ |
| 14 | off | task | on | ~~task~~ | off | task | on | ~~task~~ |
| 15 | off | task | on | ~~task~~ | off | task | on | ~~task~~ |
| 16 | (off | task) | on | task | (off | task) | on | task |
| 17 | off | task | on | ~~task~~ | (off | task) | on | task |
| 18 | off | task | on | ~~task~~ | (off | task) | on | task |
| 19 | (off | task) | on | task | off | task | on | ~~task~~ |
| 20 | off | task | on | ~~task~~ | off | task | on | ~~task~~ |
| | | | | | | **Total Intervals: 10/40** | | |
| | | | | | | **Percent Off Taks :25%** | | |

**Figure 3.3. Example data collection sheet for interval recording.**

**Momentary time sampling**. *Momentary time sampling* (MTS) can be an efficient and effective method for data collection. MTS allows the observer to record an instance of a target behavior at the end of a preset interval (e.g., at the end of every minute). For example, the observer can track a student's off-task behavior by setting an interval timer to vibrate every minute. At the end of the interval, the observer simply notes if off-task behavior occurred at that moment.

MTS is often preferred by teachers because it is not time consuming and allows them to take a snapshot of student behavior while attending to other classroom responsibilities. Like interval recording, MTS data are reported as percent of intervals.

**PLA-Check**. Similar to MTS, teachers can use a planned activity check (PLA-Check; Doke & Risley, 1972) to collect observational data on groups of students. PLA-Check is used to collect data at the end of an interval for a group of students who are engaging in the same behavior. For example, a teacher could use PLA-Check during students' independent work time as an easy way to see if the students are on task. As the interval timer signals (e.g., flashes, beeps, vibrates), the teacher observes the whole group and records how many students are engaged in the appropriate behavior. Similarly, PLA-Check can be used to measure task engagement during small group activities or class projects. Like interval recording, PLA-Check data are reported as percent of intervals.

*Figure* 3.4 shows an example data collection sheet used for MTS or PLA-Check.

Teacher: Stevenson, 5<sup>th</sup> Period Science
Date:10/12/17
Target: Completing lab work without disruption

| End-of-Minute | Group 1 | | Group 2 | |
|:---:|:---:|:---:|:---:|:---:|
| 1 | YES | NO | YES | NO |
| 2 | YES | NO | YES | NO |
| 3 | YES | NO | YES | NO |
| 4 | YES | NO | YES | NO |
| 5 | YES | NO | YES | NO |
| 6 | YES | NO | YES | NO |
| 7 | YES | NO | YES | NO |
| 8 | YES | NO | YES | NO |
| 9 | YES | NO | YES | NO |
| 10 | YES | NO | YES | NO |
| 11 | YES | NO | YES | NO |
| 12 | YES | NO | YES | NO |
| 13 | YES | NO | YES | NO |
| 14 | YES | NO | YES | NO |
| 15 | YES | NO | YES | NO |
| 16 | YES | NO | YES | NO |
| 17 | YES | NO | YES | NO |
| 18 | YES | NO | YES | NO |
| 19 | YES | NO | YES | NO |
| 20 | YES | NO | YES | NO |
| **Total "Yes"** | 18 | | 14 | |
| **Percent** | 90% | | 70% | |

**Figure 3.4. Example data collection sheet for MTS or PLA-Check**

In summary, identifying the relevant dimension of the target behavior can help determine which method of data collection is best suited to evaluate effects of an intervention (see Table 3.3). For example, if the target behavior is *quiet hand raising*, event recording would be an appropriate way to collect data. If the target behavior is *talking to peers during silent reading time*, then duration recording, partial interval recording, or MTS would be good choices.

## Table 3.3
*Dimensions Related to Data Collection*

| DIMENSION | SUGGESTED METHOD OF DATA COLLECTION |
| --- | --- |
| Count | Event recording |
| Frequency/Rate | Event recording |
| Duration | Duration recording<br>Interval recording (whole or partial)<br>Momentary time sampling<br>PLA-Check |
| Latency | Latency recording (duration) |

## ▶▶ *Displaying and Analyzing Data*

After data are collected, the teacher or therapist can visually display (usually in a graph or chart) the data to determine the day-to-day and overall effects of an intervention, adjust the intervention as needed to reach goals, and communicate progress with others.

Line graphs showing consecutive data points and bar charts showing cumulative data are effective ways to display results. Both line graphs and bar charts need to include the target student's name (or pseudonym used to protect identity), the target behavior, the intervention, and number or date of observations or sessions. Graphing software such as Microsoft Excel includes templates for designing and displaying graphs and charts (see Chapter 6). In addition, online video resources (e.g., *YouTube*) provide step-by-step instructions for constructing different types of graphs and charts. Figure 3.5 shows an example line graph and bar chart.

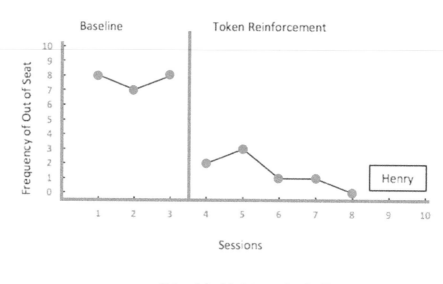

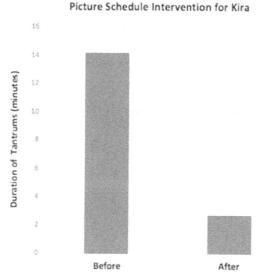

*Figure 3-5. Example line graph and bar chart.*

Graphed data points (i.e., a data path) can be analyzed by *level, trend, stability, and variability.* Level is used to describe the height of the data path (high or low). Trend is used to describe the direction of the data path (increasing, decreasing, or no trend). Stability is used to describe the close range of data points in a data path. A stable data path is one with little to no substantial increases or decreases between data points. Finally, variability (the opposite of stability) is used to describe the degree of "bounce" between data points in a data path. Figure 3.6 provides examples of data paths that show different trends, levels, stability, and variability.

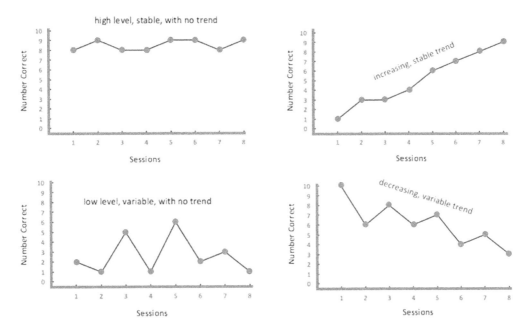

*Figure 3.6. Example of trend, level, stability, and variability.*

Using these terms in combination (e.g., decreasing variable trend) can help improve communication concerning graphed data and the individual's performance that it represents. Chapter 4 describes how data in line graphs can be arranged in a variety of behavioral research designs.

## ▶▶ *Summary*

Selecting, defining, measuring, and analyzing behavior are critical parts of any successful behavioral intervention. Behaviors targeted for intervention need to be socially acceptable and have a good chance of being maintained once an intervention is completed.

Understanding the various dimensions of behavior (i.e., count, frequency, duration, latency, magnitude, topography) can help practitioners determine appropriate data collection methods. Collected data can be graphed and displayed to analyze behavior, determine the effects of the intervention, and to communicate results to others.

# *References*

Ayllon, T., & Azrin, N. H. (1968). The token economy: *A motivational system for therapy and rehabilitation.* New York: Appleton-Century-Crofts.

Cooper, J. O., Heron, T. E., & Heward, W. L. (2007). *Applied behavior analysis* (2nd ed.). Upper Saddle River, NJ: Pearson.

Doke, L. A., & Risley, T. R. (1972). The organization of day care environments: Required vs. optional activities. *Journal of Applied Behavior Analysis, 5,* 453-454.

Hawkins, R. P., & Dotson, V. S. (1975). Reliability scores that delude: An Alice in Wonderland trip through the misleading characteristics of inter-observer agreement scores in interval recording. In E. Ramp & G. Semp (Eds.), Behavior analysis: *Areas of research and application* (pp. 359-375). Englewood Cliffs, NJ: Prentice-Hall.

O'Neill, R. E., McDonnell, J. J., Billingsley, F. B., & Jenson, W. R. (2011). *Single case research designs in educational and community settings.* Upper Saddle River, NJ: Pearson.

# USING BASIC
# SINGLE CASE DESIGNS

*Jennifer Ledford & Katherine Severini*

## KEY TERMS:

- Baseline
- Independent variable
- Maturation
- Multitreatment interference
- Non-reversible
- Drift
- Demonstrations of effect

- Behavior change
- Dependent variable
- Control
- Time-lagged
- Reliability
- Fidelity
- Visual analysis

- Experimental control
- Reversible behaviors
- History
- Covariation
- Bias
- Control variables
- Functional relation

## ▶▶ *Single-Case Design*

For about 50 years, single-case research designs have played a critical role in moving the field of ABA forward. In the first volume of *The Journal of Applied Behavior Analysis*, some of the earliest influential behavior analysts called for the practice of ABA to be *analytic*—this requires that when we implement interventions, we collect evidence regarding changes in behavior (Baer, Wolf, & Risley, 1968). However, the requirement for ABA to be analytic goes beyond simply measuring behavior change—it requires that we collect data in a way that shows that observed changes in behavior are the result of our intended interventions and not some other mediating factor (e.g., change in medication, the introduction of a home tutoring program). Single case research designs permit interventionists to collect data in such a way that it is easier to "rule out" other explanations for an observed behavior change. The two scenarios below show the weaknesses of collecting data in the absence of a single case research design.

**Aliyah and Mr. Ahmad**. *Mr. Ahmad is the classroom teacher for Aliyah, a 10-year-old girl with autism who engages in frequent problem behavior. After the first Friday in the school year, in which Aliyah engaged in problem behavior 10 times per hour, Mr. Ahmad decides to implement a reinforcement-based intervention using a token system. On Monday, he gives Aliyah a token for every activity during which she engages in no problem behavior. He collects data for four weeks, and determines that levels of problem behavior have steadily and gradually improved over time because of the token intervention. During their next parent conference, Aliyah's father reports that her behaviors at home also have improved, and seems doubtful that the token intervention is responsible since they are not providing tokens at home.*

**Declan and Ms. Matthews**. *Declan, a 6-year-old boy with a behavior disorder, has learned fewer sight words than his kindergarten classmates. Ms. Matthews, his after-school tutor, decides to use books with Declan's favorite characters to teach him sight words. After a few weeks, he has learned many of the words that he could not previously read. Ms. Matthews decides to tell Declan's teacher about the intervention (use of high-interest books). She is surprised to hear that Declan has been receiving 30 minutes of supplemental reading instruction that started at the same time as the after-school tutoring. She is now unsure that her tutoring worked at all.*

Mr. Ahmad and Ms. Matthews both collected data before they intervened (i.e., during *baseline* or "A" conditions) and while the intervention was implemented (i.e., intervention or "B" conditions). Subsequently, they compared their data across A and B conditions and determined that their students' behavior changed in a positive direction. Unfortunately, both learned that there are limitations to an A-B design when attributing improvements to their intervention. The simple A-B design does not rule out other factors that are introduced following the start of an intervention (e.g., supplemental reading instruction). In some cases, observed improvement may be deemed "good enough" in practice — Mr. Ahmad might not be concerned with whether his intervention was the reason for the behavior change — he is just happy it improved! However, without understanding the "active ingredients" that actually changed behavior, one may not be able to replicate the effects in the future.

Practitioners are important agents in research that informs the field and helps to establish practices as evidence-based. To that end, we must collect data in a way that shows not only *behavior change* (i.e., a difference in the amount of behavior that occurs), but change that we can confidently conclude is the result of our intervention procedures, and only those procedures.

When you change behavior and demonstrate that your intervention is responsible, you can say that you have demonstrated *experimental control* — a determination that you can be confident the intervention (*independent variable*) caused the change in the target behavior (*dependent variable*). We accomplish this via replication of the basic A-B effect. Each time behavior changes contingent on a change presented within a new condition (e.g., improves when we implement the intervention condition, or gets worse if we take the intervention away and return to the baseline condition), we refer to it as a *demonstration of effect*.

## Basic Design Types and Examples of Use

**A-B-A-B designs.** Withdrawal designs, also referred to as A-B-A-B designs, are among the oldest and most commonly used single case designs (Baer, Wolf, & Risley, 1968). These designs are appropriate when you are interested in changing *reversible behaviors*. These behaviors are ones that are more dependent on current contexts than on learning history; this means the behavior is likely to revert to baseline levels when an intervention is withdrawn. For example, social interactions tend to be reversible; the frequency with which we interact with others is highly dependent on context (e.g., expectations, positive or negative responses from peers). In a class, if you whisper to the person beside you and they respond favorably (e.g., whisper back, smile, nod), you are likely to continue communicating with that person. However, if the instructor begins noting your off-task behavior with raised eyebrows, you are likely to whisper less often. This describes the typical data patterns of reversible behaviors; different contingencies result in relatively fast changes in responding.

You'll remember that Mr. Ahmad collected data on Aliyah's problem behavior both before intervention and once intervention commenced. The A-B-A-B design is a simple extension of this initial A-B comparison. When this design is used, data are collected for at least three measurement occasions (sessions, days, etc.) in a baseline (no-intervention) condition, and then data are collected for at least three measurement occasions in an intervention condition. Then, the intervention is withdrawn (removed) and data are collected again. We call this removal *a return to baseline* condition, and data collected during this phase are likely to be similar to the initial baseline data. Finally, the intervention condition is reintroduced and the A-B-A-B comparison is complete. Below, you'll see data for Aliyah's problem behaviors plotted on a graph, showing an initial baseline condition ($A_1$), followed by an intervention condition ($B_1$), then a return to baseline ($A_2$), and, finally, the reintroduction of intervention ($B_2$)

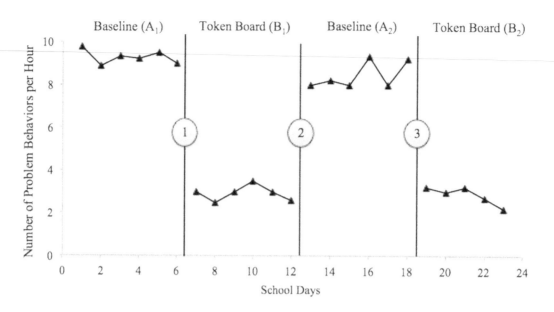

**Figure 4.1 A-B-A-B design. Numbers 1-3 on the graph indicate demonstrations of effect.**

Why does this repetition of "A" and "B" conditions give us more information than the initial A-B comparison described above? In the previous examples, other explanations for behavior change are possible. Aliyah's challenging behavior gradually and steadily improved over time, even in settings where the intervention was not implemented. This change may have been related to Mr. Ahmad's intervention, but it also may have been the result of *maturation*: gradual improvements related to the passage of time. By removing the intervention in the second baseline condition ($A_2$) and showing that behavior reverts to previous levels ($A_1$), you *control* for this threat (e.g., render the threat nonproblematic). If behavior begins to improve again when the second intervention condition is implemented, our confidence increases even further. If the behavior keeps improving even without intervention (i.e., in $A_2$), the intervention may not be the cause of the behavior change. Below is an illustration of what data would look like in an A-B-A-B design where a maturation threat is likely (e.g., Aliyah's behavior change was not the result of the intervention).

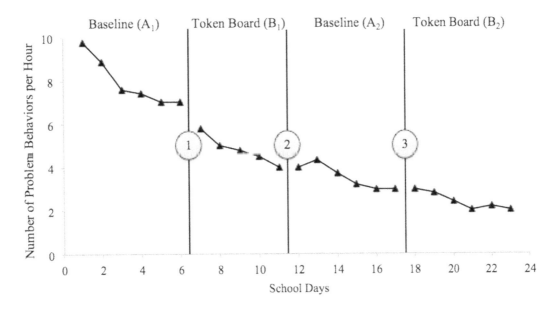

*Figure 4.2. A-B-A-B design with data showing potential maturation effects. Numbers 1-3 on the graph indicate potential demonstrations of effect because slow changes over time suggest that behavior improvements might not related to condition changes.*

The premise of the A-B-A-B design can be extended to compare two different interventions. For example, assume that, rather than assessing only one type of intervention, Mr. Ahmad was interested in whether one intervention was better than a second intervention. He might then collect data during a baseline condition, then alternate data collection in each intervention condition (an A-B-C-B-C design, with "C" referring to the second intervention).

**Alternating treatments designs.** Alternating treatments designs (ATDs; Barlow & Hayes, 1979) are also suitable for reversible behaviors (described above) that are likely to change quickly. ATDs are used to compare the effect of two or more conditions (e.g., two interventions; baseline to intervention) on the behavior of one participant. Unlike withdrawal designs, interventions in an ATD are alternated at the session level (e.g., B-C-C-B-C-B), rather than the condition level (e.g., B-B-B-C-C-C). Thus, conditions are assigned (usually randomly) to sessions or days, and comparisons are made between adjacent sessions (i.e., data points), rather than conditions (as in the A-B-A-B design, above). This session alternation allows direct comparison between intervention conditions; each condition change creates a replication of effect.

The usefulness of ATD designs can be illustrated by considering Aliyah and Mr. Ahmad again. Instead of collecting data on Aliyah's behavior during baseline and then during the use of the token intervention, Mr. Ahmad could alternate the days in which Aliyah uses the token intervention in rapid succession with days in which she does not (i.e., baseline). At the beginning of each week, he could randomly assign the token intervention to certain days of the week (e.g., Monday, Tuesday, Thursday) and baseline to the others (Wednesday, Friday); alternating between conditions would allow him to make accurate conclusions about the effectiveness of the token intervention, and whether Aliyah's behavior change is due to the token intervention and the token intervention alone. When compared to the A-B-A-B design, the ATD design is less effective at controlling for maturation effects, but allows for a demonstration of effectiveness even if maturation is present. For example, in the figure below, you see that Aliyah's behavior is slowly improving in both conditions (i.e., maturation is present). However, you can also see that she engages in many fewer problem behaviors on days when the tokens are used. The likelihood of maturation occurring in an ATD design is relatively low if there are few data points (e.g., 12, as shown below) that occur closely in time (e.g., over a three-week period).

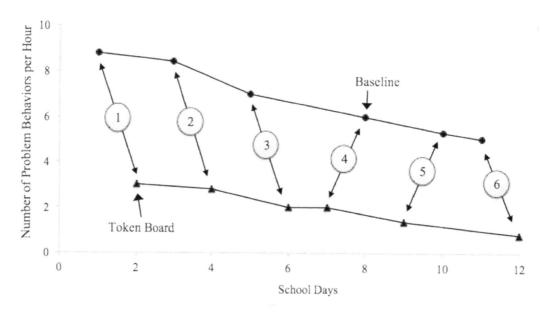

**Figure 4.3. ATD design showing potential maturation effects. Numbers 1-6 on the graph indicate demonstrations of effect (e.g., token board was shown to be superior to baseline 6 times).**

ATDs also reduce the threat of *history* effects, which are changes in participant responding due to unforeseen events that occur after the introduction of an intervention or new condition (e.g., Aliyah's family moved to a new house). In the original A-B example, if Aliyah's challenging behavior spiked for several sessions during the intervention condition, it would be unclear to Mr. Ahmad whether this was due to the intervention or external factors. However, continued differentiation between conditions, regardless of any changes in the patterns of data (i.e., sessions 5-8 in the graph below), increases our confidence in the relative effectiveness of the two conditions. That is, even though Aliyah engaged in more challenging behavior during the week following the family move, it is still clear that the token intervention resulted in lower problem behavior relative to the baseline condition.

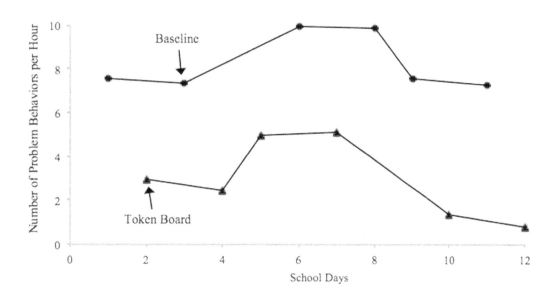

*Figure 4.4. ATD design showing potential history effects (i.e., behavior worsened in sessions 5-8, but was still higher in baseline than in the token board condition).*

When ATDs are used, it may be likely that the procedures used in one condition influence responding in the subsequent condition. This effect is referred to as *multitreatment interference.* For example, Aliyah's behavior in a baseline session on Tuesday may be influenced by procedures or contingencies that were in place during the token intervention session on Monday. The likelihood of multitreatment interference can be minimized by implementing a best alone condition at the end of the study; that is, Mr. Ahmad should continue the condition that has demonstrated greater therapeutic changes in behavior after he finishes alternating the two conditions. Given that tokens were more effective during the comparison phase, Mr. Ahmad can implement the token intervention for several contiguous sessions at the end of the study (i.e., without alternating). If Aliyah's challenging behavior remains low, the inclusion of the final token condition increases our confidence that behavior change is due to the intervention.

**Multiple baseline designs**. Another commonly used single case design is the multiple baseline of which there are three types including the multiple baseline across (a) participants, (b) behaviors, and (c) contexts. The multiple baseline across participants design is the most commonly used of all single case designs (Hammond & Gast, 2010). When these designs are employed, the same baseline and intervention conditions are conducted across multiple (usually three or four) participants. To demonstrate experimental control, we start collecting baseline data at the same time for all participants. Once data are stable and we have collected at least three data points for all participants, we start intervention with Participant 1 and continue collecting data for other participants in the baseline condition. Once behavior improves for Participant 1, we begin intervention with Participant 2 (and continue collecting data for Participant 3 in baseline). Once behavior improves for Participant 2, we begin intervention with Participant 3. We refer to data for each participant as a tier (i.e., the top panel in Figure 4 below is Tier 1, the middle panel is Tier 2, and so on) and refer to the delay in intervention implementation in later tiers as a *time-lagged* procedure.

In this design, we show experimental control when participants' behavior changes only after the introduction of the intervention. While this design might align well with clinical and educational practice (e.g., practitioners often work with more than one child who exhibits a given behavior), there are a few potential problems. First, in the case of Aliyah and Mr. Ahmad, there would have been a need for Mr. Ahmad to identify three children with problem behavior for whom token systems were likely to work in the same way. Second, if he identified three participants, but Participants 2 and 3 observed his intervention with Aliyah (Participant 1), they might have changed their behavior before he begins intervention with them. This impairs experimental control (although the improved behavior would be practically useful). Finally, as shown in the figure below, the final participant in a multiple baseline across participants design spends quite a long time in the baseline condition without intervention. This might pose ethical concerns.

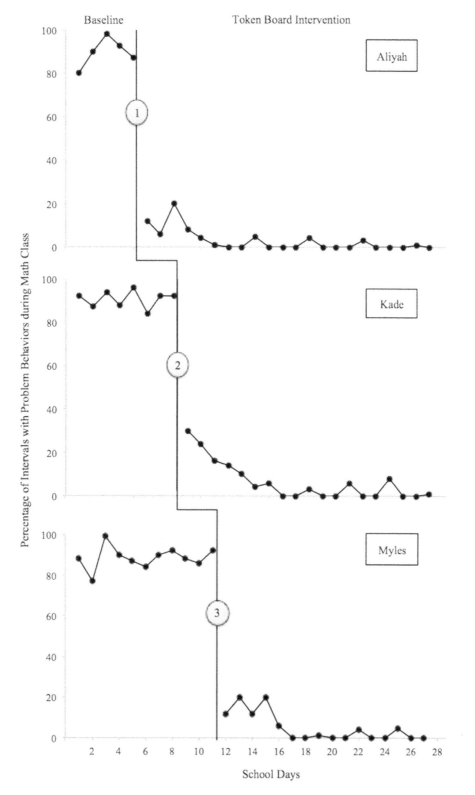

Figure 4.5. Multiple baseline across participants design. Numbers 1-3 on the graph indicate demonstrations of effect.

There are two other types of multiple baseline designs, although they are used less often than the participants variation. The first is a multiple baseline design across behaviors; these designs are typically used for increasing rather than decreasing behaviors. In Aliyah's case, Mr. Ahmad might have decided that her problem behavior was occurring because she was not able to adequately communicate when she wanted attention, needed a break from a task, or was hungry. In this case, Mr. Ahmad might decide to use a multiple baseline design across behaviors to assess the impact of using modeling and reinforcement to improve her efficacy in requesting attention (Tier 1), asking for a break (Tier 2), and asking for a snack (Tier 3; Figure 4.6).

The least common type of multiple baseline design is across contexts; when this design is used, data are collected under multiple conditions for the same participant and behavior. For Aliyah, Mr. Ahmad might have decided to evaluate the use of a token board in her classroom, during lunch, and during an after-school program. In this case, he would start collecting baseline data in all three contexts and after at least three observation periods and once data were stable, he would begin using the token board intervention in the classroom (while collecting baseline data during lunch and after school); when problem behavior decreased in the classroom, he would intervene in a time-lagged fashion in the other two contexts. In this design, covariation (changes in one tier that occur when a condition is implemented in another tier) is likely. Although this is clinically positive (e.g., in the figure below, Aliyah's behavior improved at lunch even though the token board was only implemented in the classroom), it lessens our confidence that the change is exclusively caused by the intervention and not some outside factor (e.g., a history effect).

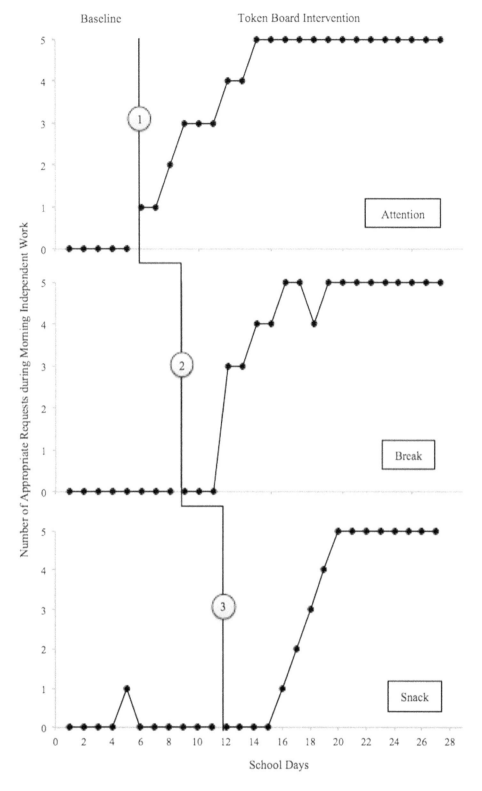

Baseline          Token Board Intervention

Attention

Break

Snack

School Days

Number of Appropriate Requests during Morning Independent Work

**Figure 4.6. Multiple baseline across behaviors design. Numbers 1-3 on the graph indicate demonstrations of effect.**

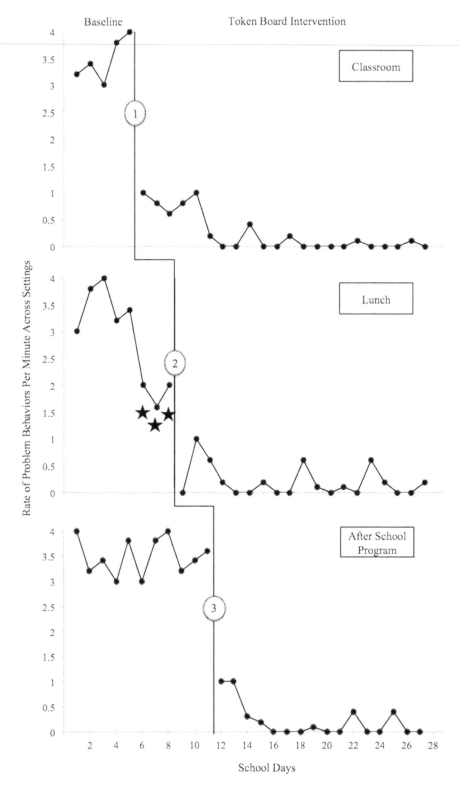

*Figure 4.7. Multiple baseline across contexts design. Covariation indicated by stars. Numbers 1-3 on the graph indicate demonstrations of effect.*

**Multiple probe designs**. In applied behavior analysis and related fields, we are often interested in *non-reversible* behaviors (i.e., behaviors that are unlikely to "reverse" once we withdraw an intervention). Consider, for example, teaching a child like Declan to read sight words or to prepare a sandwich. Once he learns to engage in these behaviors, he is unlikely to discontinue correct responding, even if you remove the intervention procedures. Thus, we need a single case design that allows for control for maturation and history when the behaviors of interest are non-reversible.

The multiple probe design, a variation of the multiple baseline design, serves this purpose. As with Aliyah's behavior change, demonstrated in the initial vignette, we cannot be sure that Declan's behavior change was due to Ms. Matthews's intervention with the high-interest books. In addition, we could not use an A-B-A-B design or an ATD design because once Declan learns a word, he is likely to continue to correctly read that word regardless of condition.

Moreover, if we used a multiple baseline design across behaviors—like the one shown in Figure 4.6 — by assigning different words to at least three tiers, there would be many baseline sessions for later tiers; however, conducting this much testing for behaviors that have not yet been taught could be interpreted as unethical (Gast & Ledford, 2014). The multiple probe design solves this issue by including the *intermittent* collection of baseline data. Thus, whether the design includes multiple participants, behaviors, or contexts, you would collect baseline data less frequently than you collect intervention data. In Figure 4.8, you can see that Ms. Matthews conducted daily intervention sessions, but only collected baseline data approximately once every third day. It is important to collect at least three baseline data immediately before you begin intervention for each tier.

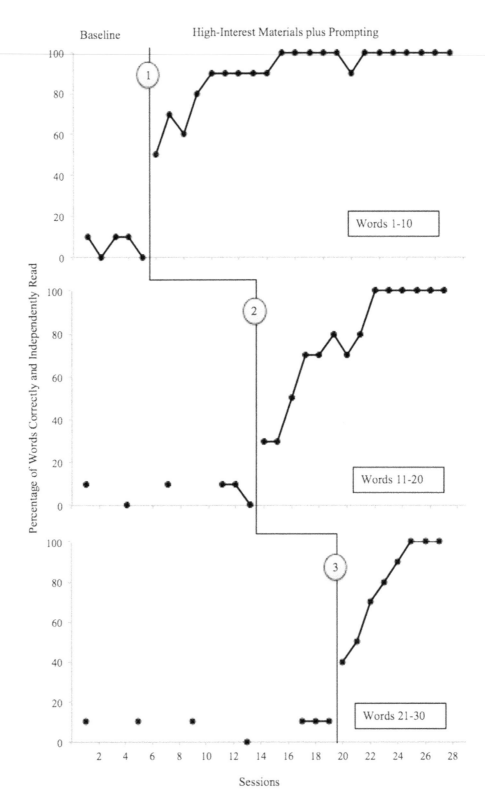

**Figure 4.8. Multiple probe across behaviors design. Numbers 1-3 on the graph indicate demonstrations of effect.**

# ▶▶ *Characteristics of Rigorous Single Case Designs*

Although a comprehensive review of quality components of single case design research is beyond the scope of this chapter, two considerations regarding measurement are critical for assessing the believability of results when a single case design is used (i.e., reliability, fidelity). Additional information on these and other single case design characteristics is available elsewhere (Council for Exceptional Children, 2015; Gast & Ledford, 2014; Horner, Carr, Halle, McGee, Odom, & Wolery, 2005).

**Reliability**. In order to show that the independent variable resulted in changes in the dependent variable, we must know whether the data were collected reliably across conditions. *Reliability* generally means *dependability*, and we typically assume it is associated with accuracy. For example, if two people can dependably record the same behaviors in the same way (i.e., are reliable), we assume both are recording the data accurately.

Two factors can hamper reliable data collection: *bias* and *drift*. Bias refers to the conscious or unconscious belief that behavior will be different under different conditions (e.g., Mr. Ahmad may believe that his token board intervention will be effective, which may impact his ability to objectively record data). This might result in the data collector making different decisions, especially in ambiguous circumstances.

For example, if Aliyah says, "No!" when Mr. Ahmad directs her to sit, but then complies with the request, it might be difficult to determine whether a challenging behavior occurred? The second possibility is drift—the likelihood that the data collector will slowly change her behavior definitions over time. For example, in the multiple baseline across behaviors example, wherein Aliyah is directly taught to request attention, Mr. Ahmad might originally count a request only if Aliyah says, "Mr. Ahmad, could you please come here?" but might inadvertently start counting similar requests that he originally did not count (e.g., if Aliyah says, "Mr. Ahmad," plus a hand gesture).

To combat these problems, you must first define your behaviors with precision (see Chapter 3). It also helps to have a different data collector intermittently collect data alongside you (or the primary data collector) to determine whether your data show similar patterns. For example, Mr. Ahmad might have a classroom assistant collect data one day per week, and then compare the data collected by the assistant with his own data.

**Fidelity**. We can only know that an intervention worked as intended if we know that the intervention was implemented as intended (i.e., was implemented with high *fidelity*). Thus, when collecting data in the context of single case designs, researchers must collect fidelity data to measure to what extent the implementers are following procedural protocols. There are two major types of fidelity failures: (a) implementers use intervention components in the baseline condition, when use *was not* planned; and (b) implementers fail to use all relevant intervention components in the intervention condition, when use was planned. The steps outlined below can prevent this from happening and detect when it does happen.

1. Write detailed protocols describing how to conduct baseline and intervention conditions. It is often helpful to use a table that describes things that will be the same between conditions (*control variables*) and things that will be different (*independent variables*).
2. Devise a data collection form that includes all of the planned steps in both conditions.
3. Present implementers with written protocols and data collection forms during training.
4. Use data collection forms to regularly collect data on the implementer's adherence to the procedural steps in each condition.
5. Re-train implementers, if necessary.

Following these steps allows you to ensure any changes in behavior are related to planned changes between conditions, allows you to re-train implementers when needed, and may help you identify components of the procedures that are difficult to implement (which may suggest that the intervention needs to be modified). In practice, having an observer watch you implement planned procedures is not always feasible, but ease of video capture using mobile devices may increase opportunities (e.g., Mr. Ahmad could video himself implementing the token board and have a paraprofessional check his fidelity).

## ▶▶ *Analyzing Single Case Data*

As shown in Figures 4.1-4.6, replication is built into all single case designs—in each design, there are multiple times when we expect behavior change to occur (i.e., every time we move to a new condition). Each of these times when behavior is expected to occur is called a potential demonstration of effect. When behavior change *does occur* it is referred to as a *demonstration of effect*. How do we know if an effect occurs between conditions (i.e., if there is a demonstration of effect)? We use *visual analysis*:  simply put, we look at the graphed data and assess whether changes occurred. Specifically, we look at three data characteristics (outlined in Chapter 3):

1. **Level:** Does the amount of behavior reliably change when intervention is implemented?
2. **Trend:** Does the direction or slope of the data change? and
3. **Variability:**  How much does the data change between measurement occasions, in the same condition (i.e., how stable are the data)?

If the answer to one or more of these questions is "yes" and the change occurs *when and only when* planned condition changes occur, we conclude that a *functional relation* exists. A functional relation suggests that we have reliably demonstrated, via replication, that the changes in the dependent variable (behavior) are functionally related to (caused by) the implementation of the independent variable.

What does a functional relation look like in each design? In A-B-A-B designs, the first demonstration is when behavior improves when intervention begins ($A^1$-$B^1$), the second is when the behavior worsens when intervention is withdrawn ($B^1$-$A^2$), and the third is when behavior improves again when the intervention is reintroduced ($A^2$-$B^2$). In multiple baseline and multiple probe designs, a demonstration of effect occurs if behavior changes when and only when intervention is introduced to each tier (e.g., the first demonstration of effect occurs when intervention is implemented in Tier 1 and behavior changes, the second demonstration of effect occurs when intervention is implemented in Tier 2 and behavior changes, and so on). In alternating treatments designs, a demonstration of effect occurs when a data point in one condition is improved (lower or higher, depending on the target behavior) relative to the adjacent paired data point.

In Figures 4.1-4.8, each demonstration of effect is identified with a circled number; note that all designs include at least three. Regardless of design type, common factors increase our confidence that our intervention (and only our intervention) is responsible for observed improvements in behavior: presence of three demonstrations of effect when conditions are changed, stability in data when conditions are not changed, and the absence of non-effects (behavior staying the same when condition changes occur). Visual analysis of our data in the context of a rigorous single case design improves practice because it decreases the likelihood that we will use ineffective interventions. This, in turn, improves the field of behavior analysis, because it allows us to build on and contribute to a growing base of knowledge.

## ▶▶ *Summary*

In sum, single-case research designs are essential to behavior analytic practice. Their use permits practitioners to assess intervention effectiveness but also to demonstrate that the intervention, not other extraneous variables, is responsible for behavior change. When using single case research designs, practitioners must select a design that matches the variables, dependent and independent, they intend to evaluate. Subsequently, they implement their intervention and use visual analysis to determine whether they have been successful or need to make changes in their intervention protocol.

# *References*

Baer, D. M., Wolf, M. M., & Risley, T. R. (1968). Some current dimensions of applied behavior analysis. *Journal of Applied Behavior Analysis*, 1, 91-97.

Barlow, D. H., & Hayes, S. C. (1979). Alternating treatments design: One strategy for comparing the effects of two treatments in a single subject. *Journal of Applied Behavior Analysis*, 12, 199-210.

Council for Exceptional Children. (2014). *Standards for evidence-based practices in special education*. Arlington, VA: Author.

Gast, D. L., & Ledford, J. R. (2014). *Single case research methodology. Applications in special education and behavioral sciences*. New York, NY: Routledge.

Hammond, D., & Gast, D. L. (2010). Descriptive analysis of single subject research designs: 1983–2007. Education and Training in Autism and Developmental Disabilities, 45, 187-202.

Horner, R. H., Carr, E. G., Halle, J., McGee, G., Odom, S., & Wolery, M. (2005). The use of single-subject research to identify evidence-based practice in special education. *Exceptional Children*, 71, 165-179.

# GRAPHING IN
# MICROSOFT EXCEL®

*Erick M. Dubuque & Emma E. Brink*

## KEY TERMS:

- Line graph
- Data points
- Data paths
- Vertical axis

- Horizontal axis
- Phase change lines
- Phase change labels
- Figure captions

Behavior analysts depend upon visual analysis of graphed data to determine the impact their interventions have on target behaviors. In behavior analysis, *line graphs* are the most common way to display data points representing quantifiable values plotted across time and conditions (see Figure 5.1). On a line graph, data are plotted on a Cartesian plane comprised of a vertical and a horizontal axis.

The *vertical axis*, also known as the ordinate or y-axis, is used to display a quantifiable dimension of behavior (e.g., frequency, rate, latency, duration, force, percentage), whereas the *horizontal axis*, also known as the abscissa or x-axis, is used to display a unit of time or the value of an independent variable (e.g., minutes, days, weeks, sessions, classes). *Data points* plotted on a line graph represent the value of the target behavior, or dependent variable, at a specified point in time. *Data paths* are used to connect consecutive data points within the same phase or condition on a line graph.

These data paths allow the behavior analyst to evaluate the level, trend, and variability of the target behavior across time and conditions. Environmental changes, such as the introduction or removal of an independent variable, are marked on line graphs using phase change or condition change lines and labels. *Phase change lines* are solid or dashed vertical lines extending from the horizontal axis to a height that matches the top of the vertical axis on a line graph. *Phase change labels* are short pieces of text used to briefly describe the environmental changes the target behavior contacted. *Figure captions*, or figure titles, are another important component of line graphs, as they are used to describe the content displayed.

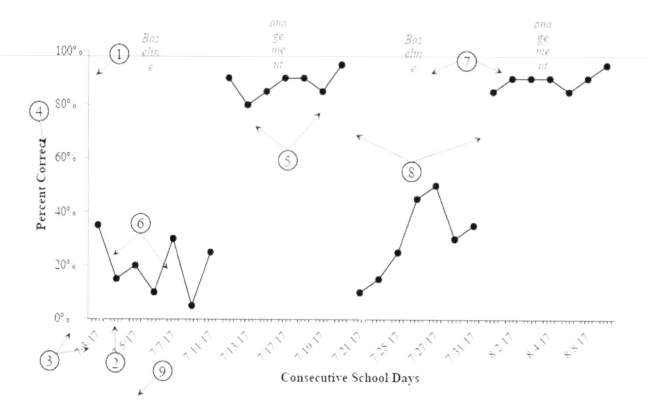

**Figure 5.1.  J.W.'s percent of time in his chair during baseline and self-management conditions.**

## COMPONENTS OF A LINE GRAPH:
1. Vertical Axis, Ordinate Or Y-Axis
2. Horizontal Axis, Abscissa Or X-Axis
3. Axis Labels
4. Axis Title
5. Data Points
6. Data Paths
7. Phase Change Labels Or Condition Change Labels
8. Phase Change Lines Or Condition Change Lines And
9. Figure Caption.

Visual analysis of graphed data is a hallmark of behavior analytic science and practice. Therefore, it is critical that behavior analysts know how to create their own graphs so they are able to evaluate changes in the dimensions of the target behaviors being measured and intervened on. The purpose of this chapter is to provide a task analysis for creating single-case graphs in Microsoft Excel® 2016 for Mac and Microsoft Excel® 2015 for PC.

## ▶▶ *Graphing Steps*

The steps involved in creating and working with these graphs are as follows.

### 1. ENTER THE RAW DATA INTO THE SPREADSHEET

*Graphs are based on the raw data entered into an Excel spreadsheet. When the raw data are changed, the graph automatically updates as long as the data remain part of the highlighted range included in the graph.*

    a. OPEN Microsoft Excel® 2016 for Mac or Microsoft Excel® 2015 for PC.

    b. Starting in cell A1, ADD the raw data from Figure 5.2 into the spreadsheet.

| Date | Percent Correct | Prompt Strength | Baseline | Least-to-Most Prompting |
|------|------|------|------|------|
| 7/3/17 | 0% | 5.0 | 1 | |
| 7/4/17 | 0% | 4.0 | | |
| 7/5/17 | 5% | 4.0 | | |
| 7/6/17 | 15% | 4.5 | | |
| 7/7/17 | 5% | 4.5 | | |
| 7/10/17 | 10% | 4.0 | | |
| 7/11/17 | 5% | 4.5 | | |
| 7/12/17 | 90% | 0.5 | | 1 |
| 7/13/17 | 80% | 1.0 | | |
| 7/14/17 | 85% | 1.0 | | |
| 7/17/17 | 90% | 0.5 | | |
| 7/18/17 | 90% | 0.5 | | |
| 7/19/17 | 85% | 1.0 | | |
| 7/20/17 | 95% | 0.5 | | |
| 7/21/17 | 10% | 4.5 | 1 | |
| 7/24/17 | 15% | 4.5 | | |
| 7/25/17 | 25% | 4.0 | | |
| 7/26/17 | 20% | 3.5 | | |
| 7/27/17 | 15% | 4.0 | | |
| 7/28/17 | 10% | 4.5 | | |
| 7/31/17 | 10% | 4.5 | | |
| 8/1/17 | 85% | 1.0 | | 1 |
| 8/2/17 | 90% | 0.5 | | |
| 8/3/17 | 80% | 1.0 | | |
| 8/4/17 | 90% | 0.5 | | |
| 8/7/17 | 90% | 0.0 | | |
| 8/8/17 | 100% | 0.0 | | |
| 8/9/17 | 95% | 0.5 | | |

**Figure 5.2. Sample withdrawal design data series.**

## 2. SET COLUMN VALUE TYPES

*Setting column value types in advance ensures consistent formatting for your graphs.*

    a. CLICK on the "A" column label to highlight the entire column.

    b. Under the *Home* tab, CLICK on the dropdown box in the top menu bar with the text, General.

    c. CLICK the on the *Short Date* option.

    d. CLICK on the "B" column label to highlight the entire column.

    e. Under the *Home* tab, CLICK on the dropdown box in the top menu bar with the text, *General.*

    f. CLICK the on the Percentage option.

    g. CLICK twice on the Decrease Decimal button located in the center of the top menu bar under the Home tab to remove the decimal places on the percentage values. To identify icon buttons without text, HOVER the mouse over the button and WAIT 1-2 seconds for the button label to appear.

    h. CLICK on the "C" column label to highlight the entire column.

    i. Under the Home tab, CLICK on the dropdown box in the top menu bar with the text, General.

    j. CLICK the on the Number option.

    k. CLICK once on the decrease decimal button located in the center of the top menu bar under the Home tab to set the decimal place value to tenths.

## 3. INSERT THE GRAPH

## 4. ASSIGN DATA SERIES TO THE SECONDARY Y-AXIS

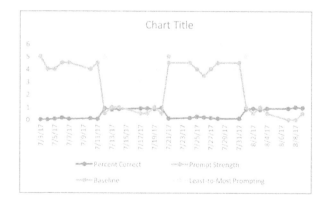

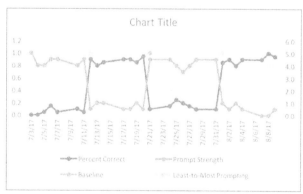

CHAPTER 5

## 5. FORMAT THE PRIMARY Y-AXIS

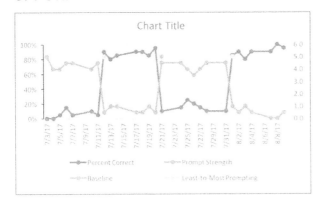

## 8. ADD AND MODIFY THE AXIS LABELS

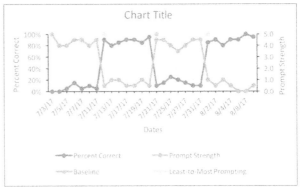

## 6. FORMAT THE SECONDARY Y-AXIS

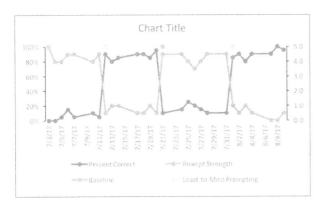

## 9. MODIFY THE CHART TITLE

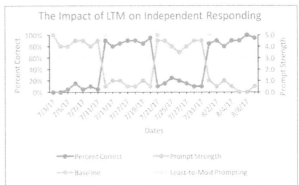

## 7. FORMAT THE X-AXIS

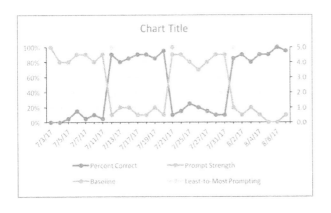

## 10. REMOVE THE GRIDLINES

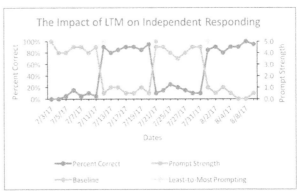

*Figure 5.3. Creating a withdrawal design graph in Microsoft Excel® (steps 3-10).*

## 11. INSERT THE GRAPH

**Figure 5.3 shows the updated graph when completing steps 3-10**

*The instructions below describe the steps for creating the initial graph.*

    a. To highlight the data, CLICK and HOLD the mouse button starting in cell A1 and moving the mouse down to E29.

    b. CLICK on the Insert tab in the top menu bar.

    c. CLICK on the Line button in Excel 2016 for Mac or CLICK on the Insert Line Chart button in Excel 2015 for PC. To identify icon buttons without text, HOVER the mouse over the button and WAIT 1-2 seconds for the button label to appear.

    d. CLICK on the Line with Markers option.

## 12. ASSIGN THE DATA SERIES TO THE SECONDARY Y-AXIS

*Use the steps below to assign the phase change line data series to the secondary y-axis OR to assign another data to the secondary axis.*

    a. RIGHT CLICK anywhere on the Prompt Strength data series in the graph and CLICK the Format Data Series... option.

    b. CLICK on the Series Options column graph icon located at the top of the sidebar.

    c. Under the Series Options settings, CLICK on the Secondary axis text to select the corresponding radio button.

    d. REPEAT these steps for the Baseline and Least-to-Most Prompting data series.

## 13. FORMAT THE PRIMARY Y-AXIS

*The instructions below describe the steps for formatting the primary y-axis line, tick marks, and values. In Excel, y-axis values automatically update unless specifically changed.*

    a. RIGHT CLICK on the primary y-axis and CLICK on the Format Axis... option.

    b. CLICK on the Axis Options column graph icon located at the top of the sidebar.

    c. Under the Axis Options settings, CHANGE the maximum Bounds value to 1 (i.e., 100%).

    d. Under the Tick Marks settings, CHANGE the Major type value to Outside and the Minor type value to None using the dropdown boxes.

    e. Under the Number settings, CHANGE the category to Percentage and the Decimal places to 0.

    f. CLICK on the Fill & Line paint bucket icon located at the top of the sidebar.

    g. Under the Line settings, CLICK on the Solid line text to select the corresponding radio button and CHANGE the color to black.

## 14. FORMAT THE SECONDARY Y-AXIS

*The instructions below describe the steps for formatting the secondary y-axis line, tick marks, and values.*

    a.  RIGHT CLICK on the secondary y-axis and CLICK on the Format Axis... option.

    b.  CLICK on the Axis Options column graph icon located at the top of the sidebar.

    c.  Under the Axis Options settings, CHANGE the maximum Bounds value to 5.

    d.  Under the Tick Marks settings, CHANGE the Major type value to Outside and the Minor type value to None using the dropdown boxes.

    e.  Under the Number settings, CHANGE the category to Number and the Decimal places to 1.

    f.  CLICK on the Fill & Line paint bucket icon located at the top of the sidebar.

    g.  Under the Line settings, CLICK on the Solid line text to select the corresponding radio button and CHANGE the color to black.

## 15. FORMAT THE X-AXIS

*The instructions below describe the steps for formatting the x-axis line, tick marks, and values.*

    a.  RIGHT CLICK on the x-axis and CLICK on the Format Axis ... option.

    b.  CLICK on the Axis Options column graph icon located at the top of the sidebar.

    c.  Under the Axis Options settings, CLICK the Text axis text to select the corresponding radio button.

    d.  Under the Tick Marks settings, CHANGE the Major type value to None and the Minor type value to Outside using the dropdown boxes to place the tick marks above the x-axis labels.

    e.  CLICK on the Fill & Line paint bucket icon located at the top of the sidebar.

    f.  Under the Line settings, CLICK on the Solid line text to select the corresponding radio button and CHANGE the color to black.

## 16. ADD AND MODIFY AXIS LABELS

*The instructions below describe the steps for adding and formatting labels for the y-axes and x-axis of the graph.*

    a.  With the graph highlighted, CLICK the Chart Design tab in Excel 2016 for Mac or the Design tab in Excel 2015 for PC.

    b.  CLICK on the Add Chart Element dropdown button.

    c.  HOVER the mouse over Axis Titles and CLICK on the Primary Vertical option.

    d.  DOUBLE CLICK inside the y-axis label to CHANGE the text to Percent Correct.

    e.  With the graph highlighted, CLICK the Chart Design tab in Excel 2016 for Mac or the Design tab in Excel 2015 for PC.

    f.  CLICK on the Add Chart Element dropdown button.

    g.  HOVER the mouse over Axis Titles and CLICK on the Secondary Vertical option.

h. DOUBLE CLICK inside the y-axis label to CHANGE the text to Prompt Strength.
i. With the graph highlighted, CLICK the Chart Design tab in Excel 2016 for Mac or the Design tab in Excel 2015 for PC.
j. CLICK on the Add Chart Element dropdown button.
k. HOVER the mouse over Axis Titles and CLICK on the Primary Horizontal option.
l. DOUBLE CLICK inside the y-axis label to CHANGE the text to Dates.

## 16. MODIFY THE CHART TITLE

*The instructions below describe the steps for formatting the chart title. Alternatively, the chart title can be deleted by clicking on the chart title label and pressing the delete key. This may be preferable if a figure caption will be included later.*

a. DOUBLE CLICK twice to get inside the chart title label.
b. CHANGE the chart title text to The Impact of LTM on Independent Responding.

## 17. REMOVE THE GRID LINES

*Grid lines are often distracting when included on a line graph and need to be removed.*

a. CLICK on any of the grid lines in the graph to highlight all of the gridlines.
b. PRESS the delete key to remove the gridlines.

## 18. MODIFY THE LEGEND

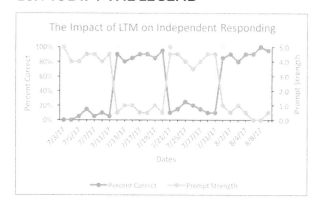

## 19. FORMAT THE DATA SERIES

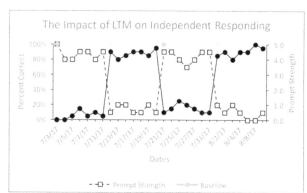

## 20. ADJUST THE BORDER AND RATIO OF THE GRAPH

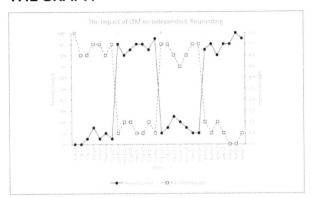

## 22. INSERT PHASE CHANGE LINES

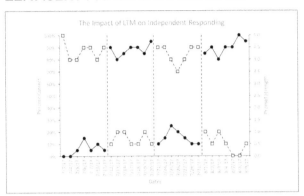

## 21. SEPARATE THE CONDITIONS

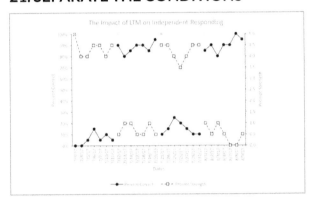

## 23. ADD PHASE CHANGE LINES

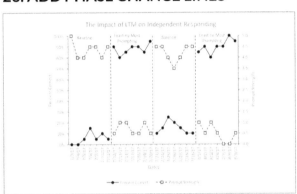

*Figure 5.4. Creating a withdrawal design graph in Microsoft Excel® (steps 11-16).*

## 24. MODIFY THE LEGEND

**Figure 5.4 shows the updated graph when completing steps 11-16**

*If a legend is used and the graph contains phase changes lines or criteria change lines, use the steps below to remove phase change line and criteria change line data series from the graph's legend.*

a. CLICK once on the legend to highlight it.

b. With the legend highlighted, CLICK once more on the Baseline data series label to highlight only that item.

c. PRESS the delete key to remove only the Baseline data series label from the legend.

d. REPEAT these steps with the Least-to-Most Prompting data series label.

## 25. FORMAT THE DATA SERIES

*Modifying the data series makes visual analysis easier. If a graph will be displayed on a printed page, it is recommended that all data are plotted in black and white with different combinations of closed (black filled data points) and open (white filled data points with black borders) data points with solid and dashed data paths.*

a.  RIGHT CLICK on the Percent Correct data series and CLICK the Format Data Series ... option.
b.  CLICK on the Fill & Line paint bucket icon located at the top of the sidebar.
c.  Under the Line settings, CLICK on the Solid line text to select the corresponding radio button and CHANGE the color to black.
a.  Under the Line settings, CHANGE the line Width value to 1 pt.
b.  CLICK on the Marker button located near the top of the sidebar.
d.  Under the Marker Options settings, CLICK Built-In and select the circle marker type and set its size to 5 pt.
e.  Under the marker Fill settings, CLICK the Solid fill text to select the corresponding radio button and CHANGE the color to black.
f.  Under the marker Border settings, CLICK on the Solid line text to select the corresponding radio button and CHANGE the color to black and the width to 1 pt.
g.  RIGHT CLICK on the Prompt Strength data series and CLICK the Format Data Series ... option.
h.  CLICK on the Fill & Line paint bucket icon located at the top of the sidebar.
i.  Under the Line settings, CLICK on the Solid line text to select the corresponding radio button and CHANGE the color to black.
j.  Under the Line settings, CHANGE the line Width value to 1 pt.
k.  Under the Line settings, CHANGE the Dash type to Dash.
l.  CLICK on the Marker button located near the top of the sidebar.
m. Under the Marker Options settings, CLICK Built-in and select the square marker type and set its size to 5 pt.
n.  Under the marker Fill settings, CLICK the Solid fill text to select the corresponding radio button and CHANGE the color to white.
o.  Under the marker Border settings, CLICK on the Solid line text to select the corresponding radio button and CHANGE the color to black and the width to 1 pt.

## 26. ADJUST THE BORDER AND RATIO OF THE GRAPH

*The instructions below describe the steps for removing the graph border and resizing the graph. When the graph size is changed, it automatically re-sizes the plot area. A ratio of 5:8 between the y-axis and x-axis is recommended for single-case research design graphs (Johnston & Pennypacker, 1980; Tufte, 1983). In Excel 2016 for Mac, dimensions are shown on the screen as the plot area size is changed. In Excel 2015 for PC, the dimensions are not shown but may be checked by viewing the dimensions of a square shape drawn directly over the plot area. Once the square is used to determine the size, it can be deleted by clicking on it once and pressing the delete key.*

    a. CLICK on the outside border of the graph.
    b. CLICK on the Format tab in the top menu.
    c. CLICK the small down arrow to the right of the Shape Outline button.
    d. CLICK on the No Outline option.
    e. CHANGE the Height value to 4.86" and the Width value to 6.31" to adjust the size of the graph.
    f. CLICK the checkbox located between and to the right of the height and width options to lock the aspect ratio of the graph.
    g. CLICK on the plot area of the graph.
    h. If necessary, use the mouse to CHANGE height and width of the plot area by dragging on the borders until the height equals 3" and the width equals 4.8" (i.e., 5:8 ratio).

## 27. SEPARATE THE CONDITIONS

*On a line graph, the data series must never cross phase change lines. Use the instructions below to eliminate the data paths crossing the phase change lines.*

    a. CLICK once on the Percent Correct data series being plotted on the graph to highlight all of the data points.
    b. CLICK once on the Percent Correct data point found at 7/12/17.
    c. RIGHT CLICK on the same data point again and CLICK the Format Data Point … option.
    d. CLICK on the paintbrush icon in the Format Data Point sidebar.
    e. CLICK on the No line text to select the corresponding radio button.
    f. With the Format Data Point sidebar still open, CLICK on the Percent Correct data point found at 7/21/17 and CLICK the No Line text to select the corresponding radio button.
    g. With the Format Data Point sidebar still open, CLICK on the Percent Correct data point found at 8/1/17 and CLICK the No Line text to select the corresponding radio button.
    h. REPEAT these steps for Prompt Strength data series.

## 28. INSERT PHASE CHANGE LINES

*Phase change lines originally included on the graph show up as data points. The steps below describe how to convert these data points into phase change lines using shadows from error bars. For an alternative version for entering phase change lines, readers may consult Dubuque (2015) or Deochand (2017).*

a. CLICK on one of the Baseline data points to highlight the series.

b. With the Baseline data points highlighted, CLICK the Chart Design tab in Excel 2016 for Mac or the Design tab in Excel 2015 for PC in the top menu bar.

c. CLICK the Change Chart Type button.

d. In Excel 2016 for Mac, HOVER the mouse over the Column label and CLICK the Clustered Column option. In Excel 2015 for PC, CLICK the Combo Button and CHANGE the Baseline chart type to Clustered Column.

e. CLICK on one of the Baseline data points to highlight the series.

f. In the top menu bar, CLICK the Chart Design tab in Excel 2016 for Mac or the Design tab in Excel 2015 for PC.

g. CLICK on the Add Chart Element button in the top menu bar.

h. HOVER the mouse over the Error Bars label and CLICK the More Error Bar Options…option.

i. In the Format Error Bars sidebar, CLICK the Error Bar Options column graph icon.

j. Under the Direction settings, CLICK the Minus text to select the corresponding radio button.

k. Under the End Style settings, CLICK the No cap text to select the corresponding radio button.

l. Under the Error Amount settings, CLICK the Percentage text to select the corresponding radio button and set the value to 100%.

m. CLICK the Effects pentagon icon located toward the top of the sidebar.

n. Under the Shadow settings, CHANGE Transparency to 0%, Size to 100%, Blur to 0 pt, Angle to 180°, and the distance to 6 pt. The distance value of the shadow will depend upon the size of the graph. The distance value used should position the phase change line between two data points and hide the initial phase change line (for the first data point in the graph) behind the y-axis. This value may need to be updated if the graph is resized.

o. CLICK on the Fill & Line paint bucket icon located near the top of the sidebar.

p. Under the Line settings, CHANGE Color to white.

q. Under the Line settings, CHANGE the width to 1 pt.

r. Under the Line settings, CHANGE Dash type to Dashed.

s. RIGHT CLICK on one of the Baseline columns and CLICK the Format Data Series… option.

t. CLICK on the Fill & Line paint bucket icon located near the top of the sidebar.

u. Under the Fill settings, CLICK the No fill text to select the corresponding radio button.

v. Under the Border settings, CLICK the No line text to select the corresponding radio button.

w. REPEAT these steps for every different phase to be included in the graph.

## 29. ADD PHASE CHANGE LABELS

*The instructions below describe the steps for adding phase change labels to a graph.*

e. CLICK on the Baseline data series. Be sure to click on data series and not the error bar. The data series can be found by hovering the mouse over the appropriate location until a label appears.

f. In the top menu bar, CLICK the Chart Design tab in Excel 2016 for Mac or the Design tab in Excel 2015 for PC.

g. CLICK on the Add Chart Element button in the top menu bar.

h. HOVER the mouse over the Data Labels option and CLICK the More Data Label Options... option.

i. In the Format Data Labels sidebar, CLICK the Label Options column graph icon.

j. Under the Label Options settings, CHECK the Series name checkbox and uncheck all of the other boxes.

k. In the graph, MOVE one of the phase change data labels to the right of the phase change line.

l. RIGHT CLICK on the data label that was just moved and CLICK on the Format Data Label... option.

m. In the Format Data Labels sidebar, CLICK the Clone Current Label button under the Data Label Series header. This step is only necessary if the phase change line is used more than once.

n. REPEAT the steps in this series with the functional communication training data series.

## 30. EXPORT THE GRAPH INTO MICROSOFT WORD®
## OR MICROSOFT POWERPOINT®.

*The instructions below describe the steps for copying and pasting a graph from Microsoft Excel® into Microsoft Word® or Microsoft PowerPoint®.*

  a. OPEN up a Microsoft Word® document or Microsoft PowerPoint® presentation.
  b. In Excel, RIGHT CLICK on the border of the graph and CLICK Copy.
  c. In Microsoft Word® or PowerPoint®, RIGHT CLICK within the document or presentation and CLICK the Paste option. To preserve the aspect ratio, do not paste the graph into a textbox in Microsoft PowerPoint®.

## 31. ADD NEW DATA TO THE GRAPH (OPTIONAL)

*The instructions below describe the steps for including new data into a graph.*

  a. Add new data in the next row under the original data set.  For example, to add new data to the sample data set included in this chapter, start by entering a new date in cell A30, a new percent correct value in cell B30, and a new prompt strength value in cell C30.
  b. CLICK on the plot area of the graph to highlight the data set.
  c. HOVER the mouse over the bottom right corner of the highlighted data set until the mouse cursor changes into an open square with two diagonal arrow heads in Microsoft Excel 2016 for Mac, or a line with two arrow heads in Microsoft Excel 2015 for PC.
  d. CLICK and DRAG the highlighted box over the new data to update the graph.

## 32. SAVE THE GRAPH AS A TEMPLATE FOR FUTURE USE

*The instructions below describe the steps for saving a graph as a template so it can be used with future data sets.*

  a. RIGHT CLICK in the plot area of the graph and CLICK the Save as Template… option.
  b. TYPE in a name for the template and CLICK the Save button. When naming the template, the file type (i.e., .crtx) must be included at the end.

## 33. APPLY THE SAVED TEMPLATE TO A NEW DATA SET.

*The instructions below describe the steps for using a saved template on a new data set.*

    a. In the spreadsheet, HIGHLIGHT the cells that contain the data to be graphed.

    b. CLICK the Insert tab in the top menu bar.

    c. In Microsoft Excel 2016 for Mac, CLICK the Insert Area, Stock, Surface, or Radar Chart icon button. HOVER the mouse over the Templates label and CLICK the name of the saved template. In Microsoft Excel 2015 for PC, CLICK the arrow box in the bottom right hand corner of the Charts options. In the dialog box that appears, CLICK the All Charts tab. CLICK on the templates folder icon. CLICK on the name of the saved template. To identify icon buttons without text, HOVER the mouse over the button and WAIT 1-2 seconds for the button label to appear.

 ## *Summary*

The purpose of this chapter was to provide a task analysis demonstrating basic graphing fundamentals in Microsoft Excel. While this chapter did not review graphing conventions for other experimental designs (changing criterion, alternating treatments design, etc.), many of the steps listed can easily be adapted to fit a variety of graphing needs.

The task analysis provided only reviews the steps involved in generating line graphs for Microsoft Excel 2016 for Mac and Microsoft Excel 2015 for PC. While many of the steps listed are the same across previous versions of Excel, enough of a difference exists to recommend readers consult earlier published works when using older versions of the software (see Carr & Burkholder, 1998; Dixon et al., 2009; Pritchard, 2009; Vanselow & Bourrett, 2012).

Microsoft Excel offers a powerful suite of tools for creating line graphs. The software is flexible enough to accommodate just about any data set for the user willing to explore and experiment with these tools. This chapter is intended to describe some of the basics which a reader can build upon with time and to provide users with examples to follow as they learn to use the program to create graphs to help with the analysis of their data.

# *References*

Carr, J. E., & Burkholder, E. O. (1998). Creating single-subject design graphs with Microsoft Excel™. *Journal of Applied Behavior Analysis*, 31, 245-251.

Deochand, N. (2017). Automating phase change lines and their labels using Microsoft Excel®. *Behavior Analysis in Practice*, Advance online publication. doi:10.1007/s40617-016-0169-1

Dixon, M. R., Jackson, J. W., Small, S. L., Horner-King, M. J., Mui Ker Lik, N., Garcia, Y., Rosales, R. (2009). Creating single-subject design graphs in Microsoft Excel™ 2007. *Journal of Applied Behavior Analysis*, 42, 277-293.

Dubuque, E. M. (2015). Inserting phase change lines into Microsoft Excel® graphs. *Behavior Analysis in Practice*, 8, 207-211.

Johnston, J. M., & Pennypacker, H. S. (1980). *Strategies and tactics of behavioral research, third edition*. Hillsdale, NJ: Lawrence Erlbaum.

Pritchard, J. (2009). A decade later: Creating single-subject design graphs with Microsoft Excel 2007™. *The Behavior Analyst Today*, 9, 153-161.

Vanselow, N. R. & Bourrett, J. C. (2012). Online interactive tutorials for creating graphs with Excel 2007 or 2010. *Behavior Analysis in Practice*, 5, 40-46.

Tufte, E. R. (1983). *The visual display of quantitative information*. Cheshire, CT: Graphics Press.

# PRACTICAL FUNCTIONAL (BEHAVIOR)
# ASSESSMENT OF PROBLEM BEHAVIOR

*Gregory P. Hanley & Jessica D. Slaton*

## KEY TERMS:

- Functional assessment
- Functional analysis
- Functional relation
- Interview-informed synthesized contingency analysis (IISCA)

- Ecologically relevant
- Functional communication training (FCT)
- Functional communication response (FCR)

The Centers for Disease Control (CDC) reports that approximately 1 in 68 children are diagnosed with autism (Christensen et al., 2016). In addition to challenges in the development of communication and social skills (which are core symptoms of autism), many children with autism also engage in problem behavior. *Problem behavior* refers to actions such as aggression, self-injurious behavior (SIB), property destruction, tantrums, or other behaviors that can be dangerous or disruptive. Problem behavior is not a core symptom of autism, but as many as one third to one half of children with autism are estimated to engage in problem behavior (Dominick et al., 2007; Hartley, Sikora, & McCoy, 2008).

## ▶▶ *The Issue with Problem Behavior*

Chronic problem behavior often leads to a highly restricted lifestyle: The person with the problem behavior and his caregivers may experience frequent and severe injuries, and he may be unable to participate in family, community, or educational activities. Some types of severe problem behavior (e.g., head banging) carry the risk of permanent injury. In other words, problem behavior is a common and serious issue. Further, children with autism who engage in problem behavior tend to become adults with autism who engage in problem behavior—meaning that we must not expect that a child will "grow out of" the behavior. Therefore, problem behavior should be actively addressed.

# ▶▶ *Functional Assessment*

The first step in treating problem behavior is understanding it: Why is the behavior occurring? What situations seem to "trigger" (evoke) it? What is the person accomplishing with the behavior (i.e., what are the reinforcers for the behavior)? The process by which we try to answer to these questions and discover the reinforcers for problem behavior is known as *functional assessment*. The functional assessment (i.e., functional behavior assessment) process is a critical prerequisite to developing an effective treatment.

Imagine if a medical doctor attempted to treat a patient with a sore throat without knowing whether the sore throat was caused by a cold, seasonal allergies or another condition. Each of these diagnoses requires a very different treatment. Giving allergy medicine to someone with strep throat will do nothing for them except prolong their pain and delay their access to appropriate, effective treatment.

The same logic applies to problem behavior. We cannot design an effective treatment without knowing the reason why the behavior is occurring. If problem behavior is occurring with any regularity, it must be reinforced in some way at least some of the time. If we can discover what those reinforcers are, we can use that information to design a treatment that teaches the person a better, safer way to get those same reinforcers.

The functional assessment process involves interviewing parents or other adults who are familiar with the individual's problem behavior, developing a hypothesis of why the problem behavior is occurring (based on details learned through interviewing), and then designing and conducting individualized conditions to test that hypothesis.

The testing part of the functional assessment process is known as a *functional analysis* (FA), in which we directly manipulate antecedents and consequences during brief sessions to demonstrate a functional relation between problem behavior and environmental events. A *functional relation* means that problem behavior happens *when and only* when a certain contingency is in place. For example, we may learn that problem behavior occurs when an individual is being ignored and receives attention following the problem behavior—never when the individual already has access to undivided attention—and these differences are repeatedly observed in our analysis. In this case, we would say there is a functional relation between problem behavior and attention.

An FA involves purposely arranging one or more test conditions that may evoke problem behavior, and then purposely providing reinforcement following problem behavior. If we observe that problem behavior reliably occurs during a test condition (compared to a control condition), we can be confident that we have identified reinforcers for that behavior. While information gathered from the parent/adult interview and other sources can help us identify some possible reasons why the behavior is occurring, the FA is necessary to confirm our suspicions. In the sore throat analogy we introduced above, think of the functional assessment process as the entire visit to the doctor's office, including describing your symptoms to the doctor, answering her questions, and discussing which tests might be appropriate; then think of functional analysis as the actual strep test.

## ▶▶ *A Brief History of Functional Analysis*

Behavior analysts have been conducting FAs and refining their methods for many decades. The earliest example of an FA was reported by Lovaas, Freitag, Gold, and Kassorla (1965). These authors demonstrated that the SIB of a child with schizophrenia was maintained by attention — in other words, the child engaged in SIB because this behavior reliably got the attention of adults. Similarly, Sailor, Guess, Rutherford, and Baer (1968) demonstrated that the tantrum behavior of a young girl with developmental disabilities was maintained by escape from a difficult task to an easier task.

In 1982, Iwata, Dorsey, Slifer, Bauman, and Richman published a seminal article that codified FA procedures into a comprehensive package that became the model for the majority of FAs published over the last 30 years. These authors reported FAs for nine individuals who engaged in SIB. In separate test conditions, they evaluated three possible reinforcers for SIB: positive reinforcement in the form of attention, negative reinforcement in the form of escape from demands, and automatic reinforcement (i.e., reinforcement naturally produced by engaging in the behavior, such as the sensation produced by striking one's hand against one's head).

Iwata et al.'s writings (1982/1994) marked a turning point in the assessment and treatment of problem behavior. The value of understanding problem behavior before attempting to treat it was emphasized. Prescribing treatment without first taking the time to understand the nature of the problem has since proven to be a less effective and somewhat dehumanizing way to help people who engage in problem behavior. The procedures championed by these authors brought both dignity and scientific rigor to the treatment of a vulnerable population unable to self-advocate. Second, Iwata et al. demonstrated with multiple participants that problem behavior is sensitive to environmental consequences and, therefore, is probably learned through ordinary interactions in the environment. This understanding provided the hope that severe problem behavior could be treated by adjusting the environmental consequences for the behavior.

Before the advent of functional analysis, people attempted to treat problem behavior with arbitrary punishers or reinforcers that often had little to do with the function of the behavior in question. This would be akin, perhaps, to the doctor prescribing a powerful painkiller for a sore throat, regardless of what illness the patient has and what treatment the patient needs. A painkiller may produce some improvement in the symptoms (by masking them), but it usually not solve the problem. That is, the symptoms are likely return as soon as the patient stops taking the painkiller. Similarly, using powerful punishers or arbitrary reinforcers (e.g., candy and privileges) without understanding why a behavior is occurring may produce desirable changes initially, but because skills that function similar to problem behavior are not taught, problem behavior is likely to return as soon as the arbitrary intervention is absent or discontinued. In short, functional analysis brought the treatment of problem behavior out of the realm of behavior modification (changing behavior without first understanding it) and into behavior analysis (understanding behavior prior to attempting to change it).

## ▶▶ *A Practical Model of Functional Assessment*

We have learned a great deal since 1982. The model described by Iwata et al. (1982/1994) provided a foundation upon which other researchers have built an evolving FA technology that is powerful, flexible, and adaptable to a wide range of needs. Like a stone tossed into a deep lake, Iwata et al. created ripples that are still moving outward almost 40 years later as our understanding of problem behavior and FA methods continues to grow. There are over 1,000 published examples of FAs (Beavers & Iwata, 2013; Hanley, Iwata, & McCord, 2003). Useful variations to experimental designs (cf., Bloom, Iwata, Fritz, Roscoe, & Carreau, 2011), measurement (e.g., latency instead of rate; Thomason-Sassi, Iwata, Neidert, & Roscoe, 2011), and overall analysis duration (cf., Wallace & Iwata, 1999; Northup et al., 1991) have been described. Table 5.1 presents a summary of some important things learned over the previous decades that can inform the use of FAs in practice and make these procedures viable in schools, homes, and other natural settings. These discoveries all grew from the groundwork laid by Lovaas et al. (1965), Sailor et al. (1968), Iwata et al. (1982/1994), and other early pioneers of functional analysis (e.g., Carr & Durand, 1985); they are the giants on whose shoulders behavior analytic practitioners currently stand.

# Table 6.1
*Ten Important Discoveries since Iwata et al. (1982/1994)*

| DISCOVERY | NEGATIVE REINFORCEMENT |
|---|---|
| 1. We cannot not rely on descriptive assessments (e.g., ABC data, checklists) to identify the reinforcers for problem behavior. | Reference by First Author (Year)<br>St. Peter (2005); Thompson (2007); Iwata (2013) |
| 2. Treatment based on an FA is more likely to be effective and less likely to rely on punishment than treatment that is not based on an FA. | Pelios (1999); Kahng (2002); Campbell (2003 |
| 3. FAs can yield useful information with short session durations (5 min), and sometimes even within one session. | Wallace (1999); Jessel (2016) |
| 4. Precursors to problem behavior likely serve the same function as the problem behavior. | Smith (2002); Borrero (2008); Herscovitch (2009) |
| 5. FAs with generic and isolated reinforcers are undifferentiated (i.e., are not useful) on the first attempt about 50% of the time. | Hagopian (2013); Slaton (2017); Lambert (2017 |
| 6. Problem behavior can be maintained by idiosyncratic reinforcers that do not easily fit in a generic category. | Bowman (1997); Fisher (1998); Adelinis (1999); Schlichenmeyer (2013) |
| 7. Problem behavior can be maintained exclusively by the interaction between several reinforcers. | Mann (2009); Sarno (2011); Hanley (2014); Santiago (2016); Slaton (2017) |
| 8. FAs can be successfully individualized based on information gathered from an open-ended interview. | Hanley (2014); Ghaemmaghami (2015); Santiago (2016); Jessel (2016); Slaton (2017); Jessel (2018 |
| 9. FAs designed from open-ended interviews have produced effective treatments. | Hanley (2014); Santiago (2016); Ghaemmaghami (2016); Slaton (2017); Jessel (2018) |
| 10. Many practitioners do not conduct FAs because they report FAs are too difficult, dangerous, and/or time-consuming | Ellingson (1999); Oliver (2015); Roscoe (2015) |

These 10 points combined strongly suggest the importance of an FA model that is less time-consuming and more effective (i.e., one that practitioners will use). We know that treatment designed from an FA is more likely to be effective, and that descriptive assessments, due to their correlational nature, are not likely to correctly identify the reinforcers for problem behavior. Given that FAs with multiple test conditions and generic, isolated reinforcers may only yield useful information on the first attempt about half of the time, a current alternative is to use open-ended interviews to design FAs with single test conditions that incorporate personalized reinforcers (i.e., reinforcers unique to the individual) and that emulate interactions as they occur in the individual's natural environment. By using short session durations (e.g., 2 to 5 minutes) and including precursor responses (e.g., verbal statements prior to physical aggression) in the FA, we can address concerns reported by practitioners who believe FAs may be too time-consuming or may produce levels of problem behavior that are potentially harmful. In summary, the 10 discoveries can be distilled into a practical model of functional assessment that is safe, effective, efficient, and capable of being conducted in natural settings.

We call the FA associated with this practical functional assessment format an *interview-informed synthesized contingency analysis* (IISCA). It is *interview-informed* because we use an open-ended interview to gather details that inform the design of the analysis; it is a *synthesized contingency* because we combine antecedent variables and multiple reinforcers into one contingency if they are reported to occur together; it is an *analysis* because we demonstrate a functional relation between a problem behavior and its reinforcers by alternating between a test and control condition.

The remainder of this chapter describes the steps for implementing this process and provides some answers to common questions or concerns that may arise about FAs in general. Examples of this functional assessment model and the treatments derived from the process may be found in Hanley, Jin, Vanselow, and Hanratty (2014), Jessel, Ingvarsson, Metras, Kirk, and Whipple (2018), and Santiago, Hanley, Jin, and Moore (2016). Tutorials and related materials may be accessed at this website: www.practicalfunctionalassessment.com

# Open-Ended Interview

The practical functional assessment process begins with an open-ended interview (Hanley 2012) to gather the information necessary to design individualized test and control conditions. The test condition will include a three-term contingency, each part of which is carefully planned based on qualitative details gathered in the interview: (a) some establishing operation (EO) that evokes problem behavior will be presented; (b) some type of problem behavior will occur; (c) some type of reinforcement will be delivered following problem behavior.

**Discovering EOs**. By asking questions about the situations in which the behavior is likely to occur and what seems to "trigger" it, we acquire information about the EOs relevant to the problem behavior. For example, if a parent reports that tantrums seem to happen while dinner is being prepared in which the parent tells the child to go play alone for a bit while dinner is being prepared, we could infer that perhaps the child's problem behavior is evoked by the cue to go play alone and the lack of parental attention. Support for the hypothesis that periods of time without parental attention may evoke problem behavior may come from additional reports that problem behavior is likely when the parent attempts to speak with other adults or puts the child to bed for the night. This information tells us what situations may be arranged to evoke problem behavior in the test condition.

**Discovering target responses.** By asking questions about which problem behaviors the child engages in—whether they seem to occur together as a cluster, whether they occur in a sequence, and whether there is a reliable "buildup" to problem behavior (i.e., whether there are precursors)—we can clearly identify which behaviors to include in the FA and create an operational definition for them. For example, a parent might report that a child typically crosses his arms and stomps his foot (precursor) immediately prior to more severe behavior of dropping to the floor and engaging in SIB in the forms of head banging and face slapping. This information is critical because it conveys which behaviors to reinforce during the test condition. Gathering information about precursors and non-dangerous behaviors that occur in the same situations as dangerous forms of behavior is of particular importance because if precursors and associated non-dangerous behaviors are reinforced during the test condition, it is unlikely that the individual will escalate to more dangerous problem behavior.

**Discovering reinforcers.** By asking questions about how people tend to calm the individual when problem behavior occurs and what events tend to follow the behavior, we can learn information about what reinforcers may be maintaining problem behavior. In the example above, if the parents reported that they respond to tantrums by leaving the meal preparation in the kitchen, going to comfort the child in the den, and then distracting the child with preferred toys and videos until she is calm, we may infer that perhaps the reinforcers for tantrum behavior are attention from parents and access to preferred toys and videos.

We can also gather important information about possible reinforcers by asking questions about situations in which the problem behavior *never* occurs. For instance, additional support that attention from parents and access to preferred toys are likely the reinforcers for problem behavior may be provided by parents reporting that they are confident their child will be completely calm when they play together with her favorite toys or while watching her favorite videos together. This information also helps us design our control condition.

An example of open-ended interview questions may be found in the appendix of Hanley (2012); various formats and translations of the interview may also be obtained at www. practicalfunctionalassessment.com. This interview is not a script; it is a guide. The questions need not be presented in order, questions may be omitted if deemed irrelevant based on earlier responses, and other clarifying questions not included in this interview may be asked if the need arises. A key feature of good clinical interviewing is responding thoughtfully and flexibly to information as it is shared. It is important to remember that the information gathered during the interview acts as a signpost pointing the way toward *potential* EOs and reinforcers for problem behavior. We must follow up by conducting an IISCA to directly evaluate whether we have identified a functional contingency.

# Design And Conduct The IISCA

An FA consists (at a minimum) of a test and a control condition. Many examples of published FAs include multiple test conditions that each evaluate a different reinforcer (e.g., an attention condition, an escape condition, a tangible condition). However, when an open-ended interview suggests that the individual usually experiences multiple reinforcers at once, these suspected reinforcers can be combined into a single test condition.

In the example of the tantrums during dinner preparation, there is no need to create one test condition to evaluate attention from parents and a second, separate test condition to evaluate preferred toys: The parents have already reported that they tend to provide both at the same time. If we tried to evaluate these two reinforcers separately, we would create a scenario that the child never actually experiences in daily life. Thus, the information from the interview is used to design test and control conditions that are ecologically relevant. *By ecologically relevant*, we mean conditions that emulate what happens in the child's natural daily environment; the conditions mimic actual examples from the child's life.

**Control condition.** Conduct the control condition first. This allows you to begin the analysis by confirming that you can "turn off" problem behavior (i.e., that you can arrange a situation in which problem behavior will not happen). During the control condition, provide free access to all reinforcers that are being evaluated in the test condition. If precursors or problem behavior occur, do not change anything (i.e., do not react; just keep doing what you are doing).

The control condition in the pre-dinner tantrum example would include continuous attention from the analyst or parent as well as continuous free access to preferred toys. The aim is to eliminate the EOs for adult attention or toys and thus, not evoke problem behavior.

**Test condition.** Begin the test condition by removing all of the reinforcers that were present "for free" in the control condition. Remove all reinforcers simultaneously and as quickly as possible. For example, do not remove toys by slowly cleaning them up one at a time; establish a method for swiftly removing them all at once—perhaps by having a toy bin nearby to which they can all be easily removed, while providing a signal that attention will be diverted to something or someone other than the child.

If the test condition involves presenting demands, also establish a way for these to be quickly presented. This can be accomplished in several ways. One option is to have two bins (one with reinforcers and one with demand materials) that can be easily presented and removed. Another option is to have the individual sit in a chair that can be easily turned back and forth between a table with reinforcers and a table with demand materials. By withholding all reinforcers, you are presenting EOs for those reinforcers (i.e., withholding attention is likely to evoke attention-seeking problem behavior). Continue presenting those EOs until the precursor or problem behavior occurs, and then immediately provide all reinforcers for a brief period (usually 30 seconds, but this can be flexible). This changeover needs to be quick as well.

Because you are presenting the exact same reinforcers that were included in the control condition, it is best for the reinforcement interval during the test condition to look just like the control condition. If you were to watch a video of the control condition and a video of just the brief reinforcement interval during a test condition, the difference between the two would be indiscernible. After 30 seconds have elapsed, remove all reinforcers again, wait until the precursor or problem behavior occurs again, and then deliver all reinforcers for 30 seconds again. Continue alternating withholding reinforcers (EO interval) and delivering reinforcers (reinforcement interval) for the duration of the test session. An example of the test condition from the previously discussed scenario is depicted in Figure 6.1. The analyst appears busy with some task while ignoring the child, and there are no toys available (to emulate the scenario of a parent who is busy cooking dinner and unable to play with the child). When precursor or problem behavior occurs, the analyst would immediately stop what she or he is doing and provide undivided attention and access to preferred toys for 30 seconds.

**Condition alternation.** The IISCA alternates between control and test sessions. Sessions can be short (3-5 minutes). The minimum number of alternations necessary to demonstrate a functional relation is two (i.e., two test and two control sessions). Repeatability is the key to believability; if problem behavior reliably occurs in a test session and not during a control session, repeating each of them a second time adds credibility and allows for confidence that the results did not occur by chance. You may, however, consider conducting a third test session, so that there will be three data points to use as a baseline against which to evaluate treatment effects later. Thus, one possible sequence of conditions is control, test, control, test, test. This is five total sessions, which would mean a total analysis duration of 15-25 minutes (depending on whether sessions are 3 or 5 minutes each). Sessions may be conducted back-to-back or short breaks may be inserted between sessions. For the sake of efficiency, however, conducting sessions back-to-back without breaks is generally recommended so that an intervention can be designed and implemented as soon as possible.

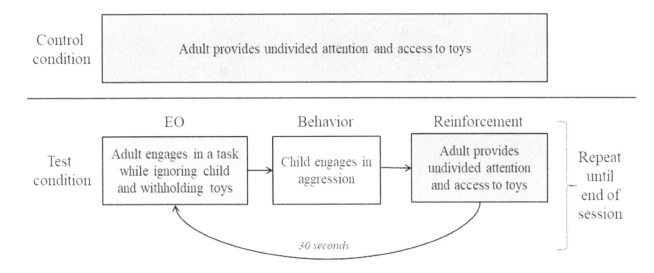

*Figure 6.1. Example of procedures in the control and test conditions of an interview-informed synthesized contingency analysis (IISCA).*

**IISCA examples.** Figure 6.2 illustrates an example of data from an IISCA. Rate of problem behavior in each of three test condition sessions is shown with the black circles and the rate of problem behavior in each of the two control condition sessions is shown with the white circles; the synthesized (i.e., combined) reinforcers evaluated in the test condition are shown in italics.

This IISCA was conducted in a school setting with a teenage boy with autism who engaged in tantrums that included severe aggression (e.g., biting), property destruction (e.g., breaking objects, damaging walls), and other disruptive behaviors (e.g., spitting, screaming). The problem behavior was evoked by any type of social interaction, including other people speaking to the boy, looking at him, or approaching him. The reinforcer for the problem behavior was an escape *from* this social interaction to independent leisure activities (e.g., watching YouTube) alone in a room.

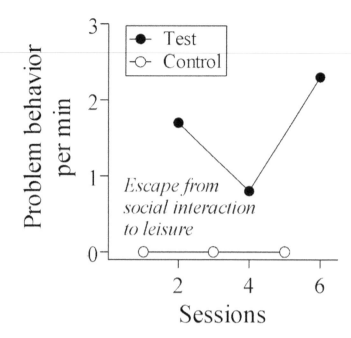

**Figure 6.2. Example of an IISCA.**

In Figure 6.2, notice that there is no problem behavior occurring in the control condition, but problem behavior does reliably occur in the test condition. When results are clearly differentiated like this, we have answered the questions necessary to begin treating problem behavior. Because we have a demonstrated a functional relation between problem behavior and the reinforcement contingency designed from the interview, we have an understanding of a situation that evokes problem behavior and the reinforcers that maintain it in that situation. We can also be confident that we know how to arrange a context in which problem behavior will *not* occur at all. (NOTE: It is important to demonstrate that we can arrange a condition in which problem behavior will not occur, because if we cannot eliminate problem behavior during the control condition, we will probably not be able to eliminate it during treatment either).

Other examples of individualized reinforcement contingencies in IISCAs may be found in Hanley et al. (2014), Jessel et al. (2016), Slaton et al. (2017), and Jessel, Ingvarsson, Metras, Kirk, and Whipple (2018). Together, these papers report 68 distinct IISCAs conducted with children and adults with autism and/or other developmental disabilities in homes, day schools, residential schools, out-patient clinics, and vocational settings. Each of the applications is unique (i.e., no two reinforcement contingencies are identical) because the open-ended interview process tends to yield rich and nuanced details about the contexts and consequences for problem behavior, despite the general categories of reinforcement being the same (e.g., escape to tangibles).

# Design Treatment From The IISCA

Results from the IISCA allow us to design individualized and skill-based interventions. That is, an intervention that focuses on the development of skills that permit an individual to obtain powerful reinforcers, learn to behave effectively when these reinforcers are unavailable, and to do both without engaging in problem behavior. Instead of using procedures that suppress problem behavior in a given context (i.e., punishment or alternative reinforcement), this skill-based approach permits the development of skills that have been shown to generalize across settings (Ghaemmaghami, Hanley, & Jessel, 2016). For example, instead of routinely placing a child in time out when he aggressively takes a toy away from a peer on the playground or distracting that same child with other toys following the problem behavior, an interventionist using a skill-based approach would spend time teaching the child to ask for the preferred toys (and a range of other items), to tolerate situations in which his requests are sometimes denied by adults and peers, and to identify and engage in other contextually-appropriate behavior while waiting for the preferred toys.

*Functional communication training* (FCT) is one of the most empirically-validated interventions for problem behavior and has been evaluated with individuals of varying ages, disabilities, communication profiles, and problem behaviors (Tiger, Hanley, & Bruzek, 2008). FCT involves teaching individuals to appropriately request the reinforcers for their problem behavior. For example, the child who engages in tantrums before dinner to get her parents' attention and to be allowed to play with preferred toys would be taught some appropriate request for this synthesized reinforcer—perhaps, "Play with me," or a similar phrase. This request is called a *functional communication response* (FCR). During FCT, the FCR produces the reinforcers that were provided in the test condition of the IISCA, and problem behavior typically no longer produces those reinforcers (i.e., problem behavior is placed on extinction). Figure 6.3 shows what the three-term contingency looks like during the IISCA vs. during FCT. Notice that the beginning and end of the chain (the EOs and reinforcers) are identical; the only part that changes is the response that produces the reinforcers.

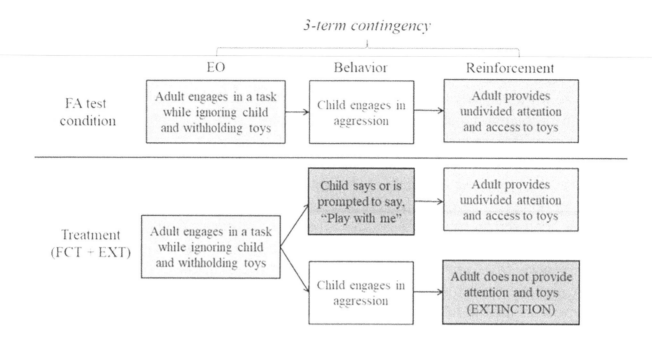

*Figure 6.3. Difference between contingencies during the FA test condition and during FCT.*

Once the individual reliably engages in the FCR (instead of the problem behavior) when presented with evocative events, it is important to thin the schedule of reinforcement, because it is not practical for caregivers to grant every single request. This thinning procedure is more thoroughly described in Hanley et al. (2014) and Ghaemmaghami et al. (2016), but may be summarized as follows: (a) begin denying some instances of the FCR (e.g., "No, I can't play with you right now,") and teach the individual an appropriate tolerance response to give when denied (e.g., the child says, "Okay"); (b) teach the individual to engage in other appropriate activities while waiting for reinforcers to become available (response chaining; e.g., teach the child to go play by herself until the parent is finished cooking dinner and ready to play).

This repertoire of communicating, tolerating, and complying is taught and maintained via intermittent and unpredictable reinforcement. By *intermittent reinforcement*, we mean that each of these different behaviors (the FCR, the tolerance response, or compliance with instructions) is reinforced immediately *some of the time*. For example, during an FCT session that includes five presentations of an evocative event, perhaps the FCR is immediately reinforced once (e.g., when toys and attention are removed, the child says, "Play with me," and the adult immediately returns the toys and attention). Perhaps the tolerance response is immediately reinforced once as well (e.g., when toys and attention are removed, the child says, "Play with me," the adult denies the request, the child gives the tolerance response of, "Okay," and then the adult immediately returns the toys and attention). Compliance with instructions is then immediately reinforced on the remaining trials. This would involve presenting different amounts and types of demands after the tolerance response (e.g., sometimes the expectation would be to complete two accurate responses following the general prompt to "Match these by color" whereas at other times the child may be instructed to clean up their toys), and then providing reinforcement once those demands have been completed. By *unpredictable reinforcement*, we mean that we do not tell the child in advance which behavior will result in reinforcement.

Figure 6.4 presents data from an example of this treatment model conducted in a home setting with a teenager with autism who engaged in tantrums that included severe SIB (head-banging), screaming, crying, and jumping hard enough to break furniture. The baseline data are the data from the test condition of his IISCA, which showed that his problem behavior was evoked when his requests (e.g., "Outside?") were denied (e.g., "No, sorry, we can't play outside right now.") or when his ritualistic placement of objects around the house was interrupted (e.g., moving his iPad to a different shelf). The reinforcers maintaining his problem behavior, therefore, were the granting of his requests and allowing him to arrange objects around the house as he chose. This young man learned a simple FCR— "*My way.*" He then learned a complex FCR — call the adult by name, pause for acknowledgment by the adult and say, "*My way, please.*" Next, he learned a tolerance response — "*All right*"— to be given when his FCR was denied, and he learned to comply with parent-directed activities such as doing chores or practicing leisure skills while waiting for his requests to be granted.

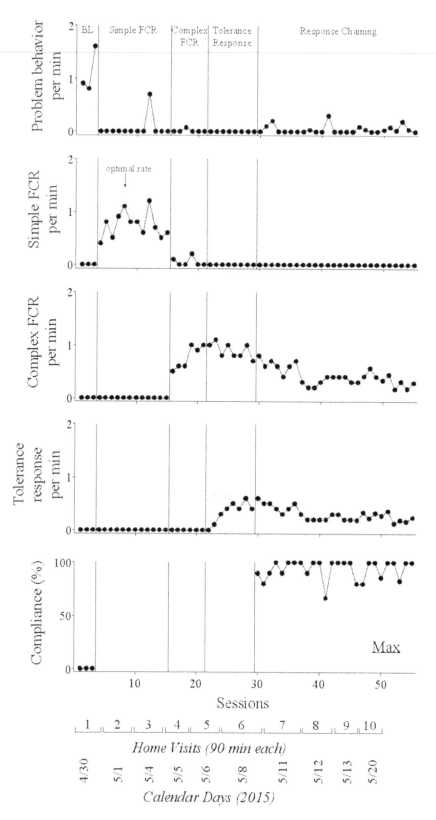

Figure 6.4. Skill-based treatment in a home setting designed from an IISCA.

## ▶▶ *Common Questions and Answers About FAs*

Several questions or concerns may arise when conducting FAs. A common question is whether we may make problem behavior worse by reinforcing it during the FA, and whether it is somehow wrong or unfair to put somebody in a test condition during which we purposely attempt to evoke the behavior. It is important to remember, in this connection, that problem behavior is *already happening regularly* and is *already being reinforced*. A helpful analogy here may be that of an allergy test. During an allergy test, the allergist purposely exposes you to potential allergens (many selected from information obtained in an interview) that may result in a small reaction. By designing test conditions to include ecologically relevant situations from the person's daily life, we are simply presenting the individual with scenarios that he or she encounters regularly; like the allergy testing, this may evoke a small reaction.

A common concern regarding FAs is that they may be dangerous, because the individual may engage in severe problem behavior. Safety is indeed the most important factor to consider when designing a functional analysis; and with careful forethought, it can be achieved through proper design of the analysis.

One way to manage safety during the FA is to reinforce all forms of problem behavior that are reported to co-occur with the most dangerous forms of problem behavior. For example, if precursor responses (e.g., foot stomping) and non-dangerous forms of problem behavior (e.g., forceful grabbing) are reinforced, it is likely that you will not observe more dangerous types of problem behavior during the FA. The overall effect of reinforcement on behavior is that it increases the future likelihood of occurrence; however, the immediate, momentary effect of reinforcement is that it causes the behavior to pause and keeps it from increasing in intensity, which is why reinforcing all behaviors with the suspected reinforcers increases levels of safety in an analysis.

Another way to increase the odds of a safe analysis is to provide all reinforcers suspected of influencing the problem behavior simultaneously in the analysis. For instance, if problem behavior is maintained by escape from instructions to an iPad, and you only provide escape from instructions in the analysis, the problem behavior may continue to occur (i.e., escalate) throughout the test sessions. Safety is achieved by quickly turning problem behavior off as soon as it begins to occur, and synthesized reinforcers are more likely to do that. Providing the reinforcers quickly following the initial problematic response is also recommended. In sum, speedy provision of all suspected reinforcers for all topographies of problem behavior that reportedly co-occur are the hallmarks of a safe analysis.

Yet another common concern is that FAs is too time-consuming and effortful. The practical functional assessment model described within this chapter addresses this issue by synthesizing reinforcers into a single test condition that emulates the naturally occurring situations that individuals typically experience. Synthesis eliminates the need for multiple test conditions, each of which can be time consuming. By using short session durations, the FA can be completed in as little as 15 minutes (or sometimes 5 minutes; see Jessel et al., 2016). By arranging conditions that emulate the individual's natural environment, the FA is no more effortful than repeating everyday interactions.

A further concern is that an FA may not seem necessary in cases in which the reinforcers for problem behavior seem obvious. Thus, it is tempting to say, "I can tell why this behavior is happening; I don't need to do an FA." There are, however, multiple reasons why the FA is still beneficial. First, the reinforcers for problem behavior may not have been correctly identified via observation alone. We know that observations, whether informal or occurring within a descriptive assessment, are not valid means identifying reinforcers because the relevance of certain events is often mistakenly inferred from the prevalence of observed events (Hanley, 2012). It is important, therefore, that we have the humility to spend 15-25 minutes verifying our hypotheses before acting on them. Second, the FA provides useful baseline data to which we can compare to our treatment data and thus determine whether the treatment is having the desired effect. Third, and perhaps most important, the FA test condition becomes the authentic teaching context in which the important skills of communicating, tolerating, and complying will be taught. This means that by conducting the FA, we are also designing the teaching context for treatment and determining whether it is a sufficiently motivating context in which to teach skills. If little or no problem behavior occurs in the FA, it is not expected that we would be able to teach appropriate communication using the same EOs and reinforcers. By contrast, when problem behavior reliably occurs during the test condition of the FA, sufficient motivation to engage in a new responses (i.e., skills) to access those reinforcers is apparent (i.e., teaching FCRs and compliance to replace problem behavior may indeed be accomplished).

A final concern is that FAs may not be appropriate for problem behavior that occurs at very low rates. Usually, problem behavior occurs at a low rate because the individual's caregivers avoid situations that they know may lead to problem behavior (i.e., the EOs are never presented), or perhaps caregivers respond immediately by delivering some reinforcers when the individual begins to escalate (i.e., precursors are reinforced). These possibilities are often discovered in interviews. Functional analyses are still effective in demonstrating functional relations despite the typical low rate of problem behavior, because EOs that are usually avoided are repeatedly arranged in the analyses.

## ▶▶ *Summary*

This chapter described a safety-and-speed-first model of functional assessment. When used as the basis for teaching life skills, it has been shown to yield socially meaningful treatment outcomes in homes, schools, and clinics (see Hanley et al., 2014; Jessel et al., 2017; Santiago et al., 2016). We encourage behavior analysts to consider applying this model to eliminate problem behavior and ultimately help families experience a higher quality of life for themselves and their children.

# *References*

Adelinis, J. D., & Hagopian, L. P. (1999). The use of symmetical "do" and "don't" requests to interrupt ongoing activities. *Journal of Applied Behavior Analysis*, 32, 519-523.

Beavers, G. A., Iwata, B. A., & Lerman, D. C. (2013). Thirty years of research on the functional analysis of problem behavior. *Journal of Applied Behavior Analysis*, 46, 1-21.

Bloom, S. E., Iwata, B. A., Fritz, J. N., Roscoe, E. M., & Carreau, A. B. (2011). Classroom application of a trial-based functional analysis. *Journal of Applied Behavior Analysis*, 44, 19-31.

Borrero, C. S., & Borrero, J. C. (2008). Descriptive and experimental analyses of potential precursors to problem behavior. *Journal of Applied Behavior Analysis*, 41, 83-96.

Bowman, L. G., Fisher, W. W., Thompson, R. H., & Piazza, C. C. (1997). On the relation of mands and the function of destructve behavior. *Journal of Applied Behavior Analysis*, 30, 251-265.

Campbell, J. M. (2003). Efficacy of behavioral interventions for reducing problem behavior in persons with autism: A quantitative synthesis of single-subject research. *Research in Developmental* Disabilities, 24, 120-138.

Carr, E. G., & Durand, V. M. (1985). Reducing behavior problems through functional communication training. *Journal of Applied Behavior Analysis*, 18, 111-126.

Christensen, D. L., Baio J., Braun K. V., et al. (2016). Prevalence and characteristics of autism spectrum disorder among children aged 8 years — Autism and Developmental Disabilities Monitoring Network, 11 Sites, United States, 2012. MMWR Surveill Summ 2016;65(No. SS-3):1-23.

Dominick, K. C., Ornstein Davis, N., Lainhart, J., Tager-Flusberg, H., & Folstein, S. (2007). Atypical behaviors in children with autism and children with a history of language impairment. *Research in Developmental Disabilities*, 28, 145-162.

Ellingson, S. A., Miltenberger, R. G., & Long, E. S. (1999). A survey of the use of functional assessment procedures in agencies serving individuals with developmental disabilities. *Behavioral Interventions*, 14, 187-198.

Fisher, W. W., Adelinis, J. D., Thompson, R. H., Worsdell, A. S., & Zarcone, J. R. (1998). Functional analysis and treatment of destructive behavior maintained by termination of "don't" (and symmetrical "do") requests. *Journal of Applied Behavior Analysis*, 31, 339-356.

Ghaemmaghami, M., Hanley, G. P., & Jessel, J. (2016). Contingencies promote delay tolerance. *Journal of Applied Behavior Analysis*, 49, 548-575.

Ghaemmaghami, M., Hanley, G. P., Jin, S. C., & Vanselow, N. R. (2015). Affirming control by multiple reinforcers via progressive treatment analysis. *Behavioral Interventions*, 31, 70-86.

Hagopian, L. P., Rooker, G. W., Jessel, J., & DeLeon, I. G. (2013). Initial functional analysis outcomes and modifications in pursuit of differentiation: A summary of 176 inpatient cases. *Journal of Applied Behavior Analysis*, 46, 88-100.

Hanley, G. P. (2012). Functional assessment of problem behavior: Dispelling myths, overcoming implementation obstacles, and developing new lore. *Behavior Analysis in Practice*, 5, 54-72.

Hanley, G. P., Iwata, B. A., & McCord, B. E. (2003). Functional analysis of problem behavior: A review. *Journal of Applied Behavior Analysis*, 36, 147-185.

Hanley, G. P., Jin, C. S., Vanselow, N. R., & Hanratty, L. A. (2014). Producing meaningful improvements in problem behavior of children with autism via synthesized analyses and treatments. *Journal of Applied Behavior Analysis*, 47, 16-36.

Hartley, S. L., Sikora, M., & McCoy, R. (2008). Prevalence and risk factors of maladaptive behaviour in young children with autistic disorder. *Journal of Intellectual Disability Research*, 52, 819-829.

Herscovitch, B., Roscoe, E. M., Libby, M. E., Bourret, J. C., & Ahearn, W. H. (2009). A procedure for identifying precursors to problem behavior. *Journal of Applied Behavior Analysis*, 42, 697-702.

Iwata, B. A., DeLeon, I. G., & Roscoe, E. M. (2013). Reliability and validity of the functional analysis scree *nalysis and Intervention in Developmental Disabilities*, 2, 3-20, 1982).

Jessel, J., Hanley, G. P., & Ghaemmaghami, M. (2016). Interview-informed synthesized contingency analyses: Thirty replications and reanalysis. *Journal of Applied Behavior Analysis*, 49, 576-595.

Jessel, J., Ingvarsson, E., T., Metras, R., Kirk, H., Whipple, R. (2018). Achieving socially significant reductions in problem behavior following the Interview-Informed Synthesized Contingency Analysis: A summary of 25 outpatient applications. *Journal of Applied Behavior Analysis*, 51, 130-157.

Kahng, S., Iwata, B. A., & Lewin, A. B. (2002). Behavioral treatment of self-injury, 1964-2000. *American Journal on Mental Retardation*, 107, 212-221.

Lambert, J. M., Staubitz, J. E., Torelli Roane, J., Houchins-Juárez, N. J., Juárez, A. P., Sanders, K. B., & Warren, Z. E. (2017). Outcome summaries of latency-based functional analyses conducted in hospital inpatient units. *Journal of Applied Behavior Analysis*, 50, 487-494.

Lovaas, O. I., Freitag, G., Gold, V. J., & Kassorla, I. C. (1965). Experimental studies in childhood schizophrenia: Analysis of self-destructive behavior. *Journal of Experimental Child Psychology*, 2, 67-84.

Mann, A. J., & Mueller, M. M. (2009). False positive functional analysis results as a contributor of treatment failure during functional communication training. *Education and Treatment of Children*, 32, 121-149.

Northup, J., Wacker, D., Sasso, G., Steege, M., Cigrand, K., Cook, J., & DeRaad, A. (1991). A brief functional analysis of aggressive and alternative behavior in an outclinic setting. *Journal of Applied Behavior Analysis*, 24, 509-522.

Oliver, A. C., Pratt, L. A., & Normand, M. P. (2015). A survey of functional behavior assessment methods used by behavior analysts in practice. Journal of Applied Behavior Analysis, 48, 817-829.

Pelios, L., Morren, J., Tesch, D., & Axelrod, S. (1999). The impact of functional analysis methodology on treatment choice for self-injurious and aggressive behavior. *Journal of Applied Behavior Analysis*, 32, 185-195.

Roscoe, E. M., Phillips, K. M., Kelly, M. A., Farber, R., & Dube, W. V. (2015). A statewide survey assessing practitioners' use and perceived utility of functional assessment. *Journal of Applied Behavior Analysis*, 48, 830-811.

Sailor, W., Guess, D., Rutherford, G., & Baer, D. M. (1968). Control of tantrum behavior by operant techniques during experimental verbal training. *Journal of Applied Behavior Analysis*, 1, 237-243.

Santiago, J. L., Hanley, G. P., Moore, K., & Jin, C. S. (2016). The generality of interview-informed functional analyses: Systematic replications in school and home. *Journal of Autism and Developmental Disorders*, 46, 797-811.

Sarno, J. M., Sterling, H. E., Mueller, M. M., Dufrene, B., Tingstrom, D. H., & Olmi, D. J. (2011). Escape-to-attention as a potential variable for maintaining problem behavior in the school setting. *School Psychology Review*, 40, 57-71.

Schlichenmeyer, K. J., Roscoe, E. M., Rooker, G. W., Wheeler, E. E., & Dube, W. V. (2013). Idiosyncratic variables that affect functional analysis outcomes: A review (2001-2010). *Journal of Applied Behavior Analysis*, 46, 339-348.

Slaton, J. D., Hanley, G. P., & Raftery, K. J. (2017). Interview-informed functional analyses: A comparison of synthesized and isolated components. *Journal of Applied Behavior Analysis*, 50, 252-277.

Smith, R. G., & Churchill, R. M. (2002). Identification of environmental determinants of behavior disorders through functional analysis of precursor behaviors. *Journal of Applied Behavior Analysis*, 35, 125-136.

St. Peter, C. C., Vollmer, T. R., Bourret, J. C., Borrero, C. S., Sloman, K. N., & Rapp, J. T. (2005). On the role of attention in naturally occurring matching relations. *Journal of Applied Behavior Analysis*, 38, 429-442.

Thomason-Sassi, J. L., Iwata, B. A., Neidert, P. L., & Roscoe, E. M. (2011). Response latency as an index of response strength during functional analyses of problem behavior. *Journal of Applied Behavior Analysis*, 44, 51-67.
Thompson, R. H., & Iwata, B. A. (2007). A comparison of outcomes from descriptive and functional analyses of problem behavior. *Journal of Applied Behavior Analysis*, 40, 333–338.

Tiger, J. H., Hanley, G. P., & Bruzek, J. (2008). Functional communication training: A review and practical guide. *Behavior Analysis in Practice*, 16-23.

Wallace, M. D., & Iwata, B. A. (1999). Effects of session duration on functional analysis outcomes. *Journal of Applied Behavior Analysis*, 32, 175-183.

# ASSESSING
# PREFERENCES

*Helen Cannella-Malone*

## KEY TERMS:

- Preference
- Reinforcer
- RAISD
- Single-stimulus assessment
- Selection
- Multiple-stimulus-without-replacement assessment

- Choice
- Preference assessment
- Sampling
- Paired-stimulus assessment
- Eye gaze
- Free-operant assessment

In our daily lives, we make dozens of choices. Am I going to wear a blouse or a sweater today? Will I exercise this morning or this afternoon? Do I want eggs or cereal for breakfast, or do I want both?

Although other contextual variables may influence the decisions we make, at least part of each of these decisions is related to our current preference. That is, at this time, what do I want? Preferences can shift for a number of reasons, including, but not limited to, satiation (i.e., having enough of some reinforcing thing), deprivation (i.e., not having enough), and other constantly shifting environmental variables such as the temperature, or the presence of people in the environment. To express our preferences—and shifts in those preferences— we make choices. I choose to wear a blouse. I choose to exercise this morning. I choose to have eggs and cereal for breakfast. It is through these choices that we demonstrate to those around us what we like and who we are.

# ▶▶ *Expressing Preferences and Making Choices*

For most people, expressing preferences and making choices happens with little effort and often with little consequence. However, for people who have significant intellectual and developmental disabilities associated with limited communication skills, the act of choosing is monumental. That is, it is through these choices—which often require careful environmental structuring on the part of a communication partner—that a person with significant disabilities can express his preference.

Imagine if you were unable to communicate consistently or systematically with those around you (e.g., no clear speech, no writing or typing, no signing, no augmentative or alternative communication system). Now imagine that as a child, you expressed signs of happiness (e.g., smiled, laughed, paid attention) when given a particular food. Because you expressed this happiness, the people around you believe that this particular food, whatever it is, is your favorite food. Now imagine that it is five years later, and everyone still believes this food is one of your favorites. Maybe it is, but maybe it is not. Because you have no systematic way of telling the people around you whether you like or do not like that food any more, they keep giving it to you. If you don't like the food, you may begin to engage in challenging behavior (e.g., refusing the food, screaming, becoming highly agitated) to escape the food, though the people around you may not know that it is that particular food that you no longer like.

This is an issue faced by many children with intellectual and developmental disabilities who struggle to communicate with those around them. The example demonstrates the importance of providing choices. It also highlights one reason why it is essential to explore the preferences of a person with significant disabilities. Without systematically examining their preferences, it is less likely that they will be provided with activities and stimuli that they enjoy and find engaging.

Another reason why it is important for people with disabilities to be able to identify their preferences is that the most effective way to change behavior is to change the environment around it by manipulating either antecedent or consequence variables. *Reinforcers* – those stimuli (e.g., tangible items, people, places, smells, activities) that a person prefers – may be used to increase the future occurrence of a given behavior, and they are. Reinforcers are a type of consequence. In many cases, when attempting to change behavior, we can simply ask somebody what they prefer, and they can tell us. For example, in many classrooms, the teacher asks students what they would like to work for, and they can tell the teacher. When they cannot easily tell us, we must use other means to identify their preferences so that those stimuli can be used to systematically change behavior.

In this chapter, we will present information on why conducting systematic preference assessments is important, describe the assessments available and for whom they are most appropriate, provide basic guidelines for conducting such assessments, and discuss how the results from such assessments can be used in the instructional design for the individual.

## ▶▶ *What Is a Preference Assessment?*

Many students with severe intellectual and developmental disabilities go through their school years with no or limited means of communicating with those around them. To identify reinforcers for these students, instructors could ask those who have frequent contact with the student. However, this alone is not sufficient, as research suggests that in nearly 50% of instances, those who work closely with the student identify stimuli that are not reinforcing (cf. Cannella, O'Reilly, & Lancioni, 2005). Moreover, merely asking may result in overlooking idiosyncratic reinforcers (e.g., watching someone sneeze).

Fortunately, there are ways to overcome such obstacles. A structured preference assessment gives instructional teams a systematic means to assess what a student prefers at a particular moment in time. Research (cf. Cannella et al., 2005; Tullis et al., 2011) provides ample support that the stimuli identified as preferred through preference assessments can be used as reinforcers to change the behavior of individuals with the most severe disabilities. At least five types of preference assessments may be used with a wide array of students with significant disabilities, including those who can make a choice from a large array to those who can only access one item at a time: single-stimulus, paired-stimulus (with physical or eye-gaze selection), multiple stimulus with or without replacement, and free-operant assessments.

## ▶▶ *What Is a Preference Assessment?*

The first step in conducting any systematic preference assessment consists of gathering stimuli to include in the assessment. Gathering information from those who spend the most time with the individual is important. One tool that has been used to help respondents with severe intellectual disability and physical or sensory impairments is the Reinforcer Assessment for Individuals With Severe Disabilities (RAISD; Fisher, Piazza, Bowman, & Amari, 1996). This questionnaire guides the respondent through the various sensory inputs with examples, then asks if the person with significant disabilities likes anything in that modality. A few examples of questions included in the RAISD are presented in Table 7.1.

# Table 7.1
*Sample Questions From the RAISD*

| |
|---|
| 1. Some children really enjoy looking at things such as a mirror, bright light, shiny objects, spinning objects, TV, etc. What are things you think ___ likes to watch? |
| 2. Some children really enjoy physical play or movement such as being tickled, wrestling, running, dancing, swinging, being pulled on a scooter board, etc. What activities like this do you think ___ most enjoys? |
| 3. Some children really enjoy touching things of different temperatures, cold things like snow or an ice pack, or warm things like a hand warmer or cup containing hot tea or coffee. What activities like this do you think _____ most enjoys? |

*Note. From "Reinforcer Assessment for Individuals with Severe Disabilities" (Fisher, Piazza, Bowman, & Amari, 1996).*

Information about other items to include in the assessment may be gathered by observing the student's same-age typically developing peers to see what types of stimuli (e.g., activities, items) with which they engage. For example, we once observed a young man who had a severe intellectual disability. He engaged in such high rates of challenging behavior that he was often required to wear arm splints or a helmet to protect his body. During one of our first observations, we noted that this young man had nearly 12 copies of well-worn *Good Housekeeping* magazines available. When we asked his teachers why those particular magazines, they said that they had a subscription, so they brought them in when they had read them because the student appeared to enjoy flipping through the pages. Although we did observe the student turning the pages, he did not seem attentive to the pictures, and often tore out pages and ripped them up.

We went to a local high school and asked some of the boys what types of magazines they enjoyed reading. The consensus was exercise and motorcycle magazines. We then purchased a few magazines from these categories and asked permission to give them to the target student. When we did, he actively engaged with the new magazines and did not return to the *Good Housekeeping* magazines. As illustrated, although this student did not appear to be opposed to flipping through a *Good Housekeeping* magazine, he did demonstrate a clear preference for the types of magazines recommended by his peers.

Once stimuli are identified, it is important to consider the practicality of including them in the assessment. Remember that a primary function of conducting a preference assessment is to identify possible reinforcers to be used to change behavior. As such, some items might need to be removed from the assessment. For example, if several people suggest that a student loves trips to the zoo, this may be a great activity to plan around, but would be a poor reinforcer due to its impracticality. That is, it would not be possible to take a student to the zoo following each instructional trial. However, items related to the zoo could easily be incorporated into a preference assessment to be used as potential reinforcers such as stories about animals, zoo animal figurines, or videos with animals.

After deciding which items to include, a decision about what to present to the student needs to be made. The physical items do not need to be used in the preference assessment (e.g., snacks, toys, books). Rather, people and activities may be included in preference assessments by teaching the student that selecting a representation of the person or activity will result in access to that person or activity. Pictures of people or activities, or a part of the activity (e.g., ball from playground, a piece from a game), can be used in the preference assessment to represent the person or activity. For example, we worked with a young man who reportedly liked going for walks. We included a picture icon for "walk" in his array. When he chose that icon, we took him for a short walk.

A final consideration before beginning a preference assessment is the student will be *sampling* the items. When the actual item is used in the assessment, prior to the start of a given set of sessions, it is best to give the student the opportunity to try each item (e.g., eat some of the food, play with the toy). When pictures or object representations are used, show them to the student, then give immediate access to the person or activity represented. Providing access to the items prior to the assessments gives the student the opportunity to engage with each item outside of the context of the preference assessment.

## ▶▶ *Preference Assessments*

In the following sections, we will describe each type of assessment and for whom it is most appropriate, the number of items that can reasonably be assessed, the ease of the assessment, and what can be learned using the assessment. Blank data sheets and additional information on each assessment may be found in Cannella-Malone, Sabielny, Jimenez, and Miller (2013).

**Single-stimulus preference assessment.** The *single-stimulus preference assessment* was designed primarily for students who do not make a choice when given more than one option, but who will attend to a single item (Pace, Ivancic, Edwards, Iwata, & Page, 1985). Although up to 16 stimuli can be included before this assessment becomes overly cumbersome, it is more reasonable to include six items in the assessment. With six stimuli, if each is presented five times in one session, the assessment will take at least an hour to complete. Although the procedures for conducting this assessment are fairly simple, it becomes time intensive as more stimuli are included.

As the name suggests, each trial of this assessment includes only one stimulus, and the student has the opportunity to engage (or not) with the item. During this assessment, the person conducting the assessment will look for indications that the student is engaging with the item.

For example, the student might look at the item, lean towards it, physically play with it, or even show a calming response. On the other hand, if a student is not interested in the stimulus, he might not look at the item, push it away, or become agitated and upset until it is removed. Those items that the student engages with will be considered preferred, and those that are not engaged with or actively avoided would be considered to not be preferred.

*Figure* 7.1. In a single-stimulus preference assessment, the teacher presents one item at a time to the student, who has the opportunity to engage with each item individually.

Unlike most of the other types of assessments, the single-stimulus preference assessment only provides information about each item individually. As such, no information about preference relative to other stimuli in the assessment can be gathered. However, the information gleaned about each item can provide perspective about which items a student prefers or does not prefer, and items that the student engages with more than others can be used as potential reinforcers in subsequent instructional programming.

**Paired-stimulus preference assessment.** In the *paired-stimulus preference assessment* (Fisher et al., 1992), each stimulus is paired with every other stimulus being assessed, and the student chooses one item from each pairing. The paired-stimulus assessment was designed for students who reliably make a choice when two items are presented, but are unable to choose reliably with more than two. Although up to 16 stimuli can be included in this assessment, it is more common to include six. To complete this assessment with six stimuli, at least 45 minutes are needed. Because each item has to be paired with every other item, the time added to the assessment with additional stimuli can be substantial.

*Figure* 7.2. In the paired-stimulus preference assessment, the teacher provides the student with two items to choose from. The student selects one of the two options.

In this assessment, preference is determined by the choices the student makes. For each pair presented, the student either chooses one of the two options or neither. In other words, the assessor presents two options and asks the student to choose one; the student then has the opportunity to take or point to one of the options. The student is allowed to engage with the chosen item for a short period of time (e.g., 30 s–1 min). Although the primary source of data is *selection* (i.e., the choice the student makes), it is helpful for the assessor to attend to the student's response to the chosen item and note whether the student engages with the item or not. If the student regularly chooses a certain item, but then exhibits behaviors suggesting a dislike of the item (e.g., throwing the item, dropping it as soon as it is chosen, showing distress when the other item is removed following the choice), such behaviors may suggest a need to provide the student with an opportunity to sample each item for a more extended period of time prior to the assessment.

A variation of the paired-stimulus assessment allows the student to make choices using *eye gaze* (Cannella-Malone, Sabielny, & Tullis, 2015). The procedures are identical to those of the paired-stimulus assessment, except that rather than reaching out and selecting an item, the student uses her eyes to choose an item by focusing the gaze on her choice. This assessment is quite cumbersome and time-consuming, but the available data suggest that it is effective in identifying reinforcing stimuli that can be used in teaching new skills to students with the most significant intellectual and physical disabilities.

Based on information gathered through this assessment, a hierarchy of preferences is identified. However, once a skill is past initial acquisition or an initial decrease, the reinforcers may be changed to some of the more moderately preferred items to avoid satiation. It is also possible, and often recommended, to give the student a choice of which of the top three items from the hierarchy he would like to work for at the start of a set of trials.

*Multiple-stimuli-without-replacement preference assessment.* For students who reliably make choices from an array of three or more items, the *multiple-stimuli-without-replacement assessment* (MSWO) is the most time-efficient preference assessment available (DeLeon & Iwata, 1996). Unlike in the previous types of assessments, including up to 16 items in the array does not increase the assessment time significantly, though small increases do occur as more items are added. When six items are assessed across five sessions in the MSWO, the assessment takes approximately 20 minutes.

*Figure* 7.3. In an MSWO preference assessment, the teacher presents the student with an array of items. After the student selects one item and has an opportunity to engage with the item, the array is presented again but with the chosen item removed.

Unlike the previous assessments, the student makes choices from a diminishing array of options. In the first trial, all of the stimuli are present. Once the student has made a choice, all stimuli but the initial choice are presented again. This process continues until all of the stimuli have been selected or the student stops making choices.

DeLeon and Iwata (1996) also explored a multiple-stimuli-with-replacement (MSW) assessment, where the initial selection was replaced in the array, but students often selected that initial choice over and over again, resulting in the potential masking of other preferences. Therefore, the standing recommendation is to conduct an MSWO (not an MSW) if a student chooses from an array of items.

As with the paired-stimulus assessment, the MSWO results in a hierarchy of preferred items. With the MSWO, more items may be assessed without adding significant time to the process; therefore, it is possible to gather more information with this assessment than with the others. With the additional information afforded by this assessment, it may be possible to increase the kinds of opportunities provided for making choices because the number of identified preferred items may be greater.

**Free-operant preference assessments**. Each of the previously described assessments is highly structured and provides a specific set of information to the assessor about potentially reinforcing stimuli. There are times, however, when an instructional team may want to make adjustments to the available stimuli quickly, but are not sure which items to use as reinforcers. In such moments, conducting a brief free-operant preference assessment might be worthwhile (Roane, Vollmer, Ringdahl, & Marcus, 1998). In this type of assessment, stimuli are placed on a table, and the student is given unrestricted access to all of the items for 5 minutes. During this time, the assessor monitors which items the student engages with the most, and these are considered to be more preferred.

*Figure* 7.4. In the free-operant preference assessment, the student has noncontingent access to an array of stimuli that he can engage with freely for a set period of time. The assessor simply observes and notes which items the student engages with and the duration of the engagement.

## ▶▶ *How Often Do Preference Assessment Need to Be Completed?*

In many ways, this question is tricky. If the student's environment is rich with opportunities to make choices, shifts in preference are likely accounted for by the choices she makes. In this type of environment, a systematic preference assessment may only need to be completed on a biannual basis. If, however, the student's environment is barren with respect to choice, shifts in preference are likely to be missed, and, as a result, systematic preference assessments need to be conducted on a regular basis.

The need for new preference assessment also may be indicated when student responding decelerates. Although there are a myriad reasons for shifts in responding to occur, one possibility to consider is that the item being used as a reinforcer has lost power. This can be tested easily by changing the reinforcer. If this results in a change in responding, it would likely be worthwhile to conduct a new preference assessment with new stimuli to identify new reinforcers.

## ▶▶ *Summary*

In this chapter, we presented information on the importance of identifying the preferences of individuals with significant intellectual, developmental, and physical disabilities, as well as several methods for systematically assessing preference. When a person's preferences can be identified, and the information gleaned can be used to change the behavior of a student, we have the potential to improve the overall quality of his life. Although this is only one tool among many in the behavior change process, a clear awareness of the role preference plays in an instruction plan can improve the overall instructional planning and implementation, making potential behavior change happen more quickly.

# *References*

Cannella, H. I., O'Reilly, M. F., & Lancioni, G. (2005). Choice and preference assessment research with people with severe to profound developmental disabilities: A review of the literature. *Research in Developmental Disabilities*, 26, 1-15.

Cannella-Malone, H. I., Sabielny, L. M., & Tullis, C. A. (2015). Using eye gaze to identify reinforcers for individuals with severe multiple disabilities. *Journal of Applied Behavior Analysis*, 48, 680-684.

DeLeon, I. G., & Iwata, B. A. (1996). Evaluation of a multiple-stimulus presentation format for assessing reinforcer preferences. *Journal of Applied Behavior Analysis*, 29, 519-533.

Fisher, W. W., Piazza, C. C., Bowman, L. G., & Amari, A. (1996). Integrating caregiver report with systematic choice assessment to enhance reinforcer identification. *American Journal on Mental Retardation*, 101, 15-25.

Fisher, W., Piazza, C. C, Bowman, L. G., Hagopian, L. P., Owens, J. G., & Slevin, I. (1992). A comparison of two approaches for identifying reinforcers for persons with severe and profound disabilities. *Journal of Applied Behavior Analysis*, 25, 491-498.

Pace, G. M., Ivancic, M. T., Edwards, G. L., Iwata, B. A., & Page, T. J. (1985). Assessment of stimulus preference and reinforce value with profoundly retarded individuals. *Journal of Applied Behavior Analysis*, 18, 249-255.

Roane, H. S., Vollmer, T. R., Ringdahl, J. E., & Marcus, B. A. (1998). Evaluation of a brief stimulus preference assessment. *Journal of Applied Behavior Analysis*, 31, 605-620.

Tullis, C. A., Cannella-Malone, H. I., Basbagill, A. R., Yeager, A., Fleming, C. V., Payne, D., & Wu, P. (2011). A review of the choice and preference assessment literature for individuals with severe to profound disabilities. *Education and Training in Autism and Developmental Disabilities*, 46, 576-595.

# SCHEDULES OF REINFORCEMENT:
## APPLICATIONS IN THE REAL WORLD

*Monica E. Delano*

## KEY TERMS:

- Positive reinforcement
- Continuous reinforcement
- Intermittent reinforcement
- Ratio schedule
- Interval schedule
- Ratio requirement
- Response rate
- Rate of reinforcement
- Fixed schedule
- Variable schedule
- Fixed ratio schedule
- Variable ratio schedule
- Fixed interval schedule

- Variable interval schedule
- Post-reinforcement pause
- Ratio run
- Ratio strain
- Limited hold
- Fixed interval scallop
- Schedule thinning
- Extinction
- Extinction burst
- Spontaneous recovery
- Differential reinforcement of lower rates
- Differential reinforcement of higher rates
- Concurrent schedules of reinforcement

[1]Names in this chapter have be changed to protect the privacy of interventionists, children and animals.

Eve Burrhus is a beginning teacher and an amateur dog trainer. On a hot May afternoon, she watched her students playing basketball during recess. They were drenched in sweat, but continued to run up and down the court attempting to make baskets. Henry, one of her youngest and smallest students, had been playing for the whole period, but hadn't made a basket. Still, he sprinted up and down the court and took his shots. Ms. Burrhus was amazed by his persistence. Then, just before the class bell rang, Henry caught the ball and began dribbling down the court. He slid by two much taller boys and ended up in the key with no one guarding him. Quickly and with what seemed like all his might, Henry shot the ball towards the basket and, much to Ms. Burrhus' surprise, it went in. Ms. Burrhus had never before seen Henry with such a wide grin. She reflected on this sequence of events. She had taken an introductory course in applied behavior analysis and surmised that this was an example of positive reinforcement.

In technical terms, *positive reinforcement* is the contingent presentation of a particular stimulus after the occurrence of a target behavior that increases the probability that the target behavior will occur in the future (Alberto & Troutman, 2013). Essentially, it is what happens when an individual emits a behavior immediately followed by some favorable consequence that results in the individual emitting that behavior again in the future. In this case, Henry threw the ball many times before his taking a shot was reinforced by scoring a basket. The future probability of Henry throwing the ball at the basket increased after he made a basket.

This was different from what happened when Ms. Burrhus was training her dog Shaggy to sit. When training Shaggy, she gave the command, "Sit." Shaggy sat, and Ms. Burrhus provided a small treat. Shaggy's sitting was continuously followed by a treat. In other words, each of Shaggy's responses resulted in reinforcement. This is an example of *continuous reinforcement*, in which each response results in reinforcement (Ferster & Skinner, 1957). However, in most environments, behaviors are not reinforced all of the time. Henry took many shots at the basket before he scored. Only occasionally did his shot go into the basket and score points. This is an example of *intermittent reinforcement*, because Henry's response resulted in reinforcement (e.g., making a basket) only occasionally (Whaley & Malott, 1971, p. 102).

This chapter introduces the four basic intermittent schedules of reinforcement and the types of behavior they may produce during reinforcement. Practical examples of reinforcement schedules from everyday life are provided. Finally, factors which may affect an individual's performance on particular reinforcement schedules are also discussed.

## ▶▶ *Schedules of Reinforcement*

Think of a schedule of reinforcement as a rule that specifies the conditions under which a behavior produces reinforcement (Cooper, Heron, & Heward, 2007; Mazur, 2017). The schedule of reinforcement depends on the time elapsed between responses, the number of responses, or some other characteristic of the response (Whaley & Malott, 1971). In other words, a schedule of reinforcement describes the timing of the delivery of a reinforcer following a response. In the above example, Ms. Burrhus uses two types of intermittent schedules of reinforcement in her classroom and at home training Shaggy: ratio schedules of reinforcement and interval schedules of reinforcement.

**Ratio schedules of reinforcement**. *Ratio schedules of reinforcement* are arranged by the number of responses made by an organism (Ferster & Skinner, 1957). In other words, ratio schedules specify the number of responses that must be emitted before one response will result in reinforcement (Cooper et al., 2007). For example, Ms. Burrhus requires Henry to correctly solve five word problems before she provides him with access to his favorite comic book for two minutes. Correctly solving the fifth problem results in reinforcement. The longer Henry procrastinates, or if he works slowly to complete the ratio requirement of five correct responses, the longer it will take for reinforcement to occur. That is, if Henry stays on task and works quickly and accurately, he will meet the ratio requirement and reinforcement will occur sooner. Thus, when a ratio schedule of reinforcement is applied, the response rate controls the frequency, or rate of reinforcement (Cooper et al., 2007).

At home, Ms. Burrhus has noticed that differences in Shaggy's response rate depend on a variety of factors. For example, she requires Shaggy to drop her toys into a toy box at the end of the day. The ratio requirement is two correct responses. After Shaggy drops the second toy in the box, Ms. Burrhus provides a small treat. On cool fall evenings, Shaggy sprints around the yard and can drop two toys in the box in 20 seconds, so she receives a treat three times in a minute. On humid summer evenings, she crawls around the yard, and it takes her a full minute to meet the ratio requirement of dropping two toys in the box, so she receives one treat per minute.

A variety of factors can impact performance on various types of reinforcement schedules. Later in this chapter, we will discuss typical patterns of responding under different reinforcement schedules. At this point, it is important to remember that ratio schedules specify the number of responses that must be emitted before a response results in reinforcement (Cooper et al., 2007). Therefore, the faster the response rate, the sooner reinforcement will occur. A second type of schedule of intermittent reinforcement is an interval schedule; this is discussed next.

**Interval schedules of reinforcement**. *Interval schedules of intermittent reinforcement* are dependent on the passage of time (Whaley & Malott, 1971). Reinforcement is determined by a clock (Ferster & Skinner, 1957). In other words, a specified amount of time must pass before a response is reinforced (Cooper et al., 2007). For example, if the interval requirement is two minutes, the first target response that occurs after two minutes have elapsed yields reinforcement (Cooper et al., 2007).

Ms. Burrhus uses an interval schedule of reinforcement with Shaggy when they vacation at the beach. Ms. Burrhus likes to read and relax in the sun. Shaggy loves to jump in the ocean to retrieve her frisbee. In order to give herself time to read a few pages between throws of the frisbee, Ms. Burrhus implemented a 10-minute interval schedule. The first time Shaggy drops her Frisbee at Ms. Burrhus' feet after 10 minutes have elapsed, Ms. Burrhus stands up and throws the Frisbee into the ocean. Shaggy then happily negotiates the waves and retrieves the frisbee. Unlike with ratio schedules, the frequency of responses produced does not control the rate of reinforcement (Cooper et al., 2007). Thus, Shaggy could drop the Frisbee at Ms. Burrhus' feet 20 times in 10 minutes, or only twice in 10 minutes, and Ms. Burrhus would still only throw the Frisbee once every 10 minutes (i.e., after the first time Shaggy drops the Frisbee following the expiration of the 10-minute interval).

Ms. Burrhus also uses interval schedules of reinforcement in her classroom. Henry likes to talk incessantly during class discussions. He raises his hand constantly, but Ms. Burrhus needs to call on other students in class. To change Henry's behavior, she decided to apply an interval schedule of reinforcement with a 4-minute interval requirement. After each 4-minute interval, she called on Henry the first time he raised his hand. As in the previous example, and unlike ratio schedules, interval schedules are controlled by time. The frequency with which Henry raises his hand on an interval schedule does not control how often Ms. Burrhus calls on him. Instead, reinforcement is contingent on Henry raising his hand one time after 4 minutes have elapsed. Interval schedules are dependent on time, and ratio schedules depend on the number of responses emitted (Cooper, et al., 2007).

Next, let's consider two types of contingencies that are used in ratio and interval schedules: fixed and variables schedules.

**Fixed and variable schedules of intermittent reinforcement**. An intermittent schedule of reinforcement may be described as fixed or variable. Schedules with a constant response ratio, or a constant interval requirement, are called *fixed schedules of reinforcement* (Cooper et al., 2007, p. 306). The schedules of reinforcement Ms. Burrhus used with Henry and Shaggy in the previous examples are fixed schedules, because the number of responses required, or the interval requirement, remained constant. However, variable schedules of reinforcement are often used in practice. In variable schedules of reinforcement, the response ratio requirement, or interval requirement, fluctuates, so reinforcement is provided after an average number of responses or an average duration of time (Cooper et al., 2007; Mazur, 2017).

For example, Ms. Burrhus could have used a variable interval 10-minute (VI10) schedule with Shaggy on the beach. Under this schedule, Ms. Burrhus would throw the frisbee the first time Shaggy puts it by her feet after intervals averaging 10 minutes in duration. Sometimes she throws the frisbee the first time Shaggy responds after a 5-minute interval. At other times, she reads a few more pages and throws the frisbee the first time Shaggy responds after a 15-minute interval. The point here is that the interval length varies; in this case, the average is 10 minutes.

Variable-ratio schedules are run in a similar manner. For example, Henry is training to try out for the basketball team. After school, Ms. Burrhus permits him to go to the gymnasium so he can run laps. She applies a variable ratio schedule of reinforcement. On average, after every third lap Henry runs, Ms. Burrhus gives him a slice of an orange—his favorite snack. Since the ratio is variable, sometimes Ms. Burrhus provides the reinforcer after Henry completes one lap; at other times, she waits until he has run five laps or more. A variable ratio 3 schedule (VR3) simply means that reinforcement is provided, on average, after every third response. In the next section, the delivery of reinforcement using fixed or variable contingencies is discussed in the context of ratio and interval schedules of intermittent reinforcement.

## ▶▶ *What Are the Four Basic Schedules of Intermittent Reinforcement?*

Schedules may be based on either a response ratio or an interval requirement. Schedules may be further characterized as fixed or variable. Thus, there are four basic schedules of intermittent reinforcement: fixed ratio, variable ratio, fixed interval, and variable interval. Each schedule will be described in this section, along with a discussion of typical response patterns under each schedule. To illustrate, reference will be made to Ms. Burrhus' applications of reinforcement schedules in the classroom and at home training Shaggy.

Fixed-ratio schedules of reinforcement. According to Ferster and Skinner (1957), a fixed-ratio schedule of reinforcement is "a schedule of intermittent reinforcement in which a response is reinforced upon completion of a fixed number of responses counted from the preceding reinforcement" (p. 727). In an earlier example, Henry received brief access to his favorite comic book after correctly completing five word problems. This is an example of a fixed-ratio schedule of reinforcement in which five correct responses are required for reinforcement. This schedule may be abbreviated "FR5."

Fixed-ratio schedules tend to cause recognizable patterns of responding. Individuals often respond at a fast rate, because the faster they meet the ratio requirement, the sooner reinforcement is delivered (Alberto & Troutman, 1986; Cooper et al., 2007). To avoid inappropriate fluencies and unnecessary errors (Alberto & Troutman, 1986), Ms. Burrhus is careful to specify that responses must be accurate when she uses a fixed-ratio schedule. Prior to this contingency, Henry would rush through his work (e.g., five word problems) to complete the ratio requirement (FR5), but he would make many errors. Now, when a fixed-ratio schedule is applied, and correct responding is required, Henry works at a constant, fast pace, and attends to accuracy as well.

In addition to a rapid rate of responding on a fixed-ratio schedule, a pause in responding typically occurs immediately after the delivery of a reinforcer. This is called a *post-reinforcement pause* (Cooper et al., 2007). A post-reinforcement pause is usually followed by a return to a high rate of responding until the next reinforcer is produced (Cooper et al., 2007; Mazur, 2017). This pattern of responding is known as a *ratio run* (Newman, Reeve, Reeve, & Ryan, 2003). Shaggy's mealtime behavior provides a good example of this sequence.

Shaggy has many food allergies; consequently, Ms. Burrhus feeds her very bland and tasteless dog food. However, Shaggy is not allergic to marshmallows and loves them. During mealtimes, Ms. Burrhus gives Shaggy one fourth of a cup of Boring Biscuit dog food at a time.  Shaggy wolfs it down, and Ms. Burrhus gives her a marshmallow. Shaggy eats the marshmallow, pauses for several seconds (i.e., post-reinforcement pause), and then eats the next one fourth cup of food at a fast, steady pace (i.e., ratio run) until the next marshmallow is delivered.

It is important to note that the size of the ratio affects the response rate and length of the post-reinforcement pause (Cooper et al., 2007). For example, when Ms. Burrhus required Shaggy to eat one-half cup of food instead of one fourth cup (i.e., larger ratio requirement), she noticed the duration of Shaggy's post-reinforcement pause increased. Generally, the larger the ratio, the longer the post-reinforcement pause. The smaller the ratio, the briefer the post-reinforcement pause (Cooper et al., 2007).

Ms. Burrhus wondered what would happen if she increased the ratio requirement for Henry. She hoped he would get more problems solved for each reinforcer. Instead of having access to his comic book after correctly completing five word problems, she changed the schedule to FR10, meaning Henry had to correctly complete 10 word problems before having access to his comic book. Ms. Burrhus happily noticed that with a larger ratio requirement,

Henry worked even faster to complete the problems and had only a slightly longer post-reinforcement pause. While it is often the case with fixed-ratio schedules that larger ratio requirements trigger higher rates of responding, if the ratio requirement is increased too much too quickly, responding may actually be weakened (Cooper et al., 2007; Mazur, 2017). As a result, the individual may exhibit slower responding and may pause at other times in addition to the post-reinforcement pause (Mazur, 2017). This is called *ratio strain*, and occurs when response performance declines after the schedule of reinforcement has been thinned too quickly (Alberto & Troutman, 1986; Cooper et al., 2007; Mazur, 2017).

This is exactly what happened when Ms. Burrhus changed Henry's reinforcement schedule to FR30. Not only did the duration of his post-reinforcement pause increase, he no longer worked at a quick and steady pace. Instead, he paused frequently and exhibited an increase in off-task behavior such as doodling and talking to a classmate. The FR30 was too large to maintain Henry's previous rate of responding. Ms. Burrhus quickly changed the schedule back to FR10.

In the next section, we will look at another ratio schedule of reinforcement that may be used to address some of these fixed-ratio schedule limitations. First, let us review the characteristics of fixed ratio schedules of reinforcement.

- A fixed ratio schedule is an intermittent schedule of reinforcement in which a set number of responses is required to obtain reinforcement (Cooper et al., 2007).
- Fixed ratio may be abbreviated "FR," and the number of required responses may be placed after the "FR." For example, FR20 means a fixed-ratio schedule in which every 20th response is reinforced.
- Fixed-ratio schedules typically trigger a steady, rapid rate of responding (Cooper et al., 2007).
- After the delivery of reinforcement on a fixed-ratio schedule, there is typically a post-reinforcement pause in which the individual does not respond. The duration of the pause is affected by the size of the ratio (Mazur, 2017).
- Larger ratios may cause a faster rate of response. However, if reinforcement is thinned too quickly and the ratio requirement becomes too large, ratio strain, or diminished responding, may occur (Alberto & Troutman, 1986; Cooper et al., 2007; Mazur, 2017).

**Variable-ratio schedules of reinforcement.** Ferster and Skinner (1957) defined a variable ratio schedule as a "schedule of intermittent reinforcement under which reinforcements are programmed according to a random series of ratios having a given mean and lying between arbitrary extreme values" (p. 734). In other words, the ratio requirement fluctuates in a variable-ratio schedule. For example, Ms. Burrhus used a VR5 schedule with Henry during language arts class after she noticed he was slow to respond when given a writing prompt. On the VR5 schedule, she gave Henry a token reinforcer, on average, after every fifth sentence he wrote to the prompt. Sometimes she provided the token after Henry wrote three sentences; at other times, after 10 sentences. On average, he received a token reinforcer after every fifth sentence. After class, he could exchange the tokens for a small snack. Ms. Burrhus noticed that Henry began to write more quickly. He even wrote an essay the day Ms. Burrhus was home sick, even though the substitute teacher did not use the token reinforcers. Ms. Burrhus decided that a variable-ratio schedule (in which the number of responses required for reinforcement varies) was effective at increasing the rate of Henry's responding and enabling him to respond even in the absence of reinforcement. The more sentences Henry wrote, the more likely he would obtain a token. Consequently, he continued writing without long pauses.

At home, Ms. Burrhus wondered if, unintentionally, she was reinforcing Shaggy's barking behavior on a variable-ratio schedule. Often, when Ms. Burrhus was on the phone, Shaggy started barking loudly and rapidly. Eventually, Ms. Burrhus gave in and let Shaggy have a treat. The number of barks required for a treat varied from three to nine. On average, Shaggy received a treat after every sixth bark, or on a VR6 schedule of reinforcement. And Ms. Burrhus had been wondering why Shaggy barked every time she got on the phone!

Variable-ratio schedules have anticipated effects during reinforcement. Similar to fixed-ratio schedules of reinforcement, the rate of responding is high and related to the size of the ratio requirement (Cooper, et al., 2007). The post-reinforcement pause often observed in fixed-ratio schedules does not usually occur on a variable-ratio schedule (Cooper, et al., 2007). Skinner (1953) observed that the probability of reinforcement remains constant, so the individual maintains a constant rate of responding. Since any response on a variable-ratio schedule may be reinforced, it makes sense that pausing is rare (Cooper, 2007). Indeed, that seemed to be the case for both Shaggy and Henry.

Before examining the characteristics of specific interval schedules of reinforcement, let us review.

- A variable-ratio schedule is an intermittent schedule of reinforcement. The number of responses required for reinforcement fluctuates on a variable ratio schedule (Cooper, et al., 2007).
- Variable ratio may be abbreviated "VR," and the average number of required responses may be placed after the "VR." For example, VR10 means a variable-ratio schedule in which, on average, every tenth response is reinforced.
- Variable-ratio schedules result in steady, rapid responding (Cooper et al., 2007; Mazur, 2017).
- Long post-reinforcement pauses are NOT typical of variable-ratio schedules (Cooper et al., 2007).
- The size of the ratio affects the rate of response in a variable-ratio schedule (Cooper et al., 2007).

**Fixed-interval schedule of reinforcement**. A fixed-interval schedule (FI) is an "intermittent schedule of reinforcement in which the first response occurring after a given interval of time … is reinforced" (Ferster & Skinner, 1957, p. 727). In an earlier example, Ms. Burrhus used an FI4 schedule with Henry. Under this schedule, she called on Henry the first time he raised his hand after 4 minutes had elapsed since the last time she called on him. This schedule was effective because she wanted Henry to stop raising his hand constantly and instead raise his hand after a classmate or two had spoken. On the fixed-interval schedule, Henry stopped raising his hand after he was called on. Then he started raising his hand again just before the 4-minute interval expired. Now that Henry did not constantly raise his hand, more students participated in discussions.

Although Ms. Burrhus was pleased with the effects of the fixed-interval schedule, she learned that it is not useful in certain circumstances. She assigned a research presentation to Henry's science class. Each student developed a presentation about an important scientist. Henry chose B.F. Skinner. After the students developed their presentations, Ms. Burrhus told the students they would have a week to practice their presentations in small groups. Then students would make their presentations to the whole class, receive course points, and be able to go on a class trip to the science museum. Each day, Ms. Burrhus provided students with a class period to practice. However, she did not provide reinforcement until one week had elapsed and students made their presentations to the whole class. Ms. Burrhus noticed that students were mostly off task during the first half of the week. They began to practice repeatedly at the end of the week, just before the due date, when reinforcement would be available.

The science presentation example is not a true fixed-interval schedule, because the students had to make their presentations to the class on a particular day and at a particular time, whereas in a true fixed-interval schedule the students could respond any time after the interval elapsed. Cooper et al. (2007) suggested that many textbook examples of fixed-interval schedules do not meet the requirements of fixed-interval schedules, but they are similar. In fact, examples of fixed-interval schedules are not easy to find in everyday life (Cooper et al., 2007). Mazur (2017) noted that "few real-world reinforcers occur on such a regular temporal cycle" (p. 727). However, as Whaley and Malott (1971) stated, behavior similar to behavior produced by a fixed-interval schedule may occur in situations with a set deadline.

In our example, the students demonstrated a lack of responding early in the interval (i.e., failure to practice their presentations) and rapid responding near the end of the interval. This effect is typical of fixed-interval schedules in which there is often a slow response rate early in the interval and a rapid response rate late in the interval, just before reinforcement is available (Mazur, 2017). This pattern of responding is sometimes called *scalloping, or a fixed interval scallop* (Cooper et al., 2007; Mazur, 2017; Newman et al., 2003; Whaley & Malott, 1971).

A variation of interval schedules is called a limited hold (LH). A limited hold is used to increase the rate of responding during interval schedules (Alberto & Troutman, 1986). A limited hold specifies the amount of time a reinforcer is available following the expiration of the interval (Cooper, et al., 2007). For example, an FI10 min/LH 15-sec schedule makes a reinforcer available for 15 seconds after the expiration of each 10-minute interval. In other words, after the interval elapses, the next response will produce reinforcement if it occurs before the limited hold expires (Alberto & Troutman, 1986). Interval schedules without a limited hold enable individuals to respond any time after the fixed interval expires and still get reinforcement (Alberto & Troutman, 1986).

Let's review the characteristics of fixed interval schedules of reinforcement.

- A fixed-interval schedule of reinforcement is an intermittent schedule of reinforcement in which the first response that occurs after a set interval of time is reinforced. Responses made during the interval do not result in reinforcement (Cooper et al., 2007, 1).
- Fixed interval may be abbreviated "FI," and the duration of the interval may be placed after "FI." For example, FI 30-sec schedule means a fixed-interval schedule in which the first response that occurs after 30 seconds have elapsed produces reinforcement.

- Fixed-interval schedules typically produce a slow rate of responding until near the end of the interval, when the rate increases. This is called the *FI scallop* (Cooper et al., 2007; Mazur, 2017; Whaley & Malott, 1971).
- After the delivery of reinforcement on a fixed-interval schedule, there is a post-reinforcement pause (Cooper et al., 2007; Mazur, 2017).
- The duration of the interval affects the duration of the post-reinforcement pause and the rate of responding; the longer the interval, the longer the post-reinforcement pause and the lower the response rate (Cooper, et al., 2007).
- A limited hold procedure can be used to increase the rate of responding when applying interval schedules of reinforcement. A limited hold limits the time that reinforcement is available (Alberto & Troutman, 1986; Cooper et al., 2007).

**Variable-interval schedule of reinforcement**. A variable-interval schedule is a "schedule of intermittent reinforcement in which reinforcements is programmed according to a random series of intervals having a given mean and lying between arbitrary extreme values" (Ferster & Skinner, 1957). A variable-interval (VI) schedule of reinforcement is like a fixed-interval schedule of reinforcement, in that the first response after the expiration of the interval produces reinforcement. However, unlike a fixed-interval schedule, the duration of intervals fluctuates (Mazur, 2017). For example, in a VI10 schedule, the first response that occurs after intervals averaging 10 minutes in duration produces reinforcement, sometimes after 5 minutes and at other times after 15 minutes.

Ms. Burrhus used a VI15 schedule with Henry to reinforce prosocial behaviors (e.g., compliment giving or offering encouragement) during cooperative learning activities. She set a vibrating timer for intervals, which averaged five minutes each. After an interval elapsed, she reinforced the first prosocial response Henry made with a token he could later exchange for a preferred item, such as baseball cards. Since the length of the interval varied, Henry never knew when a response might produce reinforcement. He responded at a steady rate and continued responding even after receiving reinforcement.

Henry's performance is typical for a variable-interval schedule. Rates of response under a variable-interval schedule tend to be consistent and stable with few post-reinforcement pauses (Cooper et al., 2007). Since the individual cannot predict the length of the interval, he performs at a steady rate without the scallops of a fixed interval schedule (Alberto & Troutman, 1986).

Let's review important information about variable interval schedules.

- A variable-interval schedule of reinforcement is an intermittent schedule in which the duration of the interval varies (Cooper et al., 2007).
- Variable interval may be abbreviated "VI," and the average duration of intervals may be placed after the "VI." For example, VI5 means a variable-interval schedule in which the first response after intervals averaging 5 minutes is reinforced.
- Variable-interval schedules tend to cause a steady and stable rate of responding without scalloping, with minimal post-reinforcement pauses (Cooper et al., 2007).
- To increase the rate of responding, "a limited hold procedure may be implemented with either an FI or a VI schedule" (Alberto & Troutman, 1986; Cooper et al., 2007).

## ▶▶ *How Long Schedules of Reinforcement Last*

A specific reinforcement schedule may be used temporarily to cause a rapid change in behavior (Alberto & Troutman, 1986). However, individuals must be able to function in typical environments and under the control of natural reinforcers. Therefore, after an individual has met a specific criterion under an artificial schedule of reinforcement, it is important to gradually reduce the density of reinforcement by thinning the schedule or removing reinforcement so that reinforcement more closely approximates natural conditions. In this section, we discuss two ways of thinning or removing reinforcement: schedule thinning and extinction.

**Schedule thinning.** *Schedule thinning* involves reducing the frequency of reinforcement or requiring a greater number of appropriate responses to produce reinforcement (Alberto & Troutman, 1986). In a ratio schedule, the ratio requirement is gradually increased (Cooper et al., 2007). For example, Ms. Burrhus initially provided a reinforcer after Shaggy caught a tennis ball two times (FR2 schedule). After a few sessions in which Shaggy consistently caught the tennis ball, Ms. Burrhus thinned the schedule to an FR4 schedule. Cooper et al. (2007) suggested that the transition from a dense schedule of reinforcement to a thin schedule be based upon the individual's performance. Consistent with this recommendation and based upon Shaggy's performance, Ms. Burrhus gradually continued to thin the schedule by requiring more responses from Shaggy to produce reinforcement, until Shaggy could catch the ball 10 times before receiving a reinforcer. Thus, she started with a dense schedule of reinforcement (FR2) and gradually transitioned to a relatively thin schedule (FR10) in which reinforcement was less frequent. *Gradually* is the key word in the last sentence. Remember, ratio strain may occur if the ratio requirement is changed too quickly to maintain a steady rate of responding (Alberto & Troutman, pp. 225-226). This may result in an overall weakening of responding and an increase in pauses in responding (Mazur, 2017, p. 145).

Interval schedules also may be thinned by gradually increasing the duration of the interval (Cooper et al., 2007, p. 313). For example, in a previous example, Ms. Burrhus implemented a VI5 schedule to reinforce Henry's prosocial behaviors. She initially started with a VI1 and gradually thinned the schedule to VI5. She intends to continue thinning the reinforcement schedule gradually. When she thins the schedule, she explicitly explains the schedule to Henry and reviews the definitions of responses that will be reinforced (e.g., compliment giving, offering help). She is not sure that this improves his performance. However, he has made several successful transitions to thinner schedules of reinforcement, and Cooper et al. (2007, p.313) noted that interventions may be more effective when students are given information about what behavior will result in reinforcement.

In summary, schedule thinning facilitates the transition from a dense schedule of reinforcement to a thin schedule of reinforcement. But what happens if we withhold reinforcement entirely for a response that was previously reinforced? This is discussed in the next section.

**Extinction**. *Extinction* is the withholding of reinforcement for a previously reinforced response, which results in a decrease in the rate of the behavior (Ferster & Skinner, 1957). Cooper and colleagues (2007, p. 463) made three important observations regarding resistance to extinction and schedules of reinforcement. First, intermittent reinforcement schedules like the four schedules discussed in this chapter cause the response to be more resistant to extinction than continuous reinforcement. Furthermore, variable schedules of reinforcement may be more resistant to extinction than fixed schedules. Finally, to some extent, thinner schedules of reinforcement are more resistant to extinction than dense schedules of reinforcement.

Thus, it takes longer for a response to be extinguished when it has been maintained on an intermittent schedule of reinforcement than when it has been maintained on a continuous schedule of reinforcement (Mazur, 2017). After reinforcement is withheld, the individual may continue to make the response that has been previously reinforced (Alberto & Troutman, 1986). In fact, there tends to be an increase in the rate and intensity of the behavior before there is a decline (Watson, 1967). This increase is called an *extinction burst* (Newman et al., 2003). Sometimes, even after the response is extinguished, there is a *spontaneous recovery*, in which the individual exhibits the response again even in the absence of reinforcement (Alberto & Troutman, 1986). This phenomenon is brief if extinction procedures continue to be in place (Cooper et al., 2007). It is important to note that in schedule thinning, the goal is to maintain the response, while extinction procedures are used to extinguish a response.

## ▶▶ *Other Schedules of Reinforcement?*

This chapter has focused on the four basic schedules of intermittent reinforcement. However, there are many possible schedules for delivering reinforcement. For example, Alberto and Troutman (1986) described a *differential reinforcement of low rates of behavior* (DRL) schedule that can be used to maintain behavior at a certain rate. Under a DRL schedule, reinforcement is delivered when the number of responses in a given period of time is less than or equal to a set maximum rate (Alberto & Troutman, 1986). Similarly, under a *differential reinforcement of high rates* (DRH) schedule, reinforcement is delivered when a specified minimum (or greater) number of responses occurs within a set amount of time. DRH schedules of reinforcement produce rapid responding (Mazur, 2017). Finally, simple schedules of reinforcement may be combined. For example, under *concurrent schedules of reinforcement*, two or more response options are available, and each has a particular reinforcement schedule (Mazur, 2017). These schedules allow data to be collected on the individual's possible preferences regarding schedules and responses (Mazur, 2017). Thus, there are many possible ways to schedule the delivery of reinforcement.

## ▶▶ *Summary*

This chapter defined various types of schedules of reinforcement. A continuous reinforcement schedule provides reinforcement for each correct response. One example was when Shaggy was learning to sit. However, as in life outside of the laboratory, most of the examples in the chapter involved intermittent schedules of reinforcement, in which reinforcement follows some—but not all—responses. Henry playing basketball was an example of this. Intermittent schedules may be fixed or variable and ratio or interval. The chapter also described the four basic schedules of intermittent reinforcement (FR, VR, FI, VI) and discussed typical response patterns under each schedule. Though this chapter focused on the four basic schedules of intermittent reinforcement, countless rules are possible for distributing reinforcement.

# *References*

Alberto, P. A., & Troutman, A. C. (2013). *Applied behavior analysis for teachers* (9$^{nd}$ ed.). Upper Saddle River, NJ: Prentice-Hall

Cooper, J. O., Heron, T. E., & Heward, W. L. (2007). *Applied behavior analysis* (2$^{nd}$ ed.). Upper Saddle River, NJ: Pearson.

Ferster, C. B., & Skinner, B. F. (1957). *Schedules of reinforcement.* Acton, MA: Copley.

Mazur, J. E. (2017). *Learning and behavior* (8th ed.). New York, NY: Routledge.

Newman, B., Reeve, K. F., Reeve, S. A., & Ryan, C. S. (2003). *Behaviorspeak: A glossary of terms in applied behavior analysis.* Victoria, BC: Dove and Orca.

Skinner, B. F. (1953). *Science and human behavior.* New York, NY: MacMillan.

Watson, L. S. (1967). Application of operant conditioning techniques to institutionalized severely and profoundly retarded children. *Mental Retardation Abstracts,*4, 1-18.

Whaley, D. L., & Malott, R. W. (1971). *Elementary principles of behavior.* Englewood Cliffs, NJ: Prentice Hall.

# DIFFERENTIAL REINFORCEMENT STRATEGIES FOR
# ADDRESSING CHALLENGING BEHAVIOR

*Kevin M. Ayres, Kadijah Quinland, Anna Butler, & Rachel Cagliani*

## KEY TERMS:

- Differential reinforcement
- Differential reinforcement of alternative behaviors
- Differential reinforcement of other behaviors
- Differential reinforcement of incompatible behaviors
- Differential reinforcement of low rates of behavior
- Differential reinforcement of high rates of behavior
- Extinction
- Functionally equivalent
- Functional communication training
- Thinning
- Multiple schedules

A foundational principle of applied behavior analysis is that most human behavior is maintained by contingencies of reinforcement (see Chapter 8). That is, individuals behave to access desirable stimuli (e.g., the attention of a peer) and escape undesirable stimuli (e.g., disapproval of a parent). How they "behave" to access those stimuli is a result of the well-established process of differential reinforcement, in which particular responses result in access to reinforcers and others do not. An individuals' repertoire, from their vocabulary to their choices in clothing have been selected through differential reinforcement (DR). For example, a teenager may develop a set of new favorite bands based on feedback received from peers or a child may tantrum when his mother is on the phone because typical bids for attention have not worked in the past.

## ▶▶ *Defining Differential Reinforcement*

Differential reinforcemetnt is a ubiquitous process across every aspect of life, but also can be harnessed as an intervention tool for use in home, educational, and clinical settings. For example, a therapist targeting an increase in the length of a child's vocalizations might reinforce the vocal request "Toy truck" while ignoring (i.e., putting on extinction) the response, "Toy." When teaching new skills, practitioners often use DR to provide reinforcement for correct responding while ignoring or correcting errors. During behavior reduction programs, they often place problem behavior on extinction (if possible) and reinforce appropriate responding (or absence of problem behavior). In this chapter, we will focus on the use of DR to reduce problem behavior; specifically, DR procedures that displace undesirable responding (e.g., harmful, disruptive) with socially acceptable or safe patterns of responding.

Researchers have developed and tested multiple forms of DR procedures for use across a range of contexts. DR procedures are often difficult for practitioners to differentiate and thus, implement. In this chapter, we will describe several systematic applications of DR, including differential reinforcement of alternative behaviors (DRA), differential reinforcement of incompatible behaviors (DRI), differential reinforcement of other behaviors (DRO), differential reinforcement of low rates (DRL), and differential reinforcement of high rates (DRH). Further, we will provide the reader with basic steps for implementing each procedure, examples designed to illustrate how the program would fit into classrooms or therapy contexts, and potential drawbacks to implementing each of the procedures.

## ▶▶ *Differential Reinforcement of Alternative Behavior*

Differential reinforcement of alternative behavior (DRA) is a procedure in which behaviors that serve as an alternative to or replacement for an individual's targeted problem behavior are reinforced (Athens & Vollmer, 2010; Piazza, Moes, & Fisher, 1996). As such, it allows individuals to engage in an alternative behavior to access the same reinforcers previously accessed by engaging in problem behavior. In other words, when using DRA, one reinforces a response that is *functionally equivalent* to the problem behavior.

For example, after determining to that a student engages in disruptive behavior (e.g., throwing pencils) to be removed from the classroom (i.e., negative reinforcement), a teacher chooses to reinforce the student's request for a break as an alternative behavior. Throwing pencils and requesting a break can occur at the same time; however, the teacher will only reinforce the appropriate behavior (i.e., requesting) in the absence of the inappropriate behavior (i.e., throwing pencils). She plans to initially reinforce every instance of the request behavior while—when possible—placing the problem behavior on extinction (i.e., not sending the student out of the room following disruptive behavior).

## Implementing DRA

**Selecting an alternative behavior.** When choosing an alternative behavior(s), it is important to ensure that it allows the individual access to the same type of reinforcement as that of a problem behavior. For example, if a child engages in scratching behavior maintained by access to tangible items, an alternative behavior may be used to teach an appropriate way to access the item(s). DRA is most effective when the alternative behavior is already in the individual's repertoire. For instance, if the child above uses a picture exchange system to communicate, then teaching the child to exchange the picture of the desired item(s) would be an appropriate alternative behavior.

When choosing alternative behaviors, interventionists also must consider the amount of effort required to engage in both the problem behavior and the alternative behavior. Ideally, the alternative behavior must require a response effort similar to less than that of the problem behavior. If the alternative behavior requires more effort than the problem behavior, then the individual may continue engaging in the problem behavior. For example, teaching a student to emit a sentence using manual signs instead of punching the teaching staff to access their attention might not be effective, as the formation of multiple signs often requires more effort than the single extension of his fist. Instead, it might be more appropriate to require a single sign or an approximation of a sign for access to attention.

Additionally, it is critical that the interventionist informs all parties who work with an individual to provide reinforcement when the alternative behavior occurs. A failure to clearly specify target alternative behaviors or communicate with all relevant parties may result in the limited reinforcement of the alternative behavior and a failure to displace problem behavior. For instance, if a therapist teaches a child to use sign language to request play time as a replacement for throwing toys, his parents and teachers also need to be directed to reinforce his signed requests. That is, if the other adults around the child cannot recognize the sign or are unaware of the plan to reinforce the sign, the child may revert back to throwing toys rather than using the new alternative response.

**Choosing appropriate reinforcers.** A functional assessment will direct a therapist toward the appropriate reinforcer for use during the DRA procedure. A functional assessment often referred to as functional behavior assessment (FBA) is a process for determining the purpose a behavior serves for an individual (see Chapter 6). FBA procedures generally include one or more of the following: (a) rating scales and interviews (e.g., Questions About Behavioral Functioning [QABF]; Vollmer & Matson, 1995); (b) antecedent-behavior-consequence (ABC) data collection; or (c) functional analysis (Iwata, Dorsey, Slifer, Bauman, & Richmond, 1994). After determining the function of a target behavior(s), the next step is to identify possible reinforcers. This can be completed by using preference assessments as discussed in Chapter 7. Finally, the therapist identifies the magnitude, duration, or quantity of the reinforcer to provide for the alternative response.

**Incorporating extinction.** In the DRA procedure, the alternative behavior may occur at the same time as the problem behavior. Therefore, the schedules of reinforcement for the target problem behavior and the alternative behavior must be carefully considered. Ideally, a teacher or therapist places the target problem behavior on extinction (i.e., discontinuation of reinforcement that previously followed the target behavior). When extinction is not appropriate (e.g., ignoring a student who engages in self-injury to get attention) or possible (e.g., preventing a 300-lb man from leaving his work area), the interventionist can adjust the schedule of reinforcement for the target problem behavior so that the alternative behavior results in access to reinforcement either sooner, more frequently, with a greater magnitude, or with greater quality.

**Considering the schedule of reinforcement.** Initially, interventionists must commit to reinforcing the alternative behavior each time it occurs. In other words, the alternative behavior would initially contact reinforcement on a continuous or fixed ratio of one schedule (FR1) (see Chapter 8). Providing access to a preferred reinforcer immediately every time the individual engages in the alternative behavior is rarely sustainable. Once the data reflect that the individual uses the alternative behavior regularly, it is time to begin gradually thinning the schedule of reinforcement. Specific guidelines for thinning schedules of reinforcement were described in Chapter 8, but there are specific ways that you can thin reinforcement when using a DRA procedure.

*Multiple schedules.* The schedule of reinforcement can be gradually thinned when implementing a DRA procedure by occasionally and temporarily restricting access to the identified reinforcer. A multiple-schedule arrangement can be used with a signal stimulus, alerting the individual when reinforcement is available and not available. For example, an interventionist may teach a student how to request to go outside using a form of picture exchange. Given that going outside is not always an option, the interventionist may choose to signal to the student when outside is available and not available by placing the picture card on various colored backgrounds (e.g., green – available, red – not available). Gradually, the ratio of green to red background (i.e., available to not available) is decreased until the schedule reflects that of the natural environment.

Delay to reinforcement. Another way to thin the schedule of reinforcement involves temporarily delaying access to the reinforcer. Initially, the therapist or parent may provide the reinforcer immediately upon request. Later, they may require a brief period of time to lapse after a request is made before providing access. In the example above, if the student requests to go outside, the therapist would respond by saying, "Okay, you can go outside, but you have to wait for five minutes." This type of schedule thinning closely resembles situations in the natural environment where a parent or teacher may not be able to provide the reinforcer immediately.

## ▶▶ *Common Forms of DRA*

Differential reinforcement of alternative behavior procedures are commonly applied in educational and therapeutic contexts. Two of the most common applications involve differentially reinforcing communicative responses and work or task completion.

**Functional communication training.** The response that is taught to replace problem behavior through *functional communication training* (FCT) can serve as an alternative behavior for DRA procedures (Carr & Durand, 1985). Therapists begin teaching FCT after first determining the function of the problem behavior by conducting a functional (behavior) assessment. Therefore, the alternative response is directly tied to the function of the behavior.

For example, a therapist may conduct functional assessment interview with a parent and subsequently run a brief functional analysis in the home and determine that a child's kicking and screaming behavior is maintained by access to attention. The parent reports that the behavior occurs most often when he is preparing dinner and attention, therefore, is diverted away from the child. The therapist begins FCT during meal preparation time by teaching the child to recruit attention by pressing a speech-generating device (SGD) that produces a vocalization saying, "Talk to me." The parent is then coached to provide the child with a brief period of high-quality attention and to no longer provide attention when problem behavior occurs. In this situation, the request for attention using the SGD replaced the problem behavior and served as an alternative behavior to aggression and disruption.

**Work completion**. Teachers and therapists may choose to use work completion as an alternative behavior for behaviors maintained by negative reinforcement in the form of escape from demands. Rather than the student escaping from completing the demand by engaging in problem behavior, he would escape work by completing either a set amount of questions or by working for a predetermined duration of time. For example, when a student worked on math problems, he engaged in property destruction by destroying the materials. The teacher determined that this behavior was maintained by negative reinforcement in the form of escape from demands. Rather than allowing the student to escape from demands by engaging in problem behavior, the teacher required him to complete five math problems before a break was delivered.

It is important to note that if work completion is used as an alternative behavior for escape-maintained behaviors, it may be necessary to implement a teaching procedure to ensure escape does not continue to take place. If a therapist places a demand, but the student does not comply, she is temporarily escaping from the demand. By implementing a teaching procedure (e.g., providing more information, physically guiding the student to complete the response) the teacher or therapist prevents the student from escaping from the task.

## ▶▶ *Potential Drawbacks to Using DRA*

Although DRA procedures have proven to be effective at reducing the rates of problem behavior, there are a few potential drawbacks to consider when implementing this type of intervention. In order for the alternative behavior to generalize to new settings, the interventionist must train those interacting with the individual how to recognize and respond to the alternative behavior. For instance, a child may use the vocalization "Tah" in order to access his tablet as an alternative to aggression. While this vocalization is recognizable to the staff and his parents, a substitute teacher or new caregiver may not recognize and acknowledge this request, which might lead to the resurgence of problem behavior. In addition, it may not always be possible to reinforce each instance of the alternative behavior. Instances may arise where the reinforcer is not available. For example, a child requests her favorite blanket with her SGD while riding in the car with her mother. The blanket is in the very back of the car, so her mother is unable to reinforce the request immediately.

To successfully address situations like this, it is important that interventionists are able to contrive opportunities for individuals to practice responding appropriately to rejection or a delay in reinforcement. Table 9.1 provides an overview of DRA

# Table 9.1

*Step-by-Step: Differential Reinforcement of Alternative Behaviors*

| STEPS | EXAMPLE A | EXAMPLE B |
|---|---|---|
| Define the problem behavior(s) | Hitting: any instance or attempt in which the student's hand (open or closed fist) comes into contact with another person from a distance of 6" or more (each hand is one instance). | Throwing materials: any instance or attempt in which the client holds an item in one or both of their hands and releases the item through the air a distance of 6" or greater so that it lands greater than 12" from another person (each item is one instance; does not include throwing toys or items designed to be thrown). |
| Establish baseline responding for the problem behavior | Teacher collects data across three independent work sessions, which was determined to be the specific time of concern. The teacher reports that the problem behavior occurs about 7 times per minute. | Clinician observes the student in their home on three separate occasions. The client engages in the behavior about three times per minute. |
| Determine function of target behavior(s) | Behavior analyst coaches the teacher through conducting a trial-based FA and determines that hitting is maintained by positive reinforcement in the form of attention from teachers and staff. | Behavior analyst conducts a multi-element functional analysis in the clinic and determines that throwing materials is maintained by negative reinforcement in the form of escape from demands. |

## Table 9.1

*Step-by-Step: Differential Reinforcement of Alternative Behaviors (cont.)*

| STEPS | EXAMPLE A | EXAMPLE B |
|---|---|---|
| Choose and define an alternative response(s) to reinforce | The student uses the Picture Exchange Communication System (PECS; Bondy & Frost, 1994) to communicate so the team decides on that exchanging a picture card with the staff members would be an appropriate alternative response. | The team conducted a mand modality assessment and determined the most preferred modality to be a BIGmack speech-generating device with the word "break" recorded. |
| Establish baseline responding of the alternative response | During independent work, the teacher made the picture available without training and the student did not independently request attention. | During daily living activities in the home, the parent presented the BIGmack, but the client did not independently engage in the alternative response. |
| Teach the alternative response, if needed | Teacher used system of least prompts to teach the student how to access reinforcement. The prompt levels were verbal, model, and physical. | Based on an observation, the clinician determined that a model prompt was the controlling prompt. The team used progressive time delay to teach the alternative response. |

# Table 9.1

*Step-by-Step: Differential Reinforcement of Alternative Behaviors (cont.)*

| STEPS | EXAMPLE A | EXAMPLE B |
|---|---|---|
| Set criteria to thin | Sessions were five minutes in length. After three five-minute sessions without problem behavior and independent alternative response, the teacher added a delay to reinforcement by saying, "hold on, I'll be right there" and waited five seconds. After every three consecutive five-minute sessions without problem behavior and with independent responding the delay to reinforcement was increased by five seconds. | Initially, the parent placed a demand and the clinician prompted the client to immediately prompt for a break. After the client independently requested a break three times, the client had to complete at least one step of the task analysis for various daily living skills before requesting the break. The number of demands was increased by one after every three consecutive sessions without problem behavior and with independent responding. |
| Reinforce all instances of alternative behavior | Initially, the teacher immediately reinforced all instances of picture exchange. After successful sessions the delay to reinforcement was increased in five-minute increments. | Initially, the parent reinforced all instances of speech-generating device activations. Demands were increased after successful sessions. |

## Table 9.1

*Step-by-Step: Differential Reinforcement of Alternative Behaviors (cont.)*

| STEPS | EXAMPLE A | EXAMPLE B |
|---|---|---|
| Implement and monitor | Teacher collected data during independent work sessions on problem behavior and the level of prompting required for the alternative response. | Parent collected data during daily living time in their home on problem behavior and the level of prompting required for the client to engage in the alternative response. |
| Begin thinning the schedule of reinforcement once criteria are met | Student met criteria for the initial delay to reinforcement increase after eight sessions. The behavior analyst advised that the cap for delay to reinforcement be one minute given a norm reference sample of wait times in a general education setting. | Client met criteria for the initial thinning criteria after five trials. |

## ▶▶ *Differential Reinforcement of Incompatible Behavior*

Differential reinforcement of incompatible behavior is similar to DRA in that the interventionist programs reinforcement for an alternative to a problem behavior. It differs from DRA in that the alternative and problem behavior cannot occur simultaneously. For example, a practitioner may use DRI for a child who engages in running away by reinforcing the incompatible behavior of sitting in a seat.

## ▶▶ *Implementation*

Selecting incompatible behaviors. When selecting incompatible behaviors to program for reinforcement, the teacher or therapist must consider the different contexts to which the student is exposed across the day. For instance, if a child engages in hand mouthing, the teacher may reinforce the behavior of keeping hands on instructional material during academic times, but may reinforce leaving hands in pockets when transitioning throughout the school. As with other DR procedures, it is important to put the target problem behavior(s) on extinction when possible and appropriate.

## ▶▶ *Potential Drawbacks to Differential Reinforcement of Incompatible Behavior*

In addition to sharing many potential drawbacks with DRA, DRI procedures can be challenging to design. Teachers and therapists may notice that there are certain behaviors for which it may be difficult to identify an appropriate incompatible response. For example, an incompatible response for spitting on the ground might be whistling, talking, or blowing, but each of these responses may be problematic in a classroom setting.

## Table 9.2

*Step-by-Step: Differential Reinforcement of Incompatible Behaviors*

| STEPS | EXAMPLE A | EXAMPLE B |
|---|---|---|
| Define the problem behavior(s) | Ripping materials off walls: any instance or attempt in which the student grabs an item off the wall (often occurs in the hallway; each item is one instance). | Disrupting materials: any instance or attempt in which the child holds an item in one or both of their hands and releases the item through the air a distance of 6" or greater so that it lands greater than 12" from another person (each item is one instance; does not include throwing toys or items designed to be thrown). |
| Determine the function of the target behavior(s) (not required but helpful for using extinction) | Based on the results of an indirect assessment, the teacher and behavior analyst hypothesize that the problem behavior is maintained by negative reinforcement in the form of escape from transitions. | Based on the results of a brief functional analysis, the in-home behavior analyst determined that problem behavior was maintained by access to attention. |

# Table 9.2

*Step-by-Step: Differential Reinforcement of Incompatible Behaviors (cont.)*

| STEPS | EXAMPLE A | EXAMPLE B |
|---|---|---|
| Establish baseline responding for problem behavior | Teacher collected data during each transition in the hallway across five transitions and determined that the behavior occurred approximately 0.5 times per minute. | In-home behavior analyst collected data during three work sessions and determined that disruption occurred approximately 0.3 per minute throughout work sessions when she was preparing materials for the next trial. |
| Choose and define incompatible response(s) to reinforce | Hands in pockets or down by side: having at least the thumb of both hands in pockets or hands down by side touch outer thigh. | Ready hands: having both hands on top of the table interlocked. Based on three observations, the behavior occurred an average of 5 times per minute. |
| Establish baseline responding for the incompatible behavior | The behavior occurs an average 20% of all transitions. | The behavior only occurred in between teaching trials when materials were being prepared. |

## Table 9.2

*Step-by-Step: Differential Reinforcement of Incompatible Behaviors (cont.)*

| STEPS | EXAMPLE A | EXAMPLE B |
|---|---|---|
| Conduct preference assessments (if necessary) | Teacher met with the student and gathered information on his preferences through an interview. The student prefers earning time to play basketball. | In-home behavior analyst conducted a free-operant preference assessment and determined that the client preferred bouncing on a trampoline. |
| Set criteria to thin | To start, the student accessed a token for every 30 seconds of engagement in the incompatible behavior. Each token represented a minute of basketball time at a later time. After three transitions without problem behavior, the interval of time required to access a token was increased by 30 seconds. | To start, the student accessed trampoline time for one minute after every one minute without problem behavior. After five work sessions without problem behavior the interval of time without problem behavior was increased by 30 seconds. |
| Implement and monitor | Teacher collected data during all transitions on the duration per occurrence of engagement in the incompatible behavior an occurrences of problem behavior. | In-home therapist collected data during work sessions on the occurrences of problem behavior. |

## ▶▶ *Differential Reinforcement of Other Behavior*

*Differential reinforcement of other behaviors* is a behavioral change tactic often used to reduce problem behavior (Piazza, Moes, & Fisher, 1998; Ringdahl et al., 2002). Unlike other forms of differential reinforcement, when using this procedure, the interventionist does not specify an alternative or incompatible behavior to reinforce but, instead, reinforces the absence of the problem behavior while other behaviors are occurring. In addition to providing reinforcement contingent upon the absence of problem behavior, the interventionist may choose to put the problem behavior being targeted for change on extinction.

## ▶▶ *Implementation*

Regardless of the form of DRO selected, the teacher usually starts by telling the student what is going to occur: "If you keep your hands out of your mouth for five minutes, you will earn a token." The teacher then sets the timer and observes. If the student engages in the target behavior at any time during the interval (interval DRO) or at the end of the interval (momentary DRO), the teacher resets the timer and the next interval begins (without the delivery of a reinforcer). If the teacher does not know the function of the behavior, generally, it is recommended to provide as little social attention when resetting the timer as is possible. However, knowing the function of the problem behavior and using that reinforcer to meet the response requirements increases the likelihood that DRO will be effective.

Although variations exist, if problem behavior occurs at any point in the interval, the prevailing convention is to reset the interval. If the interval is not reset, the omission criterion essentially increases. For example, if a teacher does not reset the timer when a child engages in problem behavior 30 seconds into a 60-second interval, the child potentially has to not engage in problem behavior for 90 seconds (i.e., the 30 seconds remaining in the interval and the subsequent 60 seconds).

Interventionists might find it helpful to use a visual timer to help the individual discriminate when the DRO is in effect and to provide a reminder of the response requirement (i.e., period of time in which they must not engage in the problem behavior). When beginning implementation, ongoing data collection helps guide changes to the program. If the student fails to reliably meet the DRO schedule multiple times, it may be necessary to decrease the interval duration. If, on the other hand, the student reliably accesses reinforcement without problem behavior, the DRO interval may be increased as reinforcement is thinned.

## ▶▶ *Setting the Interval*

Once the behavior is defined, the teacher or therapist must identify the initial omission interval. Baseline data are used to guide this decision. The teacher or therapist must first identify how long the student can do anything *other* than engage in the problem behavior. Cooper, Heron, and Heward (2007) suggested calculating interresponse time (IRT) by dividing the total duration of the observation by the total number of times the target behavior occurred. This provides a sense of what omission interval would permit the student to begin accessing reinforcement. Thus, an observation interval of 60 minutes, in which the behavior of interest occurs 20 times, would yield a mean IRT of three minutes (60 minutes/20 responses = 3 minutes mean IRT). This gross calculation assumes that the occurrence of behavior is evenly distributed across the observation period, but nonetheless allows for a starting point to generate an initial DRO interval. Calculating the intervals in such a way helps to ensure that the interval is short enough to enable the student to come into contact with reinforcement. During this initial period of data collection, the teacher is encouraged to conduct a preference assessment to identify likely reinforcers to use with the procedure.

## ▶▶ *Schedule of Reinforcement*

Once the problem behavior decreases at the initial interval requirement, thinning the schedule becomes a priority. The DRO schedule may be thinned by gradually increasing the length of the interval. The interval may be lengthened using two simple methods. First, using the constant-duration method, the interval may be increased by a constant period of time (e.g., five seconds). Second, the interval may be increased proportionately (e.g., 5%) (Cooper, Heron & Heward, 2007). If problem behavior worsens when the length of interval is increased, it may be because the schedule of reinforcement was increased too quickly, thus inducing ratio strain or a pause in responding due to a shift in reinforcement frequency (Reed, 2015). If ratio strain occurs, the therapist can return to the last interval duration at which problem behavior did not occur and reintroduce interval thinning in smaller increments. Developing a plan for thinning the schedule of reinforcement prior to starting a DRO program helps to ensure a seamless transition from initial programming to schedule thinning.

The major limitation of implementing a DRO procedure is that other problem behavior may inadvertently be reinforced if another problem behavior occurs at the end of the interval. This may necessitate revisiting and, in some cases, expanding, the reinforcement requirement (i.e., include the new behavior into the omission criteria). In addition, because DRO does not involve reinforcement of a specific behavior, the teacher or therapist essentially leaves to chance what behaviors will displace the problem behavior. For example, a teacher may implement a DRO targeting a child picking at his dry lips with his fingers, but then notices that the child increasingly chews and licks his lips. Consequently, reinforcement of omission may not be the most efficient means to bring about desirable social behaviors.

## ▶▶ *Variations of DRO*

Implementation of DRO typically involves reinforcing any behavior other than the problem behavior if that behavior has not occurred for a specific amount of time (interval DRO) or at a specific moment in time (momentary DRO). Interval DRO and momentary DRO may be further categorized by the schedule regularity, which is essentially whether the schedule is a fixed or variable amount of time. Combination of the omission contingency and the schedule yields four variations of DRO: fixed-interval DRO, variable-interval DRO, fixed-momentary DRO, and variable-momentary DRO.

**Fixed-interval DRO.** The fixed-interval DRO (FI-DRO) is a commonly used DRO schedule. First, the teacher or therapist establishes a set interval and programs reinforcement contingent upon the absence of problem behavior for the specified amount of time. Intervals may be long (e.g., entire day) or brief (e.g., 30 seconds), dependent upon the frequency of the target behavior. The defining feature of an FI-DRO is that the interval duration is constant until a specified criterion is met and thinning begins.

**Variable-interval DRO.** Implementation of variable interval DRO (VI-DRO) is identical to that of the FI-DRO with one exception: the VI-DRO uses intervals that vary in duration. Therefore, a VI-DRO 30-second schedule would include intervals of varying times that averaged 30 seconds (i.e., 30 seconds, 20 seconds, and 40 seconds). The variable interval is often easier for teachers and parents to implement, given the other duties and responsibilities they may have in addition to implementing the protocol.

**Fixed- and variable-momentary DRO.** Fixed-momentary DRO (FM-DRO) and variable-momentary DRO (VM-DRO) are implemented much like the interval DRO procedures; the key difference is that reinforcement is provided contingent upon the absence of the problem behavior at a specific moment in time, as opposed to the omission of behavior for an entire interval. Similar to momentary time sampling, Momentary DRO should only be used for behaviors that occur continuously. For example, during implementation of an FM-DRO 10-minute schedule, reinforcement would be provided if the behavior targeted for reduction did not occur at the end of 10 minutes. When using a VM-DRO 10-minute schedule, the teacher would record responding at the end of intervals that varied in duration, but averaged 10 minutes (e.g., eight minutes, 12 minutes, 10 minutes).

## ▶▶ *Potential Drawbacks to Differential Reinforcement of Other Behavior*

There are several drawbacks inherent in a formal or "pure" DRO procedure. First, DRO procedures generally have weaker effects on reducing problem behavior than the other DR procedures (Mulick, Leitenberg, & Rawson, 1976). Second, as mentioned earlier, an alternative behavior is not taught in place of the inappropriate behavior being put on extinction (Lindberg, Iwata, Kahng, & DeLeon, 1999); therefore, with a DRO procedure, interventionists risk reinforcing other inappropriate behavior. For example, if a student who typically screams at his teacher in order to recruit attention is provided a reinforcer for doing anything but screaming at teachers, he may engage in a myriad other inappropriate behaviors (e.g., aggression, disruption) in order to recruit attention and still meet the requirements to receive the reinforcer. Third, DRO schedules may be labor-intensive, as they require constant monitoring of the individual of interest, particularly when interval DRO schedules are being utilized (Vollmer, Iwata, Zarcone, Smith, & Mazaleski, 1993).

## Table 9.3
*Step-by-Step: Differential Reinforcement of Other Behavior*

| STEPS | EXAMPLE A | EXAMPLE B |
|---|---|---|
| Define the problem behavior | Self-injurious behavior (SIB): any instance/attempt in which the student's arm or hand makes contact with their teeth (excludes tips of fingers). | Inappropriate language: cursing (including less offensive words like hell, damn). |
| Establish baseline responding | Based on teacher data, SIB occurred about seven times per minute throughout the school day. | Based on teacher data, the student cursed at a rate of .08 across a 7.5 hour school day. |
| Conduct stimulus-preference assessment | An MSWO (Deleon & Iwata,1996) preference assessment, indicated that the iPad was the highest preferred stimulus. | Based on an interview with the student, the teacher determined that the student preferred free time with peers or preferred adults. |

141

CHAPTER 9

## Table 9.3
*Step-by-Step: Differential Reinforcement of Other Behavior (cont.)*

| STEPS | EXAMPLE A | EXAMPLE B |
|---|---|---|
| Determine form of DRO to be used | The teacher decided on a fixed-interval DRO. The set interval of time allowed for multiple staff to run the DRO with ease. | The teacher decided on a variable-interval DRO. |
| Establish interval length | The interval length began at 15 seconds which was based off of data collection of inter-response time of problem behavior. | The interval length began at five minutes which was based off of data collection of the interresponse time of problem behavior. |
| Establish criteria to thin | After three sessions without problem behavior, the interval increased by15 seconds until reaching one minute. After one minute, the interval increased by 30 seconds. The maximum interval was set at 10 minutes. | After three days without problem behavior, the interval was increased by two minutes |

## Table 9.3
*Step-by-Step: Differential Reinforcement of Other Behavior (cont.)*

| STEPS | EXAMPLE A | EXAMPLE B |
|---|---|---|
| Implement and monitor | Teacher and paraprofessionals implemented the FI-DRO across the school day and collected data on instances of SIB and the time it took to meet criteria for reinforcement | Classroom teacher implemented the VI-DRO across the school day and collected data on instances of inappropriate language and the time it took to meet criteria for reinforcement. |

APPLIED BEHAVIOR ANALYSIS FOR EVERYONE
PRINCIPLES AND PRACTICES EXPLAINED BY APPLIED RESEARCHERS WHO USE THEM

## ▶▶ *Differential Reinforcement of Various Rates*

When a somebody has an appropriate behavior in their repertoire, but engages in that behavior too often, or not frequently enough, a *differential reinforcement of lower rates of behavior* (DRL) *or differential reinforcement of higher rates of behavior* (DRH) procedure may be used to reduce or increase that behavior. The basic process with DRL is to gradually provide reinforcement for lower rates of responding until the behavior reaches an acceptable level. For example, a teacher may decide that a student asks questions too frequently. The teacher wants the student to continue asking questions, but does not want this behavior to occur as frequently.

Similarly, in a DRH procedure, the teacher or therapist aims to gradually increase responding to appropriate levels. But, conceptually, this procedure represents the inverse of DRL. The student accesses reinforcement when his rate of responding continues to meet the gradually increasing criterion. For example, a professor may determine that a student she is supervising vocalizes words too infrequently per minute. A DRH might be developed to increase the number of words the student produces per minute in order to communicate clearly. In the aforementioned scenarios, a DRO, DRA, or DRI would not be an appropriate intervention, since the end goal for those procedures is to eliminate the target behavior. The goal of DRH/L is to move the target behaviors toward a more acceptable frequency by reinforcing higher or lower rates of the behavior depending on the target goal.

## ▶▶ *Implementation*

To set up a DRL or DRH procedure, the first step is to measure an individual's baseline responding. This may require several days of data collection to establish current rates of behavior. During this time, the therapist can conduct a stimulus-preference assessment to identify potential reinforcers. After baseline data collection, the therapist has to set a terminal goal for an acceptable rate of behavior. One way to do this in a classroom context is to identify one or more students whom the teacher believes respond at appropriate rates. Referring to the aforementioned examples, the teacher would collect data on students who ask an appropriate number of questions during a lesson, or a student who speaks at an acceptable rate for fluent conversation. By collecting data on the frequency of these "model" individuals, the interventionist can establish a norm-referenced criterion to work into the program. In other contexts, the therapist may ask the stakeholders what would be a reasonable final criterion or take a sample of a group of individuals.

These types of DR procedures are commonly implemented when attempting to move a student to a setting that is less restrictive (e.g., from a self-contained special education setting to a collaborative setting). Suppose that the model students engage in the response four times per hour compared to the target student, who responds 20 times per hour, with a range of 15-22 responses per hour. Setting a final criterion at no more than four responses per hour would align the target student's responding with that of her peers. Since setting an initial criterion at four responses per hour would likely not be effective, the therapist might consider using the individual's lowest rate of responses emitted during baseline (i.e., the student's "best" day). As the student begins to receive reinforcement for the lower rate of response, the therapist can gradually shift the schedule closer to the final criterion.

## ▶▶ *Drawbacks to Differential Reinforcement of Various Rates*

Since both DRH and DRL are based upon intervals during which a certain amount of the target behavior is allowed or required to occur, both procedures may be difficult to implement within a classroom setting. First, if a response occurs at high rates, it will require that the teacher observe and record every occurrence of the response while simultaneously attending to the needs of the other students. Second, these procedures are designed to produce gradual change. Therefore, if the response is dangerous or disruptive, the DRH/DRL procedures might not be appropriate.

## Table 9.4
*Step-by-Step: Differential Reinforcement of Various Rates Behavior*

| STEPS | EXAMPLE A | EXAMPLE B |
|---|---|---|
| Define the problem behavior. | Requesting help during independent computer time: any instance in which the student mands for help by reaching for a staff member, vocally approximating help, or using his speech-generating device to request "help." | Interacting with peers: any instance in which the student initiated an interaction by vocalizing at least three words directed at a peer within one minute of a peer during recess. |
| Establish baseline responding | Behavior analyst assisting in the classroom collected data during three independent computer time and determined that the behavior occurred about two times per minute during 15-minute computer sessions. | Special education teacher determined that the behavior occurred about .06 per minutes during recess (three times during a 30-minute session). |

## Table 9.4
*Step-by-Step: Differential Reinforcement of Various Rates Behavior (cont.)*

| STEPS | EXAMPLE A | EXAMPLE B |
|---|---|---|
| Conduct a stimulus-preference assessment | Behavior analyst conducted a MSWO preference assessment and determined that the individual preferred gummies and a fidget. | Behavior analyst conducted a free-operant preference assessment with recess activities and determined that the individual preferred time on the swing alone. |
| Set final criteria for an acceptable frequency of behavior | The team determined that the acceptable frequency of behavior during the 15 minute computer time was five requests per period. | The team determined that the acceptable frequency of behavior during the 30 minutes recess time was 10 interactions. |
| Set initial criteria for accessing reinforcement | Initially, if the behavior occurred less than 12 times per session, the student accessed reinforcement. | Initially, if the behavior occurred at least five times during a 30 minute of recess, the individual could access alone time on the swing. Therefore, as soon as he interacted five times he could move toward the swing to play alone. |

## Table 9.4
*Step-by-Step: Differential Reinforcement of Various Rates Behavior (cont.)*

| STEPS | EXAMPLE A | EXAMPLE B |
|---|---|---|
| Thin reinforcement by gradually decreasing/increasing the criteria | After three sessions with less than 12 requests for help while on the computer, the number of requests was decreased by one until reaching the final level of five per session. | After three recess sessions with at least five interactions, the number of interactions required was increase by two. The number of interactions was increased by two after three recess sessions where the previous criteria was met. |

## ▶▶ Determining the Most Appropriate Differential Reinforcement Procedure

In general, the goal is to select the simplest and least intrusive intervention to achieve the desired effect. An elegant and complex procedure may have a certain aesthetic appeal but may be difficult to implement with fidelity.

Figure 9.1 provides a schematic that can assist a team in deciding which intervention options may be appropriate. Beginning with basic questions regarding the goal for the problem behavior, the decision tree will guide the team in selecting an appropriate DR procedure.

## ▶▶ Summary

Differential reinforcement is a foundational principle in behavior analysis and is responsible for the establishment and maintenance of much of each individual's behavioral repertoire. The systematic application of DR is one of the most common approaches to behavior change within the field of applied behavior analysis. This chapter described several powerful DR procedures, their steps for implementation, and potential variations and procedural drawbacks for consideration.

# *References*

Athens, E. S., & Vollmer, T. R. (2010). An investigation of differential reinforcement of alternative behavior without extinction. *Journal of Applied Behavior Analysis*, 43, 569-589.

Bondy, A. S., & Frost, L. A. (1994). The picture exchange communication system. *Focus on Autistic Behavior*, 9, 1-19.

Carr, E. G., & Durand, V. M. (1985). Reducing behavior problems through functional communication training. *Journal of Applied Behavior Analysis*, 18, 111-126.

Cooper, J. O., Heron, T. E., & Heward, W. L. (2007). *Applied behavior analysis* (2nd ed.). Upper Saddle River, NJ: Pearson.

Deleon, I. G., & Iwata, B. A. (1996). Evaluation of a multiple-stimulus presentation format for assessing reinforce preferences. *Journal of Applied Behavior Analysis*, 29, 519-33.

Iwata, B. A., Dorsey, M. F., Slifer, K. J., Bauman, K. E., & Richman, G. S. (1994). Toward a functional analysis of self-injury. *Journal of Applied Behavior Analysis*, 27(2), 197-209.

Lindberg, J. S., Iwata, B.A., Kahng, S., & DeLeon, I.G. (1999). DRO contingencies: An analysis of variable-momentary schedules. *Journal of Applied Behavior Analysis*, 32, 123-136.

Piazza, C. C., Fisher, W. W., Hanley, G. P., LeBlanc, L. A., Worsdell, A. S., Lindauer, S. E., & Keeney, K. M. (1998). Treatment of pica through multiple analyses of its reinforcing functions. *Journal of Applied Behavior Analysis*, 31, 165-189.

Reed, P. (2015). Rats show molar sensitivity to different aspects of random interval with linear feedback functions and random-ratio schedules. *Journal of Experimental Psychology: Animal Learning and Cognition*, 41, 432-443.

Ringdahl, J. E., Andelman, M. S., Kitsukawa, K., Winborn, L. C., Barretto, A., & Wacker, D. P. (2002). Evaluation and treatment of covert stereotypy. *Behavioral Interventions*, 17, 43-49.
Piazza, C. C., Moes, D. R., & Fisher, W. W. (1996). Differential reinforcement of alternative behavior and demand fading in the treatment of escape-maintained destructive behavior. I, 29, 569-572.

Vollmer, T. R., Iwata, B. A., Zarcone, J. R., Smith, R. G., & Mazaleski, J. L. (1993). The role of attention in the treatment of attention-maintained self-injurious behavior: Noncontingent reinforcement and differential reinforcement of other behavior. *Journal of Applied Behavior Analysis*, 26, 9-21.

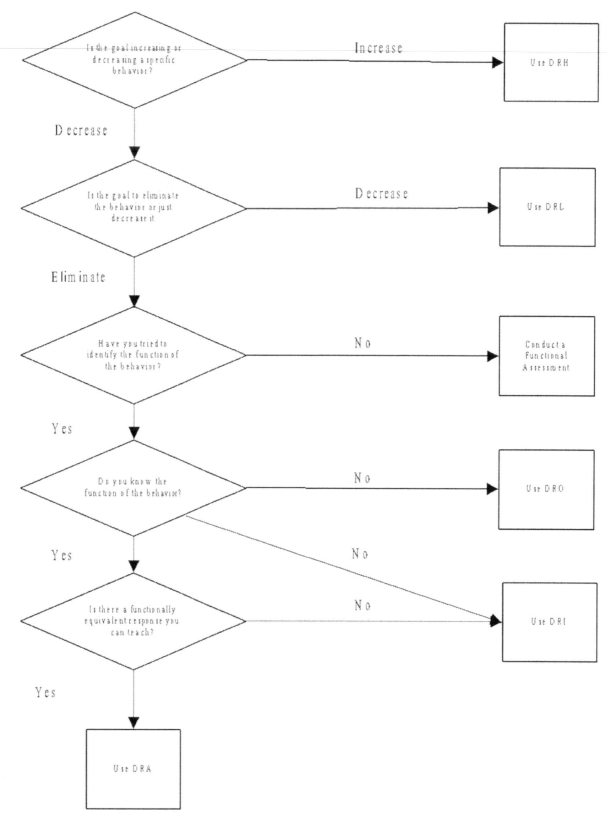

**Figure 9.1. Differential reinforcement decision tree.**

# CONSIDERATION AND APPLICATION OF
# PUNISHMENT-BASED PROCEDURES
*Rachel Cagliani, Claire Pritchet, & Kevin M. Ayres*

## KEY TERMS:

- Aversive stimuli
- Behavioral contrast
- Exclusionary timeout
- Negative punishment (Type 2 punishment)
- Positive practice overcorrection
- Positive punishment (Type 1 punishment)

- Punishment
- Response cost
- Restitutional overcorrection
- Ribbon timeout
- Seclusionary timeout
- Timeout from positive reinforcement

## ▶▶ *Technical Definition*

Colloquial use of the term *punishment* encompasses a wide range of actions that are not technically punishment. Misuse of the term can muddle communication and create confusion in intervention planning and progress monitoring. It is not accurate to say, "Punishment does not work," because the term *punishment*, as used in behavior analysis, is used to describe a relation between responding and changes in the environment. In Chapter 2, we learned that *punishment* refers to a stimulus change (e.g., presentation of an unpleasant stimulus, removal of a reinforcing stimulus) occurring immediately after a behavior that weakens the future occurrence of behavior. This weakening of behavior might be observed as a decrease in the likelihood of it occurring again, its magnitude, or its duration. Further, this weakening can be reflected as an increased latency to responding.

When a stimulus change is perceived to be unpleasant, it is often said to be *aversive*. It is important to note, however, that what functions as an aversive stimulus (i.e., punisher) for the behavior of one person may not serve the same function for another. For example, a mother might notice that when she reprimands one of her sons for playing video games instead of doing chores, he immediately puts his game controllers away and proceeds to the laundry room, but when the other is reprimanded, he just continues to play video games. While the reprimand was likely aversive for both boys, it was not bothersome enough to serve as a punisher for the second one.

When considering whether punishment has occurred, one also must carefully examine the future occurrence or nonoccurrence of behavior in similar circumstances. In the example above, though her son did not immediately stop playing his game, he might complete his chores the next evening to avoid his mother's reprimands.

In some contexts, teachers, therapists, and others purposefully arrange environments to incorporate punishment in an effort to reduce problem behavior (e.g., taking away tokens for breaking classroom rules). In other instances, they may introduce punishing events inadvertently. Consider the teacher that provides enthusiastic verbal praise to a middle school student for following the rules, but then notices that the student's rule-following behavior decreases. Though she intended her praise to serve as a reinforcer, instead, it served as an aversive stimulus to the embarrassed young man.

Punishing events also can occur as a function of the environment. Ask anyone who has ever gotten out of bed and tried walking quickly across a dark room, only to stub a toe on the corner of the wall or their dresser. The next time they get up in the dark, they will move more slowly and take shorter steps.

While punishment procedures may be used to enhance the effects of reinforcement-based procedures, doing so requires careful consideration of the negative side effects of punishment and potential infringement on individuals' human rights. In response to criticism of the systematic use of aversive stimuli in intervention programs, researchers and practitioners have emphasized the development of programs based primarily on reinforcement. We will discuss these considerations further in the next section.

## ▶▶ *Ethics and Historical Context*

Unfortunately, the field of applied behavior analysis (ABA) is often associated with the controversial and inappropriate use of programmed punishment. Several highly publicized events have obscured the countless successes attributed to behavior analytic practices. Bailey and Burch (2016) recounted one of the first examples of the inappropriate use of programmed punishment at a now closed facility in Miami, FL.

Under the auspices of behavior modification, the Sunland Training Center used various forms of punishment, including forced public sexual acts, forced washing of the mouth, paddling, and extended restraints. The training center was investigated in 1969 and was subsequently closed, but ultimately left a blemish on the field of behavior analysis and has contributed to the current regulations and guidelines concerning the use of punishment procedures.

Recently, a residential treatment center in New England garnered media scrutiny for its heavy reliance on shock therapy (Bruno, 2016). Though it is the only center of its kind in the United States, its association with behavior analysis and efforts to link itself closely with the work of B. F. Skinner may have further perpetuated negative stereotypes of behavior analytic practices.

Other contemporary events have resulted in heightened public scrutiny of punishment-based procedures (e.g., Conlon, 2017; Ladwig, 2018). Despite clear recommendations that restraint only be used to protect the safety of students and staff members, data seem to indicate that it is often used to punish problem behavior. For example, the U.S. Government Accountability Office released a document in 2009 revealing that several deaths across the country had resulted from the use of restraint and seclusion procedures. In response to these events, the U.S. Secretary of Education commissioned an investigation into the frequency of the use of restraint and seclusion. Subsequently, he issued a position statement and 15 principles for guidance on the topic (See Table 1.; U.S. Department of Education, 2012).

This unfortunate history of the abuse of punishment procedures and the resulting legislation concerning interventions for problem behavior has led to the development of ethical guidelines to emphasize the avoidance of punishment-based interventions in school and treatment contexts. The Behavior Analyst Certification Board (BACB; 2014) outlined specific considerations on the topic of punishment in the Professional and Ethical Compliance Code for Behavior Analysts. Specifically, the BACB requires that reinforcement be considered over punishment if at all possible (4.08a), and that punishment procedures be used only when behavior analysts have attempted reinforcement-based procedures or determined that a target behavior is so severe that punishment is warranted (4.08c). Additionally, when behavior change procedures require punishment, the BACB requires strict oversight on implementation, including staff training and termination of the aversive procedures when no longer necessary (4.08d). Even when punishment procedures are incorporated into behavior plans, the BACB requires that these procedures be accompanied by procedures to reinforce alternative behaviors (4.08b).

The use of punishment without accompanying reinforcement-based procedures is injudicious because some individuals may engage in problem behavior to express their wants and needs because they have not acquired a more conventional communication response. For instance, a child with limited communication skills may engage in aggression to access attention from the therapist working with her. If the therapist implemented an effective punishment procedure, the child would be left without a way to request attention and might end up engaging in another and potentially more harmful problem behavior to access attention. When practitioners commit to change a behavior that is reinforced by social consequences, they must identify an appropriate behavior to serve as a replacement for the behavior targeted for punishment. For instance, if a student destroys his work materials (e.g., pencils and worksheets) when presented with an academic demand, the teacher might teach him how to make a request for a break by holding up a picture of a break after completing a few problems independently. Such teaching of an alternate response ensures that the student is not left without a means to access reinforcers (e.g., break). Selecting a meaningful replacement behavior requires an understanding of the purpose or function that a problem behavior serves for an individual.

Ideally, when developing a behavior plan, the function of the problem behavior guides the type of intervention implemented. As discussed in previous chapters, the function of a behavior is determined through a process referred to as functional assessment (see Chapter 6). While interventionists may use punishment-based procedures without knowing the function of the behavior, function assists with the design of reinforcement-based intervention components. For example, if a problem behavior was maintained by positive reinforcement in the form of access to attention from peers, a procedure might involve communication training to teach and reinforce appropriate behavior to gain peers' attention. Knowing a behavior's function can also directly impact the selection of a punishment procedure. For example, if the therapist determines the problem behavior is maintained by access to attention, he or she might use a procedure involving restricting attention for a period of time after the problem behavior occurs instead of administering a reprimand (e.g., attention) that might inadvertently serve to reinforce the behavior. Determining the function of a problem behavior and considering that function when developing a behavior intervention plan may help to prevent other common problems when punishment-based procedures are used.

## ▶▶ *Challenges With Incorporating Aversives*

Several complications may arise when aversive stimuli are incorporated into intervention programs. For example, when using verbal reprimands, a teacher might find himself in a "criticism trap," whereby he repeatedly delivers a reprimand that results in the temporary cessation of a student's behavior, but fails to realize the reinforcing properties of that reprimand that ensure the behavior is emitted again and again (Vargas, 2013). This situation occurs frequently as teachers, caregivers, and therapists often resort to reprimanding (e.g., "Stop interrupting") or providing negative feedback (e.g., "You are interrupting, you should know better") in response to challenging behavior. While a quick reprimand may result in the immediate reduction of a past problem behavior, on closer inspection, these immediate changes are often a post-reinforcement pause (i.e., a brief cessation of responding after receiving a reinforcer) and, therefore, not lasting. Further, the use of reprimands and negative feedback fails to teach meaningful replacements for problem behavior.

Several negative side effects are associated with the use of punishment-based procedures. As with reinforcement-based procedures, individuals often learn that certain antecedent conditions are associated with punishing consequences. Consider a restaurant where you previously received poor service and disgusting food. Given this experience, the next time you consider dining options, you will choose a different restaurant to avoid the aversive stimuli in that environment (i.e., yucky food).

The same type of avoidance behavior is often observed when implementing punishment-based procedures. As the individual experiences punishing consequences, she will learn, often quickly, that it is beneficial to avoid situations (e.g., people, places, activities) associated with those consequences. This is problematic in that interventionists should strive to pair themselves as a reinforcer for their clients. Consider the likelihood of educational success by an adolescent who is frequently admonished by her teachers and punished by negative consequences associated with classroom activities (e.g., peer ridicule, negative teacher statement related to performance). Despite pleas from her parents and school counselor, she decides to drop out of school rather than facing two more years of aversive conditions. Another negative side effect of the use of punishment procedures is that it may result in an escalation of problem behavior. For example, a therapist might remove a token from a child's token reinforcement system, resulting in the child screaming and digging his nails into the therapist's forearm. Such behavior is of concern, especially when staff are not prepared for the escalation or are not equipped to support a child engaging in dangerous or aggressive behavior. Further, the choice to use a punishment procedure may set up an individual for contacting more severe consequences. For example, a student might engage in a minor challenging behavior (e.g., talking out, pencil tapping) that quickly escalates in response to a reprimand or removal of a reinforcer. Ultimately, the student is suspended from school due to a teacher's poor choice of an intervention procedure.

Finally, the use of punishment procedures may have unintended consequences in other environments. That is, if somebody is punished in one context (e.g., a specific classroom, one caregiver) for a problem behavior, that behavior may increase in another. This concept, referred to as *behavioral contrast*, can be especially problematic in instances where it may not be possible to implement punishment procedures consistently across settings. For instance, while a teacher or behavioral clinician may be equipped with the staff and resources to implement a punishment procedure, the individual may live with grandparents or in a group home setting with limited staff that is not equipped.

## *Punishment-Based Procedures*

Despite guidelines that advise restricted use of punishment procedures and careful consideration of its potentially negative side effects, these procedures may be necessary in some situations. There are two types of punishment: positive punishment (Type 1) and negative punishment (Type 2). As discussed, the terms *positive* and *negative* denote whether or not a stimulus in the environment was added or removed. In both cases, a stimulus change occurs after a behavior, and the future occurrence of that behavior is weakened. This weakening may be observed as a decrease in the frequency, magnitude, or duration of the behavior.

**Positive punishment**. *Positive punishment*, or Type 1 punishment, refers to the presentation of a stimulus immediately after a behavior occurs, resulting in a decrease or weakening of the behavior in the future. A common example of a procedure based on the principle of positive punishment is the use of verbal reprimands. When using verbal reprimands, the interventionist stands in close proximity to the targeted individual, obtains eye contact, and delivers a single reprimand using a typical volume and tone of voice. As mentioned, it is important to consider whether a reprimand may inadvertently serve to reinforce a problem behavior through the provision of attention.

Another common procedure that uses positive punishment principles is The Good Behavior Game (Barrish, Saunders, & Wolf, 1969; Donaldson, Vollmer, Krous, Downs, & Berard, 2011). In this game, teachers divide the students into teams, and when a student engages in problem behavior or breaks a class rule, the whole team receives a check mark. The team with the fewest check marks wins and receives a backup reinforcer or a non-conditioned reinforcer. Similarly, some employers institute a three-strike policy for infractions in the workplace (e.g., tardiness). When an employee accumulates three "strikes," a penalty is delivered (e.g., suspension). If the presentation of strikes decreases the future frequency of tardiness, strikes serve as a positive punisher.

Two other forms of positive punishment are *positive practice overcorrection* (PPOC) and *restitutional overcorrection* (R-OC). In PPOC, an individual is required to engage in an appropriate behavior for a set number of times contingent on an emission of problem behavior. Many people who grew up taking weekly spelling tests in school encountered PPOC as they were required to rewrite the words that they misspelled on the previous test. Similarly, teachers may require students who did not quietly transition from one classroom to the next to go back and do it again.

R-OC operates in a similar way, except that individuals who engage in problem behavior are required not only to return a disrupted environment to its original state, but to a state even better than it was before the problem occurred. For example, if a child engages in a tantrum, during which he knocks over a chair and pushes some books onto the floor, the overcorrection might involve not only picking up the chair and books, but also improving the environment by straightening all the desks and picking up any trash on the floor. Probably, the most common application of restitutional overcorrection occurs during toilet training which was derived from the seminal toilet training study by Foxx and Azrin (1971), where participants had to clean themselves, their clothing, and the area around them contingent on wetting or soiling their clothing. It is important to note that overcorrection can be difficult to implement, as the interventionist must stop what she is doing to oversee the overcorrection process; she also must ensure that the individual completes the overcorrection.

**Implementing negative punishment**. *Negative punishment*, or Type 2 punishment, refers to the removal of a stimulus immediately after a behavior, resulting in a decrease or weakening of the behavior in the future. Negative punishment may be observed when a child repeatedly bangs a toy on the back of an older sister's chair, resulting in the quick removal of the toy and a decrease in future banging behavior. Another common example involves the use of fines, such as speeding tickets: Police officers issue fines that are contingent on speeding behavior with the intent of reducing the likelihood of the offending driver speeding in the future.

One of the most common systematic school applications of negative punishment is the use of a procedure referred to as *response cost*. This procedure involves the removal of a reinforcer, contingent on the occurrence of the target behavior. For example, when using a token system in which students earn tokens for appropriate behavior (e.g., working quietly), response cost may be added (i.e., tokens are removed following occurrences of problem behavior).

Several issues need to be taken into consideration when implementing response cost. First, as with any punishment procedure, the response cost is most effective when implemented immediately following the problem behavior. For example, it would not likely be effective to remove access to a field trip a week after the problem behavior occurred. Second, the interventionist must attend to the number of reinforcers delivered compared to the number removed. If students lose more tokens or reinforcers than they could possibly earn, they may have little motivation to engage in appropriate behavior. For example, in a classroom setting, a student may lose stars for every occurrence of being out of her area. She is only given 10 stars during an hour period and receives iPad time if she has seven stars left when class is over. If she loses all the stars in the first 30 minutes of the period, she will likely have no incentive to engage in appropriate behavior for the remaining class time. Thus, when using response cost, it is important to ensure that the rate of reinforcement is greater than the rate of the response cost.

**Timeout from positive reinforcement**. *Timeout from positive reinforcement*, another procedure that is based on negative punishment, occurs when an individual loses access to positive reinforcement or is denied the opportunity to earn positive reinforcement for a specific amount of time (Baer, 1962).

In order for timeout from positive reinforcement to be effective, the individual must be denied positive reinforcement. Caregivers, teachers, and therapists often use timeout procedures, but fail to consider the context under which the problem behavior is occurring. For example, a young parent issues a timeout (e.g., sitting on the bench) for a child's tantrum during a shopping trip, but does not notice that the child is tired of shopping and that the break might serve to strengthen future occurrences of tantrums. Similarly, a teacher sends a child out of the room in response to the child's use of obscene language, but fails to notice that the removal also prevents the student from completing a difficult work assignment. Again, the struggling student might welcome the "break" from the aversive context.

 If problem behavior increases following the use of timeout, it may not been implemented correctly, and instead has served to reinforce the problem behavior. Effective implementation of timeout procedures requires an understanding of the purpose or function of a behavior; therefore, it is recommended that a functional assessment be completed prior to the use of timeout procedures.

Exclusionary and seclusionary timeout are types of timeout from positive reinforcement. *Exclusionary timeout* refers to loss of the opportunity to access reinforcement contingent on the target behavior occurring (i.e., the person is excluded from earning reinforcers). The individual remains in the same environment, but the setting is manipulated in such a way that she is denied access to positive reinforcement. Coaches in physical education classes do this frequently by making students sit and observe their peers play a game.

An example of exclusionary timeout involves the application of a *ribbon timeout*. When using this procedure, an individual is given a ribbon or a tangible item to signal that reinforcement (e.g., earning tokens) is available. That is, if the individual has the ribbon or item, she is able to earn positive reinforcement for appropriate behavior; however, if the ribbon or item is removed, the opportunity to earn reinforcement is gone for a specific amount of time. For example, a student may wear a bracelet at school to signal that he has access to teacher praise and preferred items, but when he engages in a disruptive talking out, the teacher removes the bracelet for one minute, during which time, the student cannot access teacher praise or preferred items.

A variation of this procedure involves the use of signaled restrictions to reinforcers. For example, in a classroom, when students have their marble jar on the edge of their desks with the top off, it signals that they are able to earn tokens (marbles). If a student engages in problem behavior, the teacher puts the lid on the student's jar and starts a five-minute timer. All other students can earn marbles during this time. This allows the offending student to witness other students engaging in appropriate behavior and receiving reinforcement.

Unlike exclusionary timeout, *seclusionary timeout* removes the individual from the environment and typically places him in a context free of any stimulation or social interaction. Individuals usually remain in the secluded—but supervised—environment for a brief period of time, and must engage in a certain appropriate behavior to exit (e.g., sitting quietly, standing inside a square). Since seclusionary timeout removes the individual from daily activities (e.g., learning opportunities) and may present an increased risk for harm as he is transitioned to a separate location, practitioners must follow state and organizational regulations during implementation.

## ▶▶ *Other Considerations Before Incorporating Punishment*

At times when reinforcement-based procedures are insufficient to bring about the desired behavior change, punishment-based procedures may need to be added. Gaylord-Ross (1980) outlined a list of considerations to be addressed before implementing punishment procedures: reevaluating the assessment, the schedule of reinforcer delivery, curriculum, and all critical environmental variables.

For example, the team may want to reevaluate the functional (behavior) assessment to ensure that it was implemented accurately and provided sufficient data to identify a clear function. Further, the team may decide that additional procedures are necessary. It is also important to evaluate the strength and delivery of reinforcers that have been used within the current intervention program. For example, the team may need to conduct preference assessments to identify additional reinforcers or increase the rate at which reinforcers are delivered. Finally, it may be necessary to examine other aspects of the instructional environment. For instance, if a daily curriculum provides students with a range of difficult tasks that have little meaning and are devoid of reinforcing properties, any intervention is likely to fail.

In the event that a team decides to use punishment procedures, they must ensure that individuals have ample opportunity to access reinforcers for other responses. That is, punishment procedures are to be considered an additional tool for helping individuals discriminate between appropriate and inappropriate behavior so that they may access reinforcers in the natural world. Further, the team must commit to strong oversight of the intervention program, with special attention paid to procedural fidelity and progress monitoring.

In light of the potential side effects of punishment, it is important that procedures are implemented correctly and for the shortest amount of time possible. Therefore, if the team notices that an individual fails to respond to a punishment procedure within a short period of time, the team must reconvene to modify or terminate the intervention. Finally, it is important that the entire team is trained to implement punishment procedures consistently and immediately following a problem behavior. Intermittent or delayed application of punishment is generally less effective than delivering the aversive consequences immediately following the targeted problem behavior. For example, if a student acts inappropriately at the lunch table, immediately losing the opportunity to sit with his peers is preferable to denying him access to recess two hours after the incident. Reducing the time between the behavior and the consequence also reduces the likelihood of inadvertently punishing another behavior.

## ▶▶ *Summary*

In the real world, punishment happens as students stop giggling with their peers when their teacher admonishes them, children avoid climbing on the furniture after a hard fall, and adults stop answering calls from telephone numbers they recognize as being those of telemarketers.

As a procedure, punishment is often applied unknowingly or without an understanding of the parameters under which it is most effective. However, carefully designed and monitored punishment procedures can play a critical role in intervention programming and can be helpful when a reinforcement-based intervention program fails to achieve a sufficient reduction in problem behavior. A foundational knowledge of the principles of punishment and the procedures based on those principles can help intervention teams use programmed punishment for reducing problem behavior that can help improve the quality of life for individuals across school, community, and home settings.

# *References*

Azrin, N. H., & Foxx, R. M. (1971). A rapid method of toilet training the institutionalized retarded. *Journal of Applied Behavior Analysis*, 4, 89-99.

Baer D. M. (1962). Laboratory control of thumb sucking by withdrawal and re-presentation of reinforcement. *Journal of the Experimental Analysis of Behavior*, 5, 525-528.

Bailey, J. S., & Burch, M. R. (2016). *How we got here. Ethics for behavior analysts* (3rd ed., pp. 5-9). Abingdon, United Kingdom: Routledge.

Bruno, D. (2016, November 23). An electric shock therapy stops self-harm among the autistic, but at what cost? *The Washington Post*. Retrieved from https://www.washingtonpost.com/lifestyle/magazine/an-electric-shock-therapy-stops-self-harm-among-the-autistic-but-at-what-cost/2016/11/21/b9b06c44-8f2c-11e6-9c85-ac42097b8cc0_story.html?utm_term=.7bb16a174d68

Conlon, K, (2017, April). Schools removes time-out box after News10 investigates. Retrieved from https://www.wtsp.com/article/news/school-removing-timeout-box-after-10news-investigates/67-434888674.

Donaldson, J. M., Vollmer, T. R., Krous, T., & Downs, S. (2011). An evaluation of the good behavior game in kindergarten classrooms. *Journal of Applied Behavior Analysis*, 44, 605-609.

Ladwig, B. (2018, June). Physical restraints use rising in Kentucky schools. InsiderLouisville. Retrieved from https://insiderlouisville.com/education/physical-restraint-use-rising-in-kentucky-schools-spiking-at-jcps/.

U.S. Department of Education. (2012). *Restraint and seclusion resource document*. Retrieved from https://www2.ed.gov/policy/seclusion/restraints-and-seclusion-resources.pdf

United States Government Accountability Office, Testimony Before the Committee on Education and Labor, House of Representatives. (2009). *Seclusions and restraints: Selected cases of death and abuse at public and private schools and treatment centers*. Retrieved from http://www.gao.gov/new.items/d09719t.pdf

Vargas, J. (2013). *Behavior analysis for effective teaching*. Abingdon, United Kingdom: Routledge.

## Table 1.

*U.S. Department of Education's Fifteen Principles on Restraint and Seclusion*

| |
|---|
| 1. Every effort should be made to prevent the need for the use of restraint and for the use of seclusion. |
| 2. Schools should never use mechanical restraints to restrict a child's freedom of movement, and schools should never use a drug or medication to control behavior or restrict freedom of movement (except as authorized by a licensed physician or other qualified health professional). |
| 3. Physical restraint or seclusion should not be used except in situations where the child's behavior poses imminent danger of serious physical harm to self or others and other interventions are ineffective and should be discontinued as soon as imminent danger of serious physical harm to self or others has dissipated. |
| 4. Policies restricting the use of restraint and seclusion should apply to all children, not just children with disabilities. |
| 5. Any behavioral intervention must be consistent with the child's rights to be treated with dignity and to be free from abuse. |
| 6. Restraint or seclusion should never be used as punishment or discipline (e.g., placing in seclusion for out-of-seat behavior), as a means of coercion or retaliation, or as a convenience |
| 7. Restraint or seclusion should never be used in a manner that restricts a child's breathing or harms the child. |
| 8. The use of restraint or seclusion, particularly when there is repeated use for an individual child, multiple uses within the same classroom, or multiple uses by the same individual, should trigger a review and, if appropriate, revision of strategies currently in place to address dangerous behavior;8 if positive behavioral strategies are not in place, staff should consider developing them. |
| 9. Behavioral strategies to address dangerous behavior that results in the use of restraint or seclusion should address the underlying cause or purpose of the dangerous behavior. |
| 10. Teachers and other personnel should be trained regularly on the appropriate use of effective alternatives to physical restraint and seclusion, such as positive behavioral interventions and supports and, only for cases involving imminent danger of serious physical harm, on the safe use of physical restraint and seclusion |

11. Every instance in which restraint or seclusion is used should be carefully and continuously and visually monitored to ensure the appropriateness of its use and safety of the child, other children, teachers, and other personnel.

12. Parents should be informed of the policies on restraint and seclusion at their child's school or other educational setting, as well as applicable Federal, State, or local laws.

13. Parents should be notified as soon as possible following each instance in which restraint or seclusion is used with their child.

14. Policies regarding the use of restraint and seclusion should be reviewed regularly and updated as appropriate.

15. Policies regarding the use of restraint and seclusion should provide that each incident involving the use of restraint or seclusion should be documented in writing and provide for the collection of specific data that would enable teachers, staff, and other personnel to understand and implement the preceding principles.

# STIMULUS CONTROL AND
# PROMPTING STRATEGIES

*Melinda Jones Ault & Collin N. Shepley*

## KEY TERMS:

- Stimulus control
- Differential reinforcement
- Discriminative stimulus
- S-delta
- Prompt
- Stimulus prompts
- Target stimulus
- Response prompts
- Gestural prompts
- Direct verbal prompt
- Indirect verbal prompt
- Task direction
- Model prompt
- Verbal model prompt
- Video model prompt
- Physical prompts
- Full physical prompts
- Partial physical prompts
- Mixed prompts
- Natural $S^D$
- Fading
- Transfer of stimulus control
- Constant time delay
- Controlling prompt
- Intrusiveness
- 0-s delay
- Delay trials
- Most-to-least prompting
- Prompt hierarchy

We read in Chapter 2 that behavior is what people do. Behavior is affected by the consequences that follow, and occurs in the context of the stimuli that precede it. Think about some of the behaviors that people demonstrate and the stimuli that are present when a behavior consistently occurs. For example, when you see a red traffic light, you stop your car; when the doorbell rings, you go to the door; when a baby cries, you pick her up; and when you see a flashcard of 2 + 2 = ?, you say "4." In each of these instances, you can see that certain behaviors occur in the presence of particular stimuli. These behaviors can be said to be *under the control* of the stimulus. The principle of behavior known as *stimulus control* explains this phenomenon.

Stimulus control occurs when a behavior consistently and reliably occurs when a stimulus is present, and does not occur when that stimulus is absent (Cooper, Heron, & Heward, 2007). The behaviors above would be considered to be under stimulus control if you see the red traffic light and stop, but do not stop when the red light is absent (i.e., when light is green or yellow). Parents' behavior is under stimulus control when they pick up their baby when she cries, but do not pick up their baby if she is not crying.

## ▶▶ *Establishing Stimulus Control*

Let us consider how behaviors come under stimulus control. Stimulus control is established through the use of *differential reinforcement*. When using differential reinforcement, a behavior is reinforced when the stimulus is present, but the behavior is not reinforced when the stimulus is absent. For example, consider when young children are learning new words. Everyone has been in a potentially embarrassing, yet comical situation, when a young child calls a strange man "daddy." How does the child learn to refer to only their own father as Daddy? It is through differential reinforcement that the child learns to discriminate between daddy and "not daddy." The child receives reinforcement when the response occurs in the presence of the stimulus (i.e., dad) and does not receive reinforcement when the response occurs in the absence of the stimulus (i.e., no dad). The following scenario illustrates the principle.

Bader is 15 months old. His father comes home from work and approaches him. Bader runs to him and says enthusiastically, "Da-Da." Bader's father picks him up, gives him hugs and kisses, and says, "Da-Da loves you!" Bader was reinforced for saying the behavior when the stimulus was present, thus increasing his use of "Da-Da" in the future. Conversely, when Bader sees a man in the grocery store, walks up to him and says, "Da-Da!," mom and the man chuckle uncomfortably, and mom leads Bader away by the hand with no hugs and kisses. Therefore, Bader receives no reinforcement for this response.

Over time, with the consistent use of differential reinforcement, Bader learns he will receive reinforcement when he calls his father "Da-Da" and will not receive reinforcement when he uses the term with others, causing his behavior to come under stimulus control of his father only. In this example, Bader's father is the *discriminative stimulus* ($S^D$), or the stimulus that signals to Bader that reinforcement is probably going to occur. Other men, who are not Bader's father, are the *S-delta* ($S^\Delta$), or the stimulus that is present when reinforcement will not occur. The goal of teaching new behaviors is to establish stimulus control. Table 11.1 shows two examples of the use of differential reinforcement in establishing stimulus control in the context of the S ▯ R ▯ C notation.

## Table 11.1
*Two Examples of Differential Reinforcement Paradigm*

| Antecedent/Stimulus | Learner Behavior/Response | Consequence |
|---|---|---|
| **EXAMPLE 1** <br> $S^D$    2 + 2 = ___ <br> (Target stimulus is present) | "4." | "Fantastic! 2+2 equals 4!" (Reinforcement occurs) |
| $S^\Delta$    4 + 4 = ___ <br> (Target stimulus is absent) | "4." | "Wrong, the answer is 8." (No reinforcement occurs) |
| **EXAMPLE 2** <br> $S^D$    Dog in a yard <br> (Target stimulus is present) | "Doggie." | "Yes, that is a dog! Want to pet?" (Reinforcement occurs) |
| $S^\Delta$    Goat in a pen <br> (Target stimulus is absent) | "Doggie." | "That's a goat." (No reinforcement occurs) |

## ▶▶ *Prompting*

Differential reinforcement is used to establish stimulus control, but what if the behavior we are trying to establish never occurs? How can we differentially reinforce a behavior in the presence of the $S^D$ if the behavior never happens? For example, what if Bader never says, "Da-Da," when he sees his father? What if learners never say, "4," when they see the problem 2 + 2? In these instances, it would not be possible to use differential reinforcement, because the behavior does not occur. Therefore, we must have strategies in place to help learners exhibit the behavior so that it can be differentially reinforced.

Think about when you needed to learn something you had never done before. How did you learn to ride a bike? Most likely, someone held you, ran along beside you, and supported you until you could ride by yourself. The support you received was an example of prompting. *Prompts* are the assistance that learners receive to help them perform a new behavior correctly. The prompt increases the likelihood that the learner will engage in the behavior when the $S^D$ is present. Two categories of prompts are *stimulus prompts and response prompts*.

**Stimulus prompts**. Stimulus prompts are prompts that are added to the stimulus (S$^D$), increasing the likelihood that the learner will respond correctly to the stimulus. Stimulus prompts involve some change to the antecedent stimulus. An example follows.

Marianne's preschool teacher wants to teach her to say her name when she sees it written (target stimulus). At first, Marianne is unable to do this when she sees her name alone, but she can say, "Marianne," when she sees a photo of herself. Therefore, the teacher begins instruction by including a stimulus prompt of adding Marianne's photo above her written name (target stimulus). Over time, as Marianne responds correctly to the stimulus, the teacher will gradually fade the photo until Marianne can say her name when she sees the written stimulus only, without the photo.

Figure 11.1 shows the progression of the steps of using stimulus prompts to establish stimulus control. Using differential reinforcement, Marianne is reinforced each time she responds correctly to the stimulus and is not reinforced when she responds incorrectly. When she consistently responds correctly at each step, the teacher presents the next step until she can respond correctly to the stimulus alone.

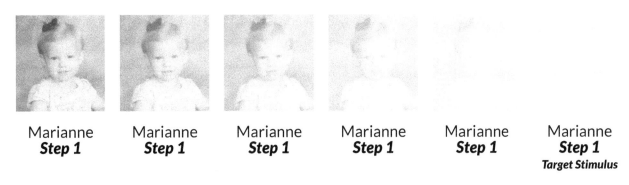

Marianne
**Step 1**

Marianne
**Step 1**

Marianne
**Step 1**

Marianne
**Step 1**

Marianne
**Step 1**

Marianne
**Step 1**
*Target Stimulus*

*Figure 11.1. Stimulus prompt steps.*

Other examples of stimulus prompts include changing the position, the topography (e.g., form, configuration), or the size of the stimulus. Regardless of the type of change made, stimulus prompting involves reinforcing the learner's correct response in the presence of a changed stimulus, which is gradually altered until the learner is responding to the unchanged or target stimulus. Other examples of stimulus prompts are listed in Table 11.2.

## Table 11.2
*Examples of Stimulus Prompts*

| STIMULUS PROMPT | EXAMPLE |
|---|---|
| Stimulus has added color prompt | Learners are presented with an array of stimuli, with the correct stimulus in a different color than the distractor stimuli. For example, children are learning to identify the numeral "2." They are shown four numerals, with the target stimulus ("2") written in red. Over time, as the children respond correctly, the red is faded to match the color of the distractor stimuli. |
| Stimulus has added visual prompt | Mom leaves child a note once a week beside the trash can that says, "Take out trash!" Over time, as the child responds correctly, the note is shortened to, "Trash!" and eventually removed completely until the child responds to the trash can alone. |
| Stimulus has a size prompt | Learners are taught initially to button their shirt using large buttons. As they become more and more successful, the button size is gradually decreased. |
| Stimulus is changed based on position | Learners are presented with an array of stimuli, with the correct stimulus positioned closer to the learners than the distractor stimuli. For example, children are learning to pick up the oval shape from an array of three shapes. Initially, the oval is placed closest to the learners, with the other shapes farther away. As the learners become more and more successful, the oval is moved closer and closer to the same position as the distractor stimuli. |
| Stimulus is changed based on topography | Learners are working on making the sound of letters. They are shown a picture of a snake and how to make the "sss" sound. Over time, the form of the snake gradually transforms into the shape of the letter "S" as the children continue to respond correctly with the "sss" sound. |

**Response prompts**. *Response prompts* are another type of prompt, defined as actions that an individual provides to learners that increase the likelihood they will respond in the presence of the S$^D$. There are numerous types of response prompts, including gestural, verbal, model, physical, visual, and mixed prompts, as described below.

**Gestural prompts**. Gestural prompts are nonverbal behaviors used to assist a learner in completing the correct response. Pointing, nodding the head, or motioning toward the correct response are examples of gestural prompts, as illustrated in the following scenario. Teodor just bought a new car that has manual transmission. Unfortunately, he doesn't know to drive this kind of car. His sister is helping him learn. As Teodor gets ready to put the car in gear, she points to the position on the stick shift. As they drive, each time Teodor needs to change gears, his sister motions to the position to which the stick shift is to be moved.

**Verbal prompts**. Verbal prompts are spoken prompts. They can be direct or indirect. A direct verbal prompt is different from simply asking somebody to perform a behavior. If you are thirsty and you tell your friend, "Get me a water bottle, please," you are simply directing your friend to perform the task, or giving a *task direction*. A task direction does not assist the learner in completing the task, so it is not considered a prompt. But if your friend did not know where you keep the water bottle, he may need a *direct verbal prompt* that assists him in performing the task. A direct verbal prompt would be: "Get the water bottle from the basement." This statement would help your friend perform the behavior, thus it is a prompt.

An *indirect verbal prompt* is also spoken, but does not state the exact behavior to perform. Examples of indirect verbal prompts might be, "What do you do next?" "Remember where we keep the water bottles?" or, "Show me how you take your turn in the game." In other words, an indirect verbal prompt is a prompt that is spoken verbally, but does not specify the behavior that needs to be performed. An example is given in the scenario that follows.

Aiden is learning to play T-ball. He knows how to hit the ball off the "T," but does not independently run to first base. In the beginning of instruction, the coach provides a direct verbal prompt after Aiden hits the ball by saying, "Run to first base." Over time, as Aiden begins to respond well to the verbal prompt, the coach begins to use an indirect verbal prompt after Aiden hits the ball and says, "Show me where to run."

Verbal prompts can be delivered in a number of ways, including being spoken in person by an individual or being recorded and played back on an electronic device.

**Model prompts**. Model prompts involves demonstrating the exact behavior the learner is expected to perform. Model prompts can be a *physical demonstration* of a behavior (e.g., an individual showing the learner how to use a key to unlock the door, use a brush to style one's hair, or use a calculator to complete a math problem) or a *verbal model*, in which an individual models the correct verbal response (e.g., demonstrates how to read a sentence with expression, demonstrates what to say when asking a friend to play). Models can be presented in actual time or be recorded and shown on a video. Have you ever watched a video on how to cook a new dish and then prepared it? If so, you were using a *video model prompt*. An example of a model prompt is in the scenario that follows.

Malik is on vacation at the beach. He wants to learn how to surf, so he books a lesson with a surfing instructor. The instructor begins by putting a surfboard on the sand and telling Malik she is going to show him what to do before he tries it. She demonstrates, showing him how she lies on the board, paddles with her hands, puts the palms of her hands on the board below her chest, and pushes off while tucking her feet under her. This demonstration is a model prompt.

**Physical prompts**. When using physical prompts, an individual touches the learner to assist him in performing the target behavior. Your parents were providing a physical prompt when they ran beside you and held up your bike as you were learning to ride. Physical prompts may be either full or partial. Full physical prompts are those prompts in which an individual completely assists the learner in performing the behavior. Full physical prompts are also referred to as full physical guidance, or hand-over-hand guidance, because the individual holds the learner's hands and guides the learner's body to respond correctly in the presence of the $S^D$. Partial physical prompts also involve physically touching and guiding the learner, but rather than completely guiding the correct response, the individual only partially guides the learner. This may entail beginning to physically assist the learner in performing the correct response, but then removing the physical prompt and allowing the learner to complete the rest of the response independently. It may also entail changing the area of the learner's body on which the physical prompt is given. For example, rather than using hand-over-hand guidance, a partial physical prompt might be guiding a response from the learner's wrist or forearm or shoulder. The example that follows provides a scenario of physical prompting.

Sofia is being taught to discriminate between the letters of the alphabet. She is presented with an array of four letters, including the correct letter and three distractor letters. Her teacher provides a task direction of, "Touch 'b,'" and begins by taking Sofia's hand and guiding her to touch the correct letter (full physical prompt). When Sofia starts to respond correctly to the full physical prompt, her teacher begins to use a partial physical prompt by taking Sofia's hand, moving it halfway toward the correct letter, and then letting go to determine if Sofia can complete the rest of the response on her own.

**Visual prompts**. Visual prompts may be used to provide additional assistance. Examples include pictures, graphic organizers, and written reminders. We all use visual prompts in our daily lives, such as calendars to keep our schedules, reminder notes, and directions on how to assemble objects. Other examples include providing visual prompts in the form of a sequence of pictures showing how to complete a complex task, directions written in a sequence that explain how to complete a behavior, or a rule written on a poster in the classroom (e.g., "i before e except after c") that would assist a student in completing a response. The example that follows provides a scenario of the use of visual prompts (Dieruf, 2017), and Figure 11.2 shows an example of a visual prompt.

Mr. Ramirez is teaching Aditi to compare two characters in a story. While he is reading the story, he places pictures of how the characters are different and the same on the Venn diagram. Then, when Aditi is required to answer questions related to comparing the characters, such as, "Compare Kevin and Miguel in the story," she can be shown the visual prompt to assist in answering the question correctly.

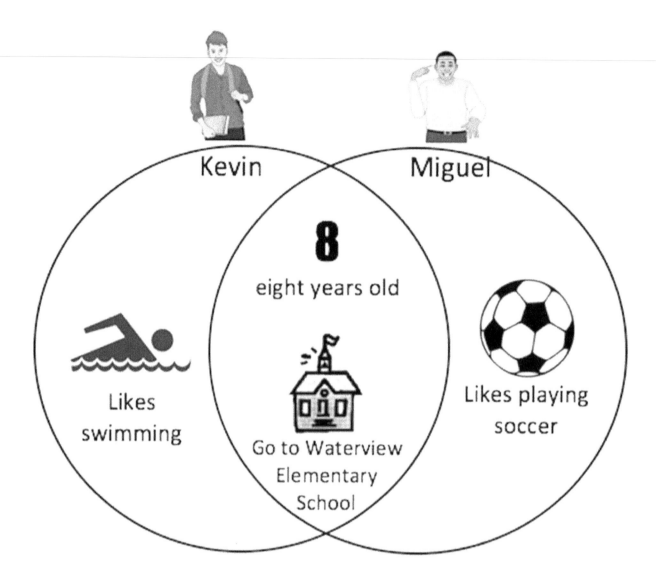

*Figure 11.2. Venn diagram as visual prompt.*

**Mixed prompts.** Sometimes a combination of one or more of the prompts we just defined are used, called mixed prompts. Table 11.3 provides examples of mixed prompts and shows target behaviors, examples of prompts delivered, and the classifications of the mixed prompts being used.

## Table 11.3
*Examples of Mixed Prompts*

| TARGET BEHAVIOR | PROMPT DELIVERED | TYPES OF PROMPTS |
|---|---|---|
| Jumping rope | "Watch me. When the rope comes, jump over like this." | Model + verbal prompt |
| Circling the current day on the calendar | Individual points to the day and says, "What should you do here?" | Gesture + indirect verbal prompt |
| Crossing the street | Individual holds the learner's forearm and guides her crossing the street while pointing both ways to look for cars and pointing when it is time to cross. | Gesture + full physical prompt |
| Completing a two-digit addition problem | Teacher says, "I'm going to show you how to complete this problem before I give you a chance to do one. First, add the numbers in the ones column and write the answer here in the ones column. Next, add the numbers in the 10s column and write the answer here." | Model + verbal prompt |
| Arriving on time to appointments | Individual points to the learner's appointment calendar | Gesture + visual prompt |

**Intrusiveness of prompts.** One consideration instructors should make in selecting prompts to be used with learners is the intrusiveness of the prompt. Prompts should be selected that are the least intrusive, yet effective. *Intrusiveness* refers to the extent to which the prompt "impinges or intrudes upon the student's body" (Wolery, Ault, & Doyle, 1992, p. 36). Given this definition, physical prompts are considered more intrusive than other types of prompts such as models or verbal prompts.

## ▶▶ *Removing Prompts*

In order to establish stimulus control to the target stimulus alone, any prompt used with a learner must be removed over time. Our goal is for a learner's behavior to be under stimulus control of either a target stimulus (i.e., the final stimulus you want the learner to respond to without prompts) or a *natural* S$^D$. A natural S$^D$ refers to the stimulus that occurs in the environment and signals a learner to respond. For example, a natural stimulus to tie your shoe would be that your shoe is untied, or a natural stimulus to refuel your car with gasoline would be a gas gauge on empty.

Removing the prompts is known as *fading* prompts. If a learner is consistently responding correctly when a prompt is delivered, the response is under stimulus control of the prompt, and we then have to transfer stimulus control from the prompt to the target stimulus. If we revisit our bicycle riding example, although you needed your parent to run beside you when you first started to ride your bike, you would not be happy if those prompts were never removed. So, as you became more fluent riding, the prompts were gradually removed, and you rode your bike without help.

We need to understand how to remove the prompts so that learners are able to respond without them. We can remove, or fade, the response prompts using response prompting procedures. There are two ways to fade prompts: (a) by delaying the delivery of the prompt by inserting an amount of time before the prompt is given, and (b) by gradually fading, using a hierarchy of prompts.

**Constant time-delay response prompting procedure**. One strategy for removing prompts involves using a delay in time. The *constant time delay* (CTD) procedure is one such strategy. To begin, the instructor identifies a *controlling prompt*, which is a prompt that the instructor knows always results in a correct response from the learner.

Once the controlling prompt is identified, the instructor begins instruction by presenting the S$^D$, immediately presenting the controlling prompt, recording the response, and delivering the consequence. This immediate presentation of the controlling prompt is known as a *0-s delay*. The notation below shows how a 0-s trial is conducted. Because a controlling prompt has been identified, it is highly likely that the learner will respond correctly to the target stimulus, because the controlling prompt is presented immediately after the stimulus.

$$S^D \xrightarrow[\textit{0-s delay}]{} Prompt \longrightarrow R \longrightarrow C$$

After a number of trials in which the learner responds correctly to the 0-s delay trials, the instructor inserts an amount of time between the stimulus and the prompt. In this way, the learner has the opportunity to respond prior to the prompt being delivered (i.e., to the $S^D$ alone) or to respond after the prompt is delivered if assistance is still needed. These are called *delay trials.*

In a CTD procedure, the amount of time is held constant for the remaining sessions until the learner can consistently respond to the $S^D$ without the need for the prompt, thus transferring stimulus control from the prompt to the stimulus. The delay interval most often used is between 3-5 s. The following notation shows how the delay trials is conducted. These trials continue until stimulus control is established to the stimulus alone.

$$S^D \xrightarrow[\text{3-s delay}]{} \text{Prompt} \longrightarrow R \longrightarrow C$$

The following is an example of how a parent might teach a child multiplication facts using CTD.

Mr. Jones is teaching his daughter, Mary Lou, the set of facts of multiplying by threes. He selects the controlling prompt of a verbal model because he knows that if he states the answer, Mary Lou can repeat it. He begins by conducting a session using 0-s delay trials, showing Mary Lou a flashcard of a multiplication fact (3 x 3) and immediately saying the correct answer (verbal model: "Nine"). Mary Lou then repeats the correct answer. When she does, her father praises her ("Great, 3 x 3 is 9!"). After he has shown her all of the flashcards using 0-s delay, he moves on to 3-s delay trials. In 3-s delay trials, Mr. Jones shows Mary Lou a flashcard, silently waits for 3 s, and then states the correct answer (gives the verbal model). In these trials, Mary Lou has a chance to say the correct answer before the verbal model or wait until Mr. Jones provides the controlling prompt, and then repeat the answer. If Mary Lou gives the correct answer either before or after Mr. Jones provides the prompt, he praises her. If Mary Lou gives an incorrect answer before Mr. Jones has a chance to provide the controlling prompt, he corrects her by stating the correct answer. These 3-s trials continue until Mary Lou is able to say each math fact correctly before hearing the controlling prompt.

**Most-to-least prompting procedure.** Another way to remove prompts is to fade prompts using a prompt hierarchy. In this procedure, the instructor identifies a series of prompts sequences them in a hierarchy, from the prompt that provides the most assistance and is most intrusive to the prompt that provides the least assistance to the learner. Based on the learner's characteristics and needs, the instructor selects individualized prompts and orders them from most to least intrusive. The first prompt that is provided is always the controlling prompt (i.e., the prompt necessary for the learner to perform the correct behavior).

The prompts are faded across the hierarchy to those that provide lesser amounts of help.

The goal is to remove all prompts and have the learner respond to the target stimulus independently. Figure 11.3 shows a series of prompts sequenced in a most-to-least sequence, with the specific prompts selected and order of intrusiveness individualized for each learner.

Verbal + Full Physical Prompt
Verbal + Model Prompt
Verbal Prompt
Target Stimulus

*Most to Least Assistance*

**Figure 11.3. Sequence of most-to-least prompts.**

Instruction begins with the instructor presenting the $S^D$ and then providing the first prompt in the hierarchy. Instruction continues using this prompt until the learner responds at a criterion predetermined by the instructor (e.g., 90% correct responding with a physical prompt). When this criterion is met, the instructor begins to fade the prompt by providing the next prompt in the hierarchy. When the learner responds at the criterion level at this prompt level (e.g., 90% correct responding using a model prompt), the instructor then fades the prompts by providing the next less intrusive prompt. This sequence continues until the learner is able to respond at criterion levels without any prompting when the target stimulus is presented.  The following is an example of how a parent might teach his child to ride a bike using most-to-least prompting.

Before teaching Lilia to ride her bike, Dad decided on a prompt hierarchy of (a) full physical guidance, (b) partial physical guidance, (c) verbal prompts, and (d) independent or no prompting. When he uses full physical guidance, he will run alongside her and hold the bike the entire time Lilia pedals. When he uses partial physical guidance, he will get her started by running alongside her and then let go as she continues on independently. When he uses verbal prompts, he will verbally remind her to, "Push off hard and keep pedaling." On the first day they practice riding the bike, Dad takes Lilia out to the sidewalk and provides full physical guidance as she rides down the sidewalk. When she is able to do that well for three days, he moves to the less intrusive prompt of partial physical guidance. He gets her started, and then lets her continue by herself. When Lilia can do that well for three days, Dad moves on to the verbal prompt, where he just tells her to push off and keep pedaling, but does not touch her. When she can do that well for three days, he then lets her ride independently without touching her or saying anything.

# ▶▶ *Summary*

Through differential reinforcement, prompting, and prompt fading, learners can acquire a vast number of new behaviors. Regardless of the specific behavior being taught (e.g., driving a stick shift, doing addition), it is critical to have a plan in place for fading prompts; otherwise, a behavior may remain under stimulus control of the prompts and never be under stimulus control of the natural stimulus (e.g., engine's RPMs exceed 4,000 to signal a gear shift needed) or target stimulus (e.g., "What is 5 + 6?"). Considering the types of stimulus prompts and response prompting procedures to use when teaching a new behavior is necessary to ensure a successful transfer of stimulus control. Further, it is important to select prompts that are individualized for a learner's characteristics and are likely to be encountered in typical settings; it is also important to highlight cues that are normally embedded in the environment. For example, to simulate real life when teaching somebody how to pay for goods at a store using a credit card, rather than an indirect verbal prompt, use a gesture prompt and point to the green arrow on the credit card machine that points to the slot for inserting a credit card, rather than saying, "What do you need to do next?" A cashier might be more likely to point to the credit card machine than verbally ask for the customer to consider their next steps.

Reflecting on the environment in which target behaviors are used can provide meaningful information for the types of prompts to provide, how to fade those prompts, and the reinforcers available. In addition, understanding a learner's ability to respond to different types of prompts can ensure time is not wasted on prompts to which the learner does not respond. For example, if a learner cannot imitate, then using a model prompt would not be appropriate.

Finally, when selecting prompt fading strategies, seek out those that work most efficiently for individual learners by evaluating how quickly they learn with a selected strategy. In addition to the CTD and most-to-least strategies described in this chapter, a number of additional prompt-fading strategies are available, and may be found in texts devoted to the subject (Collins, 2012; Wolery et al., 1992). Through careful consideration of both the learner and the environment, stimulus control can be established and new behaviors taught.

# *References*

Collins, B. C. (2012). *Systematic instruction for students with moderate and severe disabilities.* Baltimore, MD: Brookes.

Cooper, J. O., Heron, T. E., & Heward, W. L. (2007). *Applied behavior analysis* (2nd ed.). Upper Saddle River, NJ: Prentice Hall.

Dieruf, K. B. (2017). *Using a system of least prompts and a graphic organizer to teach academic content to students with moderate intellectual disabilities* (Unpublished master's thesis). Retrieved from http://uknowledge.uky.edu/edsrc_etds/40/.

Wolery, M., Ault, M. J., & Doyle, P. M. (1992). *Teaching students with moderate and severe disabilities*: Use of response prompting strategies. White Plains, NY: Longman.

# SHAPING AND
# CHAINING

*Shu Chen Tsai*

## KEY TERMS:

- Shaping
- Chaining
- Total-task chaining
- Successive approximations
- Backward chaining
- Task analysis
- Forward chaining

Many individuals have difficulty learning new skills through typical instructional approaches. For instance, some individuals may find it hard to follow verbal directions, or to imitate a model performed by someone else. For these learners, it may be prudent to use a "gradual" approach where an interventionist targets approximations or parts of a skill. This chapter focuses on two useful techniques, shaping and chaining, that can be used to gradually move individuals towards successful performance of a skill.

## ▶▶ *What Is Shaping?*

Shaping is the application of differential reinforcement (see Chapter 9) to successive approximations toward a final behavior (Cooper, Heron, & Heward, 2007). In others word, you differentially reinforce an individual's behavior each time it is one-step closer to the specified target behavior. Consider the case of Jake who never plays with his peers at recess, so his teacher plans to intervene to help him join a playgroup. The final, specified behavior for Jake would be playing with peers. His teacher first provides Jake with a reinforcer when he stays in the playground watching his peers. Once Jake meets the goal, then the teacher delivers a reinforcer to Jake only when he stands within one foot of a playgroup. After the previous goal is met, his teacher reinforces standing right next to a peer. Finally, his teacher only reinforces Jake's responses to a peer's invitation (e.g., catches the ball when a peer tosses it to him) or initiation to join in (e.g., hands a toy to a peer or runs with a peer). The steps from standing and watching, standing one foot away, and standing right next to a peer are called *successive approximations*; the whole teaching process is shaping. Figure 12.1 illustrates the concept of shaping.

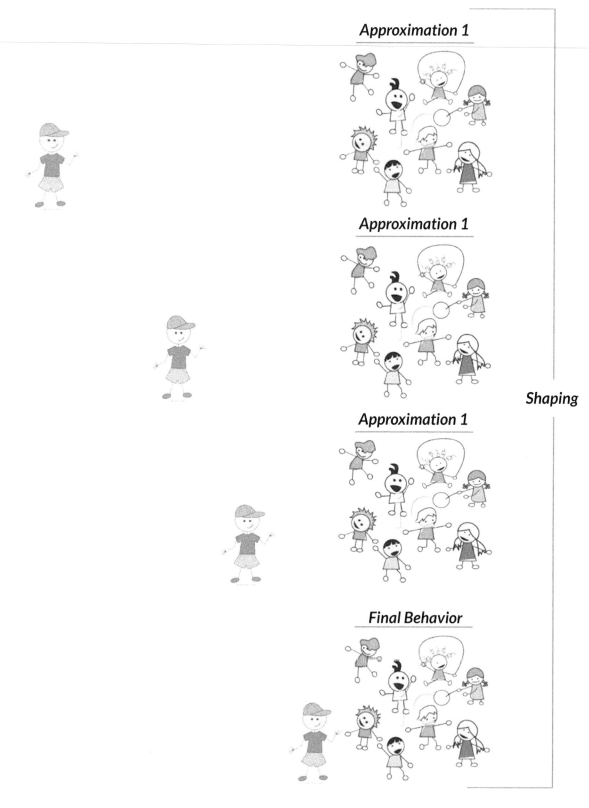

**Approximation 1**

**Approximation 1**

**Shaping**

**Approximation 1**

**Final Behavior**

*Figure 12.1. Shaping play behavior and its successive approximations.*

# ▶▶ *Using Shaping to Improve Different Dimensions of Behavior*

Shaping can be applied to different dimensions of a behavior including its (a) *topography/ form*, (b) *duration/length*, (c) *frequency*, (d) *latency*, and (e) *magnitude/force*. Below are examples of how shaping might be applied to the different dimensions of a Jake's play behavior described in the example above.

**Topography/form**. Topography refers to the form a behavior takes. In the example above, Jake's behavior was shaped from one form (i.e., standing outside the playground) to another form (i.e., joining in a playgroup).

**Duration/length**. Once Jake learned to join a playgroup, his teacher finds out that he only stays with his peers for up to 5 minutes; however, the recess is 20 minutes in duration. Using shaping, his teacher differentially reinforces his staying in the group for gradually longer periods of time until he remains for the entire 20-minute recess period.

**Frequency**. Jake has learned to stay with the group but needs some help in developing his dodgeball skills. His teacher notices that he never attempts to catch the ball, so she targets the attempting to catch the ball for the shaping. Initially, she sets a criterion for a single attempt in order to access a reinforcer. Then, she gradually increases the response requirement to catch the ball to two times, three times, four times, and finally five times during the game.

**Latency**. Watching Jake play dodgeball with peers, his teacher notices that he holds on to the ball for a minute or longer after a peer asks, "Quick, pass the ball to me." Sometimes, because Jake does not respond to this directive, another peer standing right next to him grabs the ball from him and passes it. To help him respond to a peer quickly, the teacher initially reinforces passing the ball within 50 s following a peer's request, and then gradually shortens the delay to 40 s, 25 s, 10 s, and finally 5 s.

**Magnitude/force**. On another occasion, the teacher notices that Jake only drops the ball when it is his turn to pass it, resulting in shouting by peers. She begins to deliver reinforcement after he throws the ball a distance of 2 feet, and then gradually increases the distance requirement to 4, 6, 8, and the up to 10 feet away.

## ▶▶ *Shaping vs. Other Instructional Procedures*

Shaping differs from other procedures in that it only requires the arrangement of consequences for a specified behavior. Other procedures including stimulus shaping, fading, and response prompting, require the teacher to carefully arrange the presentation of antecedent/ instructional stimuli. For example, when teaching a child to ask for a ball, the teacher might deliver a model prompt, wait for the child to respond, and then provide access to the ball. When using shaping, the teacher might present the ball and wait for the child to emit any sounds and then provide access to the ball. Gradually, the teacher would only provide access to the ball contingent on closer approximations to the word "ball."

## ▶▶ *What Is Chaining?*

Chaining is a procedure used to teach a complex skill by linking each small steps of the skill together; the former step in the sequence serves as an S$^D$ for the next step, while the later step functions as a reinforcer for the previous step. Before we can use chaining, the first thing we need to do is to break down a complex skill into several small teachable steps.

**Task analysis**. The process of breaking down a skill into small parts is called a *task analysis or a behavioral chain*. For example, we can break down brushing teeth into several steps shown as below and then teach a child step by step to complete the whole task:

1. Open the cap of a tooth paste
2. Put a drop of tooth paste on a toothbrush
3. Put the tooth brush into mouth
4. Brush front teeth
5. Brush both sides
6. Brush upper and lower parts
7. Rinse mouth

There are three ways that a practitioner can use to create a task analysis. One way is to perform the task and observe the steps needed to complete it. The second way is to observe someone else performing the task. Finally, a third way is to ask an expert for help to identify the steps needed in order to complete a specific task.

Once we have a task analysis constructed, then we can use chaining procedures to teach the skill. There are three ways of using chaining to teach a new skill: (a) *forward chaining*, (b) *backward chaining*, and (c) *total task chaining*. Below are the examples of these three chaining procedures used to teach brushing teeth:

**Forward chaining.** Forward chaining involves teaching a skill, starting with the initial step identified in a task analysis. Instruction is delivered on the first step until the child meets mastery and then proceeds to the next step and so on until the child masters the entire chain. Using our brushing teeth as an example, a forward chaining procedure would proceed like this:

| 1st DAY/TRIAL | 2nd DAY/TRIAL | 3rd DAY/TRIAL |
|---|---|---|
| 1. Open the cap of a toothpaste tube. →Receive praise, "Good job! You opened it." | 1. Open the cap of a toothpaste tube<br><br>2. Put a drop of toothpaste on a tooth brush →Receive praise, "Good job! You put toothpaste on a toothbrush." | 1. Open the cap of a toothpaste tube<br><br>2. Put a drop of toothpaste on a tooth brush<br><br>3. Put the toothbrush into mouth. →Receive praise, "Good job you putting the tooth brush with toothpaste in your mouth!" |

*Backward chaining.* When using backward chaining the teacher begins instruction with the last step in a task analysis and proceeds in reverse order. The teacher initially completes all steps in the task analysis with the exception of the last step and then teaches the child to perform the last step. Once the last step is mastered, the teachers targets the second to last step and so on. A backward chaining procedure for our tooth brushing illustrates as below (shaded parts indicate the steps completed by the trainer; bolded parts indicates the step(s) completed by the child):

| 1st DAY/TRIAL | 2nd DAY/TRIAL | 3rd DAY/TRIAL |
|---|---|---|
| 1. Open the cap of a toothpaste tube | 1. Open the cap of a toothpaste tube | 1. Open the cap of a toothpaste tube |
| 2. Put a drop of toothpaste on a toothbrush | 2. Put a drop of toothpaste on a toothbrush | 2. Put a drop of toothpaste on a toothbrush |
| 3. Put the toothbrush into mouth | 3. Put the toothbrush into mouth | 3. Put the toothbrush into mouth |
| 4. Brush front teeth | 4. Brush front teeth | 4. Brush front teeth |
| 5. Brush both sides | 5. Brush both sides | 5. Brush both sides |
| 6. Brush upper and lower parts | 6. Brush upper and lower parts | 6. Brush upper and lower parts |
| 7. Rinse mouth→ Receive praise, "You did it!" | 7. Rinse mouth→ Receive praise, "You did it!" | 7. Rinse mouth→ Receive praise, "You did it!" |

**Total-task chaining.** When using total-task chaining, the teacher provides an opportunity for the learner to perform every step of the task during training. When students approach a step they are unable to complete independently, the teacher administers a prompt to assist them and ultimately those prompts are faded. This is an example of using total-task chaining to teach brushing teeth (P = Prompt; I = Independent):

| STEPS | 1st DAY/TRIAL | 2nd DAY/TRIAL | 3rd DAY/TRIAL |
|---|---|---|---|
| 1. Open the cap of a toothpaste tube | P | P | I |
| 2. Put a drop of toothpaste on a toothbrush | P | I | I |
| 3. Put the toothbrush into mouth | I | I | I |
| 4. Brush front teeth | I | I | I |
| 5. Brush both sides | I | I | I |
| 6. Brush upper and lower parts | I | I | I |
| 7. Rinse mouth | P | I | I |
|  | I | I | I |
|  | Receive praise, "Good job! You brushed your teeth with some help." | Receive praise, "Good job! You brushed your teeth with little help." | Receive praise, "Good job! You brushed your teeth all by yourself." |

## ▶▶ *Clarification about Shaping and Chaining*

So far, we have discussed shaping and chaining. You may notice that shaping and chaining look alike as they both involve targeting steps closer to the performance of a final or terminal behavior. In fact, shaping and chaining are different (Kazdin, 2013). In shaping, only one target behavior is performed along successive approximations, and the later approximation replaces the previous one until the final behavior occurs. On the contrary, in chaining, multiple discrete behaviors are performed along the way, and the later step of a task analysis does not replace the previous one. In other words, at the end of chaining, the sequential steps of a task analysis must all be performed each time.

To clarify the differences between these two procedures, let's look at the following two examples. Imagine that you want to begin exercising 30 minutes daily, so you start by walking on a treadmill for 10 minutes. When you finish, you indulge in a fruit smoothie. Three days later, you increase the requirement for a smoothie to 20 minutes on the treadmill. By the end of the week, you adjust to the requirement to your terminal goal to 30 minutes. In this shaping process, you only performed one target behavior- walking, but the duration changed (i.e., the dimension of walking). After you achieve the goal of walking for 30 minutes, the previous steps or no longer relevant. On the other hand, you decide to celebrate a family member's birthday by baking a cake. You find a recipe and follow the instructions to complete your baking masterpiece. The baking process is an example of chaining. While baking the cake, cracking eggs, mixing ingredients, and putting the pan into oven are discrete behaviors that had to be completed in a particular order.

## ▶▶ *Using Shaping and Chaining Effectively*

Below are some tips for planning and implementing shaping and chaining procedures.

**Planning.** Before you start a shaping procedure, it is important to define the final behavior, then determine the initial behavior that will be reinforced and finally decide on the size of approximations. For example, a teacher is having difficulty getting her students to complete independent seat work. She sets a target at answering five word problems each day. She decides to initially reinforce the student for putting his name and the date on his paper and decide to increase his response requirement (approximation) by one problem each day. It is also important to keep in mind that a child may not progress linearly as you planned. At times, you may need to adjust the size of approximations depending on the child's needs.

Likewise, before launching a chaining program, you will first use one of the strategies we discussed earlier to construct a task analysis. Then, carefully check if the sequence of a task analysis is in a logical order and determine if any prerequisite skill required is for the learner to perform a specific step of the task analysis. If so, it is important to teach prerequisite skills before teaching the complex skill.

Shaping and chaining are rarely used in isolation. To help a learner acquire a new skill quickly during shaping and chaining training, you may consider using some of the prompting strategies you learned in Chapter 11. Finally, to help the child maintain the skills taught with shaping and chaining, it is important that you frequently reinforce the child's performance of skills even after the training is terminated.

 **Summary**

In this chapter, we discussed the two procedures for teaching new behaviors: shaping and chaining. Shaping is the differential reinforcement of successive approximations toward a final behavior and can be a useful procedure in building up a learner's performance to a desired level. Chaining involves in reinforcing the completion of sequential steps of a skill. It is a useful procedure for teaching complex skills comprised of multiple steps. Both procedures can be used in conjunction with prompting strategies to facilitate student success.

# References

Cooper, J. O., Heron, T. E., & Heward, W. L. (2007). *Applied behavior analysis* (2nd ed.). Upper Saddle River, NJ: Prentice Hall.

Kazdin, A. E. (2013). *Behavior modification in applied settings* (7th ed.). Long Grove, IL: Waveland Press.

# MAKING IT COUNT:
## PROGRAMMING FOR GENERALIZATION

*Jon Burt & Justin Cooper*

### KEY TERMS:

- Generality
- Generalization
- Stimulus generalization
- Response generalization
- Generalization across people
- Generalization across settings

- Maintenance
- Functional contingencies
- Training diversely
- Functional mediators
- Overgeneralization
- Faulty stimulus control

So far you have studied the basic principles by which we explain and understand how behavior happens. Using tactics derived from those basic principles, you have learned powerful techniques to address challenges of social importance for students or clients. And finally, you have learned how to collect, display, and analyze data within single-case experimental designs to determine the extent to which your interventions are responsible for the observed behavior change.

In this chapter, we will discuss the limits of that technology on producing lasting behavior change beyond the controlled conditions of training environments. We conclude with a review of recommended strategies for overcoming those limitations and a brief discussion of potential side effects.

- A thousand times you have rehearsed with your child the hold-hands-in-a-parking-lot procedure, but when she arrives at the Jumpy Fun Park with her grandparents, she opens the door and bolts from the car towards the sidewalk.

- You practiced order of operations all year long, referencing the *Please Excuse My Dear Aunt Sally* mnemonic poster and were certain your fourth graders would ace that portion of the assessment. On the day of the test, you were directed to remove the poster from the test environment, and most of your students missed the questions.

- Three weeks in a row during in-home therapy sessions, your client with ASD replied, "Great, how are you?" when you or her parents asked her how she was doing. The fourth week, despite prompting to use a novel response, she continued to reply with the well-rehearsed, "Great, how are you?"

- You showed the first student in line how to turn off the faucet using a paper towel instead of his bare hand. You were disappointed to learn that each student required the same instruction to master the hygienic objective.

If you have experienced anything like the scenarios described above, you have encountered the frustrating limits of behavior change, and, as a result, you have likely asked the kinds of questions asked by behavior analysts since the founding of the discipline. Each scenario depicts a different aspect of the most important outcome of intervention – generalization of behavior change (Cooper, Heron, & Heward, 2007).

## ▶▶ *Generalization Defined*

Generalization is broadly defined as "the occurrence of relevant behavior under different non training conditions (across subjects, settings, behaviors, and/or time) without the scheduling of the same events in those conditions as had been scheduled in training conditions" (Stokes & Baer, 1977, p. 350). In other words, generalization involves getting individuals to do what you have taught them to do in diverse ways, under novel circumstances, and to continue doing it long after they have finished their training. In the absence of generalization, a skill cannot be said to be truly taught, as it will likely have little utility for the learner.

Failure to generalize skills to novel contexts can have dire consequences. Consider students who rehearse fire safety skills four times a year, but fail to follow the evacuation route and report to their assigned safe space amidst the chaos of an actual emergency; a young man with ASD who is trained to attend to instructions from a uniformed police officer, but ignores a plain clothes officer with only a badge as identification; or a girl who knows to immediately find an adult if she sees an unsecured firearm, but plays with a pink Hello Kitty gun discovered in her friend's parents' closet.

Whether your instructional objective involves a simple response to a task or an essential life skill, the ultimate goal is to promote the use of the skill when and where it matters most. This is the primary objective in generalization training.

## ▶▶ *Generalization of Behavioral Interventions*

*Generalization* is a broad term used to describe at least four distinct outcomes of behavior interventions. The common theme among each is that the new response (be it across settings, behavior topographies, people, or time) must occur in the absence of the full range of procedures with which it was initially trained.

To start, we will discuss perhaps the most obvious example of generalization —setting/situation generalization. *Setting/situation generalization* is simply the transfer of a behavior to a novel setting where the behavior was not trained and where different conditions are present. Consider a child with limited verbal skills who frequently cries, throws objects, and scratches her parents. The family was referred to a behavior analyst, who conducted a functional analysis in a clinical setting and determined the function of the problem behavior was to obtain food and drink. The behavior analyst, by way of functional communication training, taught the girl to use an assistive communication device to "speak" the name of the item she wanted when she was hungry or thirsty. The behavior analyst ignored all instances of problem behavior and initially prompted the use of the device with most-to-least prompting procedures. Across five clinic-based training sessions, rates of problem behavior fell to zero levels, all prompting was faded, and the girl could independently request all her preferred foods and beverages. Problem solved! Case closed!

Not so fast! The parents reported that not only did their daughter continue to throw tantrums at home when she was hungry, she now also had a new projectile in the form of her assistive technology device. That is, although functional communication training produced impressive results in the clinical settings with only the behavior analyst present, the newly acquired behavior failed to generalize to the home with the parents as communication partners. Put another way, the behavioral intervention did not produce setting/situation generalization.

To be considered setting/situation generalization, some feature of the generalization setting must be different from the intervention setting in which the behavior was initially acquired. For example, if you have taught your students the SLANT (sit up, lean in, ask questions, nod your head, track the speaker) method of active listening, do they do it in the presence of a substitute teacher? You taught your client to dial 911 from a smart phone. Could he complete the task from a basic cell phone or a landline? Your preschooler can read her name in print. Can she read her name in cursive as well?

It is difficult to imagine a behavior that you would not want to generalize, at least to some degree, to unique settings or situations. The ability to apply a skill acquired in one setting under one set of circumstances to other settings and different circumstances is a principal feature of independence; it is, therefore, an important target objective for any behavior plan.

A second generalization outcome is response generalization. *Response generalization* refers to the use of any untrained variation of the topography (i.e., form) of a trained response that serves the same purpose as the original response. You may have taught your daughter to hold the elevator door with her hand while passengers board, for example. At the next floor, without prompting, she presses and holds the *door open* button. Or, during life skills training, you teach your client to thoroughly rinse his hair under running water. During the next session, he accomplishes the same objective by submerging his head under water and shaking the soap out of his hair. In any case, response generalization occurs when the learner gets the job done in a way that is different from the one you originally trained him to use.

The importance of response generalization is often questioned by consumers of behavioral interventions, who rightfully claim that, in some cases, the behaviors acquired from systematic training are too repetitive or rigid. This is often observed in individuals with ASD, for whom narrow and restricted behavior patterns is a defining characteristic. Therefore, any intervention that teaches a single response topography to accomplish a task is likely to be considered countertherapeutic. Referencing the previous example of the girl receiving functional communication training, suppose the communication responses had successfully generalized to the home with the parents. After several days of, "Pretzels, please," "Pretzels, please," "Pretzels, please," the parents may very well opt for the crying and scratching over the monotony of the new approach.

While setting/situation generalization expands the range across which behavior is observed, response generalizations increases the number of ways a behavior is performed. A third form of generalization, called response maintenance, addresses the durability of behavior change. *Response maintenance* is continued correct responding after the removal of some or all of the training protocol. Recall the example of the fourth-grade teacher whose students missed the order of operations questions when the rules poster was removed. Had the students answered the questions correctly in the absence of teacher prompts to reference the poster, this would have been an example of response maintenance.

An example is often observed by parents who have used formal procedures to toilet train their toddlers. Initially, consistent schedules, sticker charts, candy, or other rewards, and an abundance of cheers and praise may have been used to teach the child how to urinate in the toilet. Quickly, however, these components are faded, and the natural reinforcers associated with urinating in the toilet soon assume control. What is heralded as skillful parenting when applied to a typically developing 2-year-old would be widely criticized if used with the same child (all else besides age being equal) as she enters middle school. Naturally and intuitively, we understand that we must wean the learner off our control and transfer that control to natural contingencies in order to promote independence.

To reiterate, response maintenance refers to sustained correct responding following the systematic removal of some component of the intervention package. Other sources distinguish between response maintenance as we have defined it and generalization across time, or follow-up (Cooper, Heron, & Heward, 2007). Generalization across time is the sustained correct responding over an extended period of time following the termination of formal training. The difference between the two is subtle, but important. Each time you fade a component of the intervention, and the learner continues to behave appropriately, you have observed response maintenance. However, eventually, you will arrive at terminal conditions. You will either run out of time, have nothing left to teach the student regarding a given skill, or you will have removed all remaining supports. At that point, you will begin to assess for generalization across time, or follow-up, by conducting probes of the skill at regular extended intervals.

To illustrate this distinction, let us again use the example of the two-year-old learning to use the toilet. Suppose the parents initially cued the child to use the bathroom every 30 minutes and reinforced every attempt with one gold star and every successful "potty" with two gold stars. Three gold stars would earn the child a choice among various prizes and privileges. After the child earned the first three gold stars, the "cost" of a prize or privilege was raised to five gold stars. Similarly, after the child reached five gold stars, the next prize point was set at eight. Assuming the child continued to use the toilet as instructed, even after the cost of purchasing a prize or privilege was raised, this would be an example of response maintenance, as continued correct responding was maintained after each reinforcement schedule extension. After three days of successful training, the parents began to fade their prompts, and token reinforcement was discontinued altogether. After one week, our triumphant 2-year-old got to pick out his favorite big-boy undies from the store, thus ending formal training. Generalization across time, or follow-up, would be observed if the parents waited a month, then assessed the number of accidents over the weekend and determined their son had maintained to criterion.

As a general rule, it is preferable to fade support, including care-taker prompts and artificial reinforcers, to the greatest extent possible. However, it may be appropriate in some cases to leave intervention components in place for an indefinite period. For example, if that same 2-year-old maintained low rates of toileting accidents after the removal of all parental cues and token reinforcement, but developed a bladder infection due to excessive urine retention, the supports that were faded would most certainly need to be reimplemented.

## Table 13.1
*Generalization Categories*

| CATEGORY | EXAMPLE |
|---|---|
| Setting/Situation Generalization | Using self-monitoring materials, a student is trained to recruit teacher feedback and assistance in a resource room. The materials are sent with the student to his general education class, and he successfully recruits teacher assistance and feedback as per his training. |
| Response Generalization | A child is trained to greet her peers by saying, "Hello." The child spontaneously says, "Hiya," and "What's up?" in subsequent sessions. |
| Response maintenance (generalization across time) | The first week of school, a teacher uses a group contingency to teach hand raising. The second week, without the contingency in place, the students continue to raise their hands as trained. The students continue to raise their hand appropriately three months into the school year. |
| Generalization across people | A behavior analyst trains a classroom teacher to increase positive feedback. The teacher's aide observes the improved student behavior and increases her use of positive feedback as well. |

# ▶▶ *Programming for Generalization*

We now know what generalization is, but we have yet to discuss how to make it happen. You may realize from experience that, although generalization is the goal, it often does not happen on its own. It takes the implementation of carefully planned intervention components to achieve thorough generalization. While this may sound complicated, the basic premise is not – we must teach generalization. Different strategies may be used to promote the generalization of a variety of skills; too often, however, we teach a child a specific skill or behavior in one setting, and then simply hope that the child will exhibit that and similar behaviors in other environments and situations. This approach is called *train and hope*, and it is not recommended as best practice, especially for students with disabilities or struggling learners (Stokes & Baer, 1977). Similar to academic content or social behaviors, generalization must be taught. Teaching or programming for generalization is the responsibility of the adult in charge. It requires purposeful action designed to promote the generalization of new skills (Scott, 2017).

The basic ideas behind programming for generalization have changed little over the past 40 years. In 1977, Stokes and Baer summarized the most promising generalization and maintenance strategies found in the behavioral literature at that time in an article titled *An Implicit Technology of Generalization*. Stokes and Osnes (1989) subsequently organized those strategies into three general categories: (a) take advantage of current functional contingencies, (b) train diversely, and (c) incorporate functional mediators (see Table 13.2 for a summary of the strategies).

# Table 13.2
*Generalization Programming Strategies*

| STRATEGY | RECOMMENDATION |
|---|---|
| Exploit Current | Target behaviors that will likely be reinforced naturally |
| Functional | Actively solicit the help of those in the generalization setting to reinforce the target behavior and teach the learner to recruit reinforcement as well. |
| Contingencies | Minimize reinforcement for competing behaviors using differential reinforcement and extinction procedures.<br>Actively assess and reinforce any appearance of generalized responding. |
| Train diversely | Include exemplars representing the full range of stimulus conditions during training.<br>Teach a variety of functionally equivalent responses.<br>Vary training conditions to the greatest extent possible without sacrificing instructional control.<br>Use intermittent and delay schedules of reinforcement to make contingencies less apparent. |
| Incorporate Functional | Include common physical features of the generalization setting in the training setting. |
| Mediators | Recruit people from the generalization setting to assist with instruction in the training setting.<br>Send mediating materials with the learner to the generalization setting. |

*Adapted from Stokes, T. F., & Osnes, P. G. (1989). An operant pursuit of generalization. Behavior Therapy, 20, 337-355.*

The strategies recommended under each category are still relevant today. Let us first explore what it means to take advantage of current functional contingencies. Remember that a contingency is the relation between the circumstances that lead to a behavior (antecedents), the events that follow a behavior (consequences), and the behavior itself. Therefore, if we wish to accomplish behavior change in a generalization setting, we must pay attention to the contextual variables already in play in that setting and use them or change them to our advantage.

The first recommendation within this principle is to target behaviors that will likely encounter natural communities of reinforcement. Specifically, this requires teaching students relevant behaviors that will work when they return to their natural settings. For example, when we teach a student with social skills deficits to greet his peers, we must first observe what type of greetings are used among the peers in a natural setting. If a student's peers greet each other with a "Wassup?" and fist bumps, then teaching our student to offer a handshake and say, "Good afternoon," probably will not work. Why? Because the natural community does not reinforce formal greetings. When programming for generalization, it is often easier to figure out what behaviors go with the flow of the current contingencies than trying to change the contingencies to accommodate new behaviors.

To take this a step further, not only can we teach our students behaviors that have a high probability of succeeding in the natural setting, we can also teach them to actively seek out reinforcing social consequences if none occur naturally. Alber and Heward (2000) presented a helpful review of various techniques used to train students to recruit teacher praise and feedback following completion of an academic task. They offered a set of general guideline for recruitment training that included (a) select target students that could benefit from learning to recruit praise and feedback, (b) select target behaviors for which students will recruit praise, (c) teach students to self-assess their work before recruiting attention, (d) teach appropriate recruiting behaviors, (e) teach students an appropriate recruiting rate, (f) model and role play the complete recruiting sequence, and (g) promote generalization across classrooms.

The popular saying would have us believe that no good deed goes unpunished; however, in the typical classroom, it is perhaps more accurate to say that most good deeds go unnoticed. A teacher simply does not have the energy and resources to identify and give feedback for every correct response from every student. Therefore, it would benefit both the student and the teacher if the student could self-select responses for which she would like feedback and signal to the teacher that help, feedback, or encouragement is needed.

Despite selecting behaviors likely to be reinforced and teaching students to recruit natural consequences, in many instances, the contingencies that are maintaining undesirable behavior are so strong that we must intervene with the counterproductive contextual variables to make room for new behaviors. This requires the interventionist to adjust the parts of the environment that may be evoking and reinforcing undesirable behavior. A functional (behavior) assessment (FBA), presented in Chapter 6, is an indispensable tool for this purpose. If problem behavior of a similar form occurs in multiple settings, an FBA must be conducted across all settings to ensure the behaviors belong to the same functional class. If they do not, an intervention that works in one setting will likely not lead to generalized behavior change in the next.

To illustrate, suppose a student with an emotional behavior disorder frequently curses in class. Indirect assessments reveal this happens most frequently in general education language arts, and secondarily in a resource math class. An FBA is conducted in the student's reading class; it appears that cursing occurs during independent reading of long passages, resulting in escape from the academic task. The intervention involves using coupons to request shortened reading passages and access to preferred content.

A similar intervention is implemented in the student's math class. Rates of cursing immediately drop in the reading class, but surge in the math class. How could that be? A follow-up assessment reveals that cursing was never maintained by escape from academic tasks in the math class. Rather, the student frequently zipped through his independent math work and cursed to obtain attention from the teacher and peers. You can see how the coupon intervention would be fruitless in the math class, because escape from difficult or boring tasks was never the issue. An FBA incorporating all settings targeted for generalization is necessary to ensure that intervention components address the various functions of problem behavior in each setting.

The final strategy related to exploiting functional contingencies reminds us that it is sometimes necessary to directly prompt and reinforce occurrences of generalization. If and when generalization – in whatever form – does occur "by randomness and good fortune," we should make a big deal of it (Stokes & Osnes, 1989, p. 243). However, if it does not occur naturally, we can increase the odds in favor of generalization simply by directing the student to use the new skill in a generalization setting and reinforcing its occurrence.

The second principle proposed by Stokes and Osnes (1986) is to *train diversely*. This principle reminds us to arrange instructional conditions to cover a range of possibilities that may be found in the generalized settings. The first strategy is to use sufficient stimulus exemplars. This means training for multiple stimuli to control the desired behavior. This may entail providing instruction in multiple settings or under different conditions.

Another strategy is to use sufficient response exemplars. This means teaching the student a range of appropriate responses to a particular stimulus, and then reinforcing the student for using them. For example, can a child recognize that he may need to respond differently to a question, depending on who poses the question? A student might respond one way when a friend asks him how he is doing, but he may need to respond in a more formal manner if that same question is posed by a teacher or a school principal.

A third strategy under this principle is to *train loosely*. This requires the person providing instruction to use the loosest, yet effective, instructional environment possible. Examples of teaching loosely include having two or more teachers provide instruction, teaching in multiple locations, varying the reinforcers used, varying time of day for trainings, and teaching with varying noise and light conditions (Baer, 1999). This will help students to be successful when they move to other environments where instructional conditions may be different.

The next two strategies under this principle have been mentioned previously. First, *indiscriminate contingencies*. This means thinning the reinforcement over time by using an intermittent schedule of reinforcement. Recall that when the student first acquires the new behavior, we are likely to use a continuous schedule of reinforcement (i.e., reinforce every time the behavior occurs). However, over time, if we thin that reinforcement schedule to every other time, or even every third time, the behavior occurs, we promote generalization of that behavior.

Second, reinforce *unprompted generalization*. This simply means that you watch for the target behavior to occur in generalized settings, and provide reinforcement when the student demonstrates the target behavior without being prompted. This increases the probability of the target behavior occurring more frequently in the generalized natural setting.

The final principle for promoting generalization offered by Stokes and Osnes (1986) is to incorporate functional mediators. This involves using physical stimuli, social stimuli, and self-mediated verbal stimuli to transfer stimulus control from the training environment to the generalization setting. This is a fancy way of saying the training setting needs to look and feel like the generalization setting to the greatest extent possible. Using common physical stimuli simply means to make sure that physical stimuli that may act as a discriminative stimulus to the desired behavior are present in all settings where you want the behavior to generalize. For example, a communication technology device that allows a child to make a request during instruction needs to be present in other environments where you wanted the student to be able to make similar requests. More important, the presence of that device may be the discriminative stimulus that sets the occasion for the student to exhibit the behavior in generalized settings. In other words, the student may exhibit the behavior not only while the interventionist is present during instruction; she might do the same thing without the presence of the interventionist in another environment simply because the technology device is present in the generalized setting.

A second recommendation is to use common social stimuli. This means that you might want to have other children or adults present during training; these same children or adults might then be present in the other settings where you want generalization to occur. This is especially useful when you are training a skill that requires interaction with peers.

Another strategy is to teach students to use self-mediated stimuli. This entails having the student either carry or self-deliver stimuli that will help prompt a particular response. You could think of this as self-prompting. This could range from having the student wear a rubber band on the wrist to prompt a particular response, to the student internalizing a strategy that prompts them to respond a particular way to a certain stimulus. If you can get a student to be able to self-mediate, it can be very effective; it is much less intrusive in terms of intervention, and it provides a tool that the student can draw on independently in a variety of setting conditions.

## ▶▶ *Special Considerations*

The strategies presented here offer a host of potentially powerful techniques to facilitate generalized responding. As with all behavioral technology, however, one must be mindful of all potential intervention outcomes. Two possible scenarios present challenging side effects of generalization programming procedures. The first is called overgeneralization.

*Overgeneralization* occurs when a learner overextends a new behavior to an inappropriate setting/context or exhibits an inappropriate form of the response. Parents of small children are constantly addressing the overgeneralization of their children's disclosure of the need to use the restroom. We cheer when our child tells us they need to go to the bathroom when we are at home. But the same response displayed loudly in the middle of a church service is met with shushes and red-faced apologies from the parents. Cases like this show that the child has not learned when not to tell his parents he must use the facilities.

Overgeneralization also occurs when someone uses an inappropriate response form or topography to accomplish a task. To stick with the bathroom example, we praise a child for wiping with toilet paper. What do we do if she uses the monogrammed hand towels? The point is, for every setting/situation or response form we wish to see generalized, there are at least as many, if not more, that we wish would not generalize.

A second consideration when planning for generalization is faulty stimulus control. *Faulty stimulus control* occurs when a behavior is evoked by an irrelevant stimulus not meant to acquire stimulus control. If overgeneralization can be summarized by right behavior/wrong place and time, or wrong behavior/right place and time, then faulty stimulus control can be summarized by right behavior, place, and/or time for the wrong reasons. If left unchecked, this would eventually lead to overgeneralization, as illustrated by the earlier example of the client with ASD learning to discern police officers from other people.

To teach a student to whom it is appropriate to disclose personal information, you may conduct the following skill training protocol. First, you show a picture of a uniformed municipal police officer and ask the student, "If he asks, 'What is your name and where do you live?' what should you say?" The student correctly and appropriately identifies himself and discloses his address. You show a picture of another man in plain clothes and ask the student the same question. The student correctly and appropriately ignores the request. You repeat the procedure, this time with a highway patrolman in a different uniform. The student responds appropriately among various examples of uniformed officers and nonuniformed individuals.

Later that day at the gas station, the service attendant says to the student, "Hey, bud, what's your name?" According to his training, unintentional as it was, he learned that it is okay to tell anyone with a name on his shirt your personal information. In this case, the student was able to ace your assessment for the wrong reasons. The name on the officer's uniform acquired faulty stimulus control instead of the host of other stimuli (e.g., badge, belt, gun, uniform) you had hoped would have collectively controlled the response. Being aware of these potential generalization problems during instruction can help you to control for, or at least adjust, your instructional procedures for promoting generalization in an effort to produce desirable outcomes for your students and clients.

## ▶▶ *Measuring Generalization*

Once a skill or behavior has been taught using effective, purposeful instruction, including specific generalization programming procedures, it is necessary to measure or assess the degree of generalization of a desired behavior. When assessing generalization, our primary concern is the extent to which behaviors generalize to untrained stimuli and conditions. The specific method for assessing if this has happened is to conduct generalization probes before, during, and after instruction (Cooper, Heron, & Heward, 2007). These probes involve brief direct observations using natural or contrived trials to see if the behavior is occurring under different antecedent stimuli and in different settings, and to ensure that overgeneralization or faulty stimulus control is not present. In essence, this means that after teaching the learner how to respond to as many potential stimulus and response examples as possible, you assess him on as many untrained examples as possible to test for generality of the behavior.

Figure 13.1 offers a sample generalization probe sheet for the social skills instruction of reciprocal greetings for a young child with ASD. First, we ask where and under what circumstances this skill is applicable. The skill is useful at school with a familiar friend, as well as at home with family members, and even in the community under certain circumstances. However, we do not want our client to respond to unsolicited greetings from an adult if she is ever isolated in public, even if only for a moment. This is listed in black as a nonexample, or opportunity for overgeneralization. Every two weeks, we conduct a probe of the scenario described. Again, special consideration and careful planning are warranted for the overgeneralization probe in this case, as a trustworthy adult unknown by the child would need to be recruited.

With these data, we can adjust our instruction according to client responses. As indicated in the data in Figure 13.1, it appears that by week two our client responded to a greeting by a stranger in the community. We would then target overgeneralization with additional training in subsequent sessions. Conversely, she has yet to respond appropriately to greetings by unfamiliar staff at school. Perhaps we need to better differentiate our instruction regarding when it is appropriate to respond to a greeting from an unfamiliar adult and when it is not.

| | Where and under what circumstances is this skill applicable? | | | | | | | |
|---|---|---|---|---|---|---|---|---|
| | School w/ familiar friend | School w/ unfamiliar peer | School w/ familiar staff | School w/ unfamiliar staff | Home w/ parent | Home w/ sibling | Community w/ service provider (e.g., cashier) | Community alone w/ stranger |
| Baseline | 0 | 0 | 0 | 0 | 0 | 0 | 0 | 0 |
| Week 2 | X | 0 | X | 0 | X | X | 0 | X |
| Week 4 | X | X | X | 0 | X | X | X | 0 |

*Figure 13.1. Setting generalization probe sheet.*

We would also want to monitor our client's type of responses to ensure varied responding is occurring. Figure 13.2 shows another sample probe sheet that prompts us to again ask ourselves how many ways the targeted skill can be performed. We could list several variations we have heard other students say and leave space for as-yet undefined responses. As before, with setting/situation generalization, we monitor at regular intervals to determine if the new responses have been emitted. If overly repetitive patterns emerge, we might consider targeting response generalization in subsequent training sessions.

| | How many ways can this task be performed? | | | | | | |
|---|---|---|---|---|---|---|---|
| | Hi | Heya | How's it going | How're you | *<response>* | *<response>* | *<response>* |
| Baseline | | | | | | | |
| Week 2 | X | X | | | | | |
| Week 4 | X | | X | | | | |

*Figure 13.2. Response generalization probe sheet.*

Another way to measure generalization is in the form of behavioral objectives. Horner, Bellamy, and Colvin (1984) recommended that successful generalization be included as a behavior goal within intervention plans. The learner's ability to perform the behavior in different settings, including a natural setting, for another adult or peer, and in response to different antecedent stimuli, indicated a completed objective. Failure on any of these criteria would mean the behavior has failed to generalize, and the objective has not been met. While there is no way to monitor every situation that a student might encounter or every form a response may take, including several examples within each category is often sufficient to ensure generalization is an active focus of the treatment plan.

## ▶▶ *Summary*

In this chapter, you have been introduced to the concept of generalization and can now define four separate generalization outcomes. You have been introduced to Stokes and Osnes' (1989) classification of generalization promotion strategies, and you have been provided guidelines on how to measure generalization. Now it is up to you to generalize these concepts and skills and apply them where it matters most – with your clients, students, and children.

Given our goal to promote independence among our learners, the ability to act appropriately in a variety of environments in the absence of intervention and training procedures/ materials and to sustain that performance long after formal training has ended are essential criteria of successful interventions. Given the importance of the ability to generalize new skills and behaviors to the settings in which the behaviors are necessary for those in our care, it is critical that teachers and interventionists take the time and make the effort to systematically plan for how generalization will be taught and specifically programmed into the instructional process.

We cannot leave to chance that our learners will be able to take what they have been taught in one setting or under very specific conditions and apply that behavior or skill to another setting. We must teach it. And remember, if it does not generalize, it means that it was not taught!

# *References*

Alber, S. R., & Heward, W. L. (2000). Teaching students to recruit positive attention: A review and recommendations. *Journal of Behavioral Education*, 10(4), 177-204.

Baer, D. M. (1999). *How to plan for generalization* (2nd ed.). Austin, TX: Pro-Ed.

Cooper, J. O., Heron, T. E., & Heward, W. L. (2007). *Applied behavior analysis* (2nd ed.). Upper Saddle River, NJ: Pearson.

Horner, R. H., Bellamy, G. T., & Colvin, G. T. (1984). Responding to the presence of non-trained stimuli: Implications of generalization error patterns. *Journal of the Association for Persons with Severe Handicaps*, 9(4), 287-295.

Ingersoll, B., & Wainer, A. (2013). Initial efficacy of project ImPACT: A parent-mediated social communication intervention for young children with ASD. *Journal of Autism and Developmental Disorders*, 43(12), 2943-2952.

Kerr, M. M., & Nelson, C. M. (2010). *Strategies for addressing behavior problems in the classroom* (6th ed.). Upper Saddle River, NJ: Pearson.

Neef, N. A., Lensbower, J., Hockersmith, I., DePalma, V., & Gray, K. (1990). In vivo versus simulation training: An interactional analysis of range and type of training exemplars. *Journal of Applied Behavior Analysis*, 23, 447-458.

Scott, T. M. (2017). *Teaching behavior: Managing classrooms through effective instruction.* Thousand Oaks, CA: Corwin.

Stokes, T. F., & Baer, D. M. (1977). An implicit technology of generalization *Journal of Applied Behavior Analysis*, 10, 349-367.

Stokes, T. F., & Osnes, P. G. (1989). An operant pursuit of generalization. *Behavior Therapy*, 20, 337-355.

# A BEHAVIOR ANALYTIC APPROACH TO
# TEACHING COMMUNICATION

*Matt Tincani & Ashlee Lamson Temple University*

## KEY TERMS:

- Applied behavior analysis
- Assessment of basic language and learning skills
- Autism spectrum disorder
- Discrete trial teaching
- Echoic
- Verbal behavior
- Intraverbal
- Mand
- Natural environment teaching

- Picture exchange communication system
- Pivotal response training
- Speech-generating device
- Tact
- Three term contingency
- Verbal behavior
- Verbal Behavior Milestones Assessment and Placement Program

The importance of communication to success in everyday life is universally recognized. Communication helps us to make friends, connect with loved ones, and navigate relationships at school, work, and in the community. Unfortunately, many individuals with *autism spectrum disorder* (ASD) and other disabilities do not learn to communicate naturally. Thus, they benefit from specialized strategies to help them learn to communicate functionally, which can improve their quality of life across different environments.

The purpose of this chapter is to overview strategies to teach communication to learners with ASD based in the science of *applied behavior analysis* (ABA). Although we will focus on intervention for individuals with ASD, the strategies have been effective in teaching learners with a range of disabilities. Our intent is to provide a basic overview of communication within the ABA framework, types of communicative behaviors, and information on empirically supported assessments and interventions to teach communication skills.

# What Is Communication?

The ABA framework for understanding communication comes from B. F. Skinner's (1957) seminal book, *Verbal Behavior*. Skinner defined communication, or *verbal behavior*, as "behavior reinforced through the mediation of other persons" (p. 2). Skinner's definition is important because it emphasizes three critical components of communication. First, communication is *behavior*, or a response that a person actively performs. Second, communication is *social* in that it is directed toward another person (i.e., a listener) or persons (i.e., an audience). Third, communication is behavior that is *learned* through contact with the environment, as when another person provides reinforcement to the speaker for communicating.

Consider the following scenario. Madison looks at her mother and says, "Can I have some juice, please?" Her mother walks to the refrigerator, takes out a juice box, and hands it to Madison, who takes a sip. Madison's behavior of asking her mother for juice is communication because (a) it is behavior, (b) it is directed toward another person, and (c) reinforcement is provided by the other person — her mother — in the form of handing Madison a juice box. In contrast, if Madison simply walked to the refrigerator and got a juice box herself, this would not be communication, because the behavior is not directed toward or reinforced by another person. In the former example, the type of communicative response that Madison performs is a request, or mand. We will explore the mand and other types of verbal responses later in the chapter.

# The Communication Needs of People With ASD

ASD is a lifelong neurological and developmental disorder that affects an individual's social communication skills and results in restricted and repetitive behaviors (American Psychiatric Association, 2013). In recent years, great strides have been made in early screening, diagnosis, and development of educational strategies to teach important skills (Wong et al., 2015).

Nevertheless, many individuals with ASD lack important functional communication skills. For example, they may have difficulty making their basic wants and needs known to others through speech; or, if they do speak, they may have difficulty navigating basic social interactions with peers, teachers, and other important people. Effective functional communication training has the potential to increase their involvement in the community, to improve their educational experiences, and to help them sustain employment in adulthood.

The science of ABA gives us the tools necessary to understand communication and the ability to change the environment to teach communication. This can lead to development of academic skills, greater independence across settings, and other improved life outcomes, such as getting a job and living independently (Sundberg & Michael, 2001).

## ▶▶ *Verbal Operants*

In ABA, behavior is analyzed according to the *three-term contingency* (see Chapter 2). As illustrated in Figure 14.1, the components of the three-term contingency are: the antecedent, which motivates the individual to perform the behavior or evokes the behavior; the behavior itself; and a consequence, which reinforces the behavior.

Each *verbal operant*, or unit of language, is uniquely controlled by a different three-term contingency or set of controlling relations. In this section, we will explore the four primary verbal operants that are essential to everyday communication exchanges—*the mand, echoic, intraverbal, and tact*—along with examples of their corresponding controlling relations.

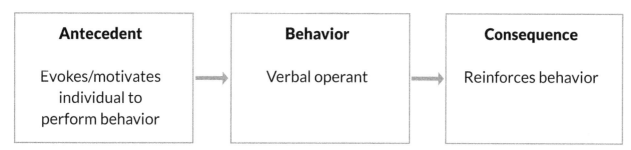

**Figure 14.1. Three-term contingency.**

## ▶▶ *Mand*

The mand is one of the first verbal operants that young children learn. And it is often the first verbal operant targeted for instruction in individuals with ASD, because it is the only operant that results in direct reinforcement, or reinforcement that benefits the speaker. Therefore, individuals with ASD are often highly motivated to engage in mands. You may notice the word *mand* is similar to that of *command* or *demand*; this is purposeful, as mands are also referred to as requests. More technically, a mand is a verbal operant that is under direct control of a motivating operation (see Chapter 2), and is reinforced by a specific, direct consequence that benefits the speaker. The response form of the mand usually specifies its reinforcement. For example, a young child who is deprived of liquids utters the word, "juice," and receives a juice box from his teacher. In this case, the form of the response—the word "juice"—specified the reinforcer—a container of juice.

An individual can not only mand for simple, tangible items, but also for information, attention, assistance, and so on. For instance, the question, "Have you seen my wallet?" may be deemed a mand, as the speaker is requesting information regarding the location of his wallet. Table 14.1 contains some everyday examples of motivating operations, behaviors and consequences of the mand.

## Table 14.1
*Mand: Three-term Contingency Examples*

| ANTECEDENT | BEHAVIOR | CONSEQUENCE |
| --- | --- | --- |
| Food deprivation | "Can we have dinner?" | Dad gives son a plate of dinner food. |
| Missing keys | "Have you seen my keys, honey?" | Wife says, "Yes, they are on the kitchen table." |
| Coloring activity; missing green crayon | "Can I have a green crayon, please?" | Teacher gives student a green crayon. |
| Crowded, noisy cafeteria | "Can we leave, please?" | Teacher guides student into the empty, quiet hallway. |

## ▶▶ *Echoic*

The *echoic* is a verbal operant evoked by a prior verbal stimulus with which it bears point-to-point correspondence. Echoic behavior is also known as verbal imitation. For example, a parent says, "Ball," and the child says, "Ball." An important distinction between the echoic and the mand is that the echoic results in social or educational reinforcement, whereas the mand results in direct reinforcement. Thus, in the prior example, the parent would not provide the child with a ball, but would say, "Yes, it's a ball," or provide some other form of social recognition or praise. Table 14.2 lists examples of echoics from everyday life.

## Table 14.2
*Echoics: Three-term Contingency Examples*

| ANTECEDENT | BEHAVIOR | CONSEQUENCE |
|---|---|---|
| Parent says, "Keys." | Child utters, "Keys." | Parent praises child. |
| Teacher says, "Green." | Student says, "Green." | Teacher gives student a high five. |
| Babysitter says, "I want to go outside." | Child repeats, "I want to go outside." | Babysitter says, "Nice talking!" |

Echoic behavior may be used to teach new communication behaviors. For example, if a parent is teaching her daughter how to mand for preferred items, she might take advantage of her daughter's echoic skills to prompt manding for specific items (e.g., "Say, 'I want *ball*!'"). Once her daughter learns to say, "Ball," in order to receive a ball, the verbal operant is no longer an echoic, but a mand, because receiving the ball is direct rather than social reinforcement. Therefore, when we observe a child engage in any particular verbal response, we must also understand the contingencies or controlling relations for the response in order to identify the kind of verbal operant she is performing.

## ▶▶ *Intraverbal*

The *intraverbal* is similar to the echoic, except that in the intraverbal, the response lacks point-to-point correspondence with the prior verbal stimuli that evoked it. Intraverbal behavior is also known as conversation. In its most basic form, a speaker says something, and the listener says something different. For instance, a speaker says, "How are you today?" and the listener responds with, "I am fine. Thank you." Small talk, asking questions, reciting the alphabet, and discussion of scientific phenomena are common examples of intraverbal behavior. Like the echoic, the intraverbal is maintained by social or educational reinforcement. For instance, a conversation is continued, an answer to a question is praised, or attention is maintained.

Acquiring intraverbal skills can be particularly challenging for individuals with ASD, because intraverbals do not produce direct reinforcement, and individuals with ASD may be infrequently exposed to the kind of naturalistic conversational exchanges that tend to yield robust intraverbal skills. Nonetheless, as we will learn shortly, a variety of empirically supported interventions may be used to teach intraverbal skills. Table 14.3 provides some examples of everyday intraverbal exchanges.

## Table 14.3
*Intraverbal: Three-term Contingency Examples*

| ANTECEDENT | BEHAVIOR | CONSEQUENCE |
|---|---|---|
| Teacher says, "What is the weather today?" | Student answers, "It's sunny and warm." | Teacher says, "I have been waiting for the warm weather!" |
| Parent asks, "How was school today?" | Child responds, "It was OK." | Parent says, "That is good, dear." |
| Friend 1 says, "What is your favorite color?" | Friend 2 says, "Green." | Friend 1 says, "Mine, too!" |

# Tact

In certain cases, the physical environment, or some aspect of it, functions as an antecedent for verbal behavior. The word *tact* is derived from *contact*, meaning *to come into contact* with the physical environment. Therefore, the tact is a verbal operant evoked by an object, event, or property, or an object or event.

Tacts are sometimes referred to as *expressive labeling*, because they involve the speaker identifying some aspect of the physical environment. For instance, a toy truck is present on a kitchen table; the boy says, "Truck," and his mother says, "Right, it's a truck." Like the echoic and intraverbal, the tact is reinforced by social or educational consequences, such as verbal praise or some other acknowledgement of the speaker's response. Skinner (1957) described the tact as a verbal operant that benefits the listener, since the speaker is providing the listener with certain information about the physical environment in the verbal exchange. For example, a speaker emits the following tact about the weather: "It's extremely hot outside." This information may benefit the speaker by occasioning him to dress accordingly (e.g., wearing shorts and short sleeves). Examples of everyday tact relations are given in Table 14.4.

## Table 14.4
*Intraverbal: Three-term Contingency Examples*

| ANTECEDENT | BEHAVIOR | CONSEQUENCE |
|---|---|---|
| An airplane is flying in the sky. | Child looks up and says, "Look, Mom, an airplane!" | The parent responds, "Yes, that is an airplane!" |
| Teacher holds up a red flashcard and says, "What color is it?" | Child responds, "Red." | Teacher says, "It is red! Great job!" |
| Doorbell rings. | Child says, "Doorbell!" | Parent says, "I'll get it." |

To review, Table 14.5 lists antecedents, behaviors, consequences, along with an example for each of the four verbal operants: the mand, echoic, intraverbal, and tac.

## Table 14.5
*Examples of the Four Verbal Operants*

| Verbal Operant | Antecedent | Behavior | Consequence | Example |
|---|---|---|---|---|
| Mand (Request) | Motivating operation (MO); Examples: Food deprivation, aversive stimulation | Verbal behavior (VB); response specifies its consequence | Direct; benefits the speaker | When food-deprived, child says, "I want a snack," and Mother gives her a snack. |
| Echoic (Verbal imitation) | Verbal stimulus | VB; form of response is identical to the antecedent | Social; educational | Teacher says, "Pop," and child says, "Pop." Teacher says, "Good job." |
| Intraverbal (Conversation) | Verbal stimulus | VB; type of response form is different than the antecedent | Social; educational | Teacher says, "How are you?" and child says, "Very well." Teacher says, "Good to know!" |
| Tact (Comment; expressive identification) | Nonverbal stimulus; object or event | VB | Social; educational | Fire truck goes by; child says, "Truck!" Father says, "Right, it's a truck!" |

## ▶▶ Assessing Communication

When we develop comprehensive programs to teach verbal behavior to children with ASD, the first step is to assess their current communication skills. This is an important step, because we must first understand which skills a child is lacking in order to know where teaching needs to begin.

Two standardized assessments based in Skinner's (1957) verbal behavior framework, the *Verbal Behavior—Milestones Assessment and Placement Program* (VB-MAPP) (Sundberg, 2008) and *Assessment of Basic Language and Learning Skills—Revised* (ABLLS-R) (Partington, 2008), are widely used to assess children's communication and related skills for the purpose of instructional program development and progress monitoring. Each will be described below.

## ▶▶ *Verbal Behavior—Milestones Assessment and Placement Program (VB-MAPP)*

The VB-MAPP is an observational assessment that can be used as a curriculum guide to develop comprehensive verbal behavior programs for children with ASD. Comprised of five components to evaluate the child's skills and keep track of progress during instructional programming, the VB-MAPP Milestones Assessment tests the child's ability to engage in 170 skills that are categorized according to developmental level. These skills include the basic verbal operants (e.g., mand, echoic, intraverbal, tact), along with receptive language, imitation, play, and other skills.

The VB-MAPP Barriers Assessment helps identify common learning barriers, such as problem behaviors, that interfere with learning. The VB-MAPP Transition Assessment helps evaluate the child's progress and readiness for instruction in less restrictive environments, while the VB-MAPP Task Analysis and Skills Tracking enables teachers to monitor the child's acquisition of skills targeted through assessment. Finally, the VB-MAPP Placement and IEP Goals section enables the educational team to make placement recommendations and provides direction for development of the child's educational goals.

## ▶▶ *Assessment of Basic Language and Learning Skills—Revised (ABLLS-R)*

The ABLLS-R is also based on Skinner's analysis of verbal behavior. The ABLLS-R is extensive as it assesses 544 discrete skills within 25 skill categories (e.g., cooperation and reinforcer effectiveness, intraverbals, early academic skills, motor imitation). The authors purport the ABLLS-R can be used to assess skills that are often obtained by learners without disabilities prior to entering kindergarten.

Like the VB-MAPP, the ABLLS-R also includes an IEP development guide for helping families and practitioners identify critical instructional targets and design a comprehensive curriculum for teaching language. Further, it can be used a skill tracking system to help monitor learners' progress and assist in making instructional decisions. The ABLLS-R assessment has been used widely in behavioral programming since its publication in 1998.

## ▶▶ *Empirically Supported Interventions to Teach Communication*

*Augmentative and alternative communication* (AAC) systems may be helpful in teaching communication to nonvocal learners by using specialized equipment and devices to support communication as an alternative to speech.

Two types of AAC, the *Picture Exchange Communication System* (PECS) (Frost & Bondy, 2002) and *speech-generating devices* (SGD), have strong empirical support for children and youth with ASD (Wong et al., 2015). PECS was developed in consideration of Skinner's analysis of verbal behavior and seeks to establish mands, tacts, intraverbals, and other operants through specialized teaching techniques. SGDs can be employed in a similar fashion to teach verbal operants to children and youth with ASD within Skinner's framework (Lorah, Parnell, Whitby, & Hantula, 2015).

## ▶▶ *Picture Exchange Communication System (PECS)*

PECS was developed by Andy Bondy, Lori Frost, and their colleagues at the Delaware Autism Program, a public school program for students with ASD (Frost & Bondy, 2002). PECS is comprised of six teaching phases, summarized in the Table 14.6.

Prior to beginning Phase I, teachers conduct a preference assessment to determine the individual's preferred items and activities. In Phase I, two trainers—one seated in front of the student acting as a listener, and the other seated behind the student providing prompts—teach the student to mand for preferred items and activities by exchanging a picture symbol from a communication book. PECS requires no prerequisite skills, such as attending to an instructor or imitating someone else's movements, to learn the basic communication skills with the system.

Phase II of PECS seeks to expand spontaneity by teaching the learner to walk varying distances to the communication book and varying distances to the listener in order to communicate. In Phase III, the learner is taught to discriminate between different picture symbols, thereby increasing vocabulary and expanding functional communication. In Phase IV, the individual is taught to mand by assembling two picture symbols that are combined to form a basic sentence frame (e.g., "I want _____."). Phase V teaches the learner to respond to the question, "What do you want?." A response results in access to a preferred item/activity; the resulting impure verbal operant is an intraverbal mand. Finally, in Phase VI, the learner is taught to respond to questions such as, "What do you see?" or "What do you have?" in the presence of different items; the resulting verbal operant in this phase is an intraverbal tact.

Recently, the developers of PECS have released an iPad app, the Phase III app, which enables a learner who has mastered Phase III of PECS to transition to the iPad for communication (for more information, visit www.pecs.com).

## Table 14.6
*Procedures and Outcomes of the Six PECS Teaching Phases*

| PECS Phase | Procedures and Outcomes |
|---|---|
| Phase I - How to Communicate | Using two trainers, student is taught to exchange a picture symbol (mand) for a preferred item. |
| Phase II - Distance and Persistence | Student learns to remove a picture from a communication board and get a communicative partner's attention at a distance. |
| Phase III - Picture Discrimination | Student is taught to discriminate between different picture symbols; vocabulary is developed. |
| Phase IV - Sentence Structure | Student learns to form a sentence with picture symbols (i.e., "I want _____."). |
| Phase V - Responding, "What do you want?" | Student is taught to answer the question, "What do you want?" |
| Phase VI - Commenting | Student is taught to answer questions (e.g., "What do you see?") in response to the environment. |

## ▶▶ *Speech-Generating Devices (SGD)*

SGDs are electronic devices with displays that contain a vocabulary of picture symbols and/or words customizable to meet the individual needs of the user (Lorah et al., 2015). When a specific picture symbol on the touch screen menu is pressed, the device emits a recording of the word that approximates a user's speech (e.g., vocalization of the word "ball"). Symbols also may be assembled to form sentences (e.g., "I want the ball, please.").

Until fairly recently, SGDs were available only as specialized electronic devices designed specifically to function as SGDs. More recently, however, with the advent and widespread use of smartphones and tablet computers, specialized apps such as Proloquo2go have been developed to make these widely available technology devices function as SGDs with functionality similar to more expensive, specialized devices.

Unlike the specific teaching strategies associated with PECS, a variety of techniques and strategies may be employed to help nonvocal individuals to communicate with SGDs using Skinner's verbal behavior as the framework. SGDs may offer a few advantages over other AAC systems, such as PECS. For example, whereas picture symbol books contain, at most, a few hundred picture symbols, SGDs can accommodate thousands of picture symbols to meet the needs of advanced users with large and sophisticated vocabularies. Furthermore, SGD apps can be customized so that picture symbols are grouped into one or more vocabulary folders (e.g., foods, toys, greetings), permitting the user to quickly and easily access a large number of picture symbols. Despite these benefits, use of SGDs entails some disadvantages. Specifically, as with any technology, SGDs require routine maintenance (e.g., battery charges, operating system updates), can be damaged, may break down, and may not be available to users with limited financial resources. Thus, SGDs may not be a viable option for all individuals with ASD.

## ▶▶ *Comprehensive Approaches*

Several empirically supported, comprehensive approaches are also available to teach communication skills to individuals with ASD that incorporate, or are complementary to, Skinner's (1957) analysis of verbal behavior. Three major approaches are *pivotal response training* (PRT), *natural environment training* (NET), and *discrete-trial teaching* (DTT).

**Pivotal response training.** Pivotal response training, developed by Robert and Lynn Koegel from the University of California, Santa Barbara, is a naturalistic, play-based and empirically validated intervention derived from the principles of ABA (Koegel & Koegel, 2006). In PRT, target skills are taught in the natural environment to optimize the development of broad or pivotal skills.

Pivotal skills targeted in PRT include motivation, initiation, self-management, and the ability to respond to multiple cues. These skills are taught as they affect a wide range of other skills, leading to generalization and spontaneity of skills and behaviors across settings (Stahmer, Suhrheinrich, Reed, Bolduc, & Schreibman, 2010).

Pivotal response training is similar to other naturalistic interventions, in that the learning environment is loosely structured, shared control exists between teacher and child, interactions between teacher and student are ongoing, explicit teaching techniques are used, and attempts to respond are also reinforced. Pivotal response training has been found most successful in teaching communication, language, play, and social skills (Stahmer et al., 2010).

The primary elements of PRT follow the three-term contingency within the principles of ABA: antecedent, behavior, and consequence. The first step consists of presenting a cue (antecedent), which can be either specific and succinct (e.g., "What shape is this?") or general (e.g., allowing a child to choose a toy from a bin of toys you have presented). The activities (e.g., play items, games) are frequently varied to allow for consistent engagement, interest, and motivation.

In addition, shared control between child and teacher is important. Essentially, this requires the child to choose the materials used and guide the session, whereas the teacher embeds learning opportunities into the chosen activity. Another important element that falls within the cue or antecedent condition involves interspersing maintenance, or previously mastered/easy tasks with target or more challenging tasks. The purpose here is to maintain motivation by increasing the probability that the child will be successful, as well as continue to access high levels of reinforcement.

After the cue is presented, consistent with the three-term contingency, the child engages in a verbal response. The child provides either a correct or an incorrect response, and the consequence, or feedback/actions from the instructor, is implemented accordingly. Following the behavior, reinforcement is applied, preferably occurring as a natural consequence that is directly related to the activity. For example, if a child spontaneously requests, "Block," during a PRT session, access to the block would be the consequence. If this is a target response, the instructor may provide access to many blocks as positive reinforcement for the appropriate request. In addition to providing reinforcement for correct responses, reasonable, goal-directed attempts are also reinforced in PRT in an effort to maintain motivation in current and future PRT sessions (Stahmer et al., 2010).

As an intervention that is child-led and focused heavily on motivation, a variety of verbal operants may be taught across sessions, including mands, tacts, echoics and intraverbals, in a naturalistic way. In fact, one of the main purposes of PRT is to pair language and social interaction with reinforcement in a way that is specific to the individual learner.

**Natural environment training.** Natural environment training (NET), also known as naturalistic teaching or natural environment teaching, is an ABA-based intervention that has been validated by several research organizations in recent years and often serves as a well-rounded component of verbal behavior programs (Wong et al., 2015).

NET is similar to PRT in that the intervention is implemented in the individual's natural environment (e.g., classroom, playground, home) using natural routines (e.g., playtime, meals, educational activities), and purposeful manipulation of the environment is used to prompt certain cues for instruction. For instance, if the target goal is for the child to request a toy car, the interventionist would ensure the play environment included a toy car.

NET also consists of shared control between the child and the instructor, with an emphasis on the adult following the child's lead wherever possible. The notion of shared control and child-led activities is embedded in the principles of motivation and natural reinforcement. Naturally occurring activities, alongside naturally occurring reinforcers, are used to shape behavior. For example, during a transitional routine from snack to play time (a highly motivating activity), a teacher might prompt, "Where are we going next?" to which a child might respond, "The play center!" The consequence for this correct response is that the child is given free access to that space. The goal for this particular child might be to label spaces or centers within the classroom setting; by using a natural opportunity, alongside the child's motivation to play, the instructor is able to evoke an effective tact response.

Due to the ubiquitous nature of language, educators must target a wide array of operants (e.g., mands, tacts, echoic, intraverbals) across a wide range of activities to facilitate the generalization of language skills across new and ever-changing contexts. Natural environment training, steeped in Skinner's verbal behavior, offers a prime example of an intervention that can be used to address this aim. Furthermore, NET can be used alongside DTT, discussed next, as a balanced approach of structured and unstructured teaching to allow for generalization of skills across environments.

**Discrete trial teaching**. Discrete trial teaching, or DTT, is a highly structured, one-to-one teaching session in which an educator utilizes the three-term contingency—antecedent, behavior, consequence—to teach predetermined skills in a systematic way.

Unlike PRT and NET, to implement DTT, the learner is typically removed from his natural environment to engage in highly structured teaching and learning. Skills are taught through repetition, in discrete or small steps and trials that have a definitive beginning and end. Positive reinforcement, prompting, shaping, and chaining, all principles or strategies with roots in the science of ABA, are used to directly teach preplanned target skills. Sessions begin with a clearly defined instruction, or discriminative stimulus (e.g., "What day is it?"); the child then engages in a target behavior (e.g., "Wednesday,"), and methods of reinforcement are used to increase correct responses (e.g., "Right, it's Wednesday!"). Data are collected for ongoing assessment of skills to gauge learners' progress and to prompt modifications to DTT programming as necessary. Skills targeted during DTT may include language skills, academic or cognitive skills, life skills, and so on. Once mastered, skills are often targeted in the natural environment to ensure generalization across environments.

## ▶▶ *Summary*

In this chapter, we have overviewed a definition of communication based on Skinner's (1957) analysis of verbal behavior, described four verbal operants that comprise many everyday communication episodes (i.e., mand, echoic, intraverbal, tact), two behaviorally oriented approaches for assessing communication (i.e., VB-MAPP, ABLLS-R), two specific, empirically-supported strategies for teaching communication (i.e., PECS, SGD), and, finally, three comprehensive approaches for teaching communication (i.e., PRT, NET, DTT). Although we have described these approaches separately, each is complementary to the others, and in many cases, effective programs must incorporate blends of approaches to produce optimal learning outcomes (e.g., PRT plus PECS, DTT plus NET). This is not an exhaustive list of empirically supported assessment and intervention strategies based in Skinner's verbal behavior theory. When teaching communication from the ABA perspective, regardless of approach, the most important element in successful programming is thoughtful and intentional incorporation of Skinner's principles, along with effective use of the three-term contingency.

# *References*

American Psychiatric Association. (2013). *Diagnostic and statistical manual of mental disorders (5ᵗʰ ed.)* (DSM-5). Washington, DC: Author.

Frost, L., & Bondy, A. (2002). *The picture exchange communication system training manual.* Newark: DE: Pyramid Educational Products.

Koegel, R. L., & Kern Koegel, L. (2006). *Pivotal response treatments for autism: Communication, social, and academic development.* Baltimore, MD: Brookes Publishing.

Lorah, E. R., Parnell, A., Whitby, P. S., & Hantula, D. (2015). A systematic review of tablet computers and portable media players as speech generating devices for individuals with autism spectrum disorder. *Journal of Autism and Developmental Disorders, 45,* 3792-3804.

Partington, J. W. (2006). *Assessment of basic language and learning skills-Revised* (ABLLS-R). Pleasant Hill, CA: Behavior Analysts, Inc.

Skinner, B. F. (1957). *Verbal behavior.* Englewood Cliffs, NJ: Prentice-Hall.
Stahmer, A. C., Suhrheinrich, J., Reed, S., Bolduc, C., & Schreibman, L. (2010). Pivotal response teaching in the classroom setting. *Preventing School Failure: Alternative Education for Children and Youth, 54,* 265-274.

Sundberg, M. L. (2008). *Verbal behavior milestones assessment and placement program guide.* Concord, CA: AVB Press.

Sundberg, M. L., & Michael, J. (2001). The benefits of Skinner's analysis of verbal behavior for children with autism. *Behavior Modification, 25,* 698-724.

Wong, C., Odom, S. L., Hume, K. Cox, A. W., Fettig, A., Kucharczyk, S., & Schultz, T. R. (2014). *Evidence-based practices for children, youth, and young adults with autism spectrum disorder.* Chapel Hill, NC: The University of North Carolina, Frank Porter Graham Child

Development Institute, Autism Evidence-Based Practice Review Group. Retrieved from http://autismpdc.fpg.unc.edu/sites/autismpdc.fpg.unc.edu/files/2014-EBP Report.pdf

# BEHAVIORAL SKILLS
# TRAINING

*Erick Dubuque & Molly Dubuque*

## KEY TERMS:

- Behavioral skills training
- Task analysis
- Instruction
- Modeling
- Generalized imitation
- In vivo modeling
- Video modeling
- Video self-modeling
- Rehearsal
- Feedback
- In situ assessment
- In situ training

## ▶▶ *Translating Instruction Into Action*

In education, two common misconceptions adversely impact how skills are taught to learners. The first is the idea that when a teacher tells a student how to do something, the student will be able to perform that skill (e.g., when a teacher expects her students to wash their hands in accordance with the instructions given or written above the sink). The second misconception is that skills can be evaluated by asking a learner *how* to perform the skill (e.g., when a teacher determines whether a student is capable of washing their hands correctly by asking them to list or write the steps involved in handwashing).

Both of these assumptions are problematic because they falsely equate the description of an action with the action itself (Kantor, 1953). However, talking about a skill is not the same as performing it. In other words, to determine whether a student is capable of washing his hands, the teacher must observe him doing it. While didactic instruction can help establish skills in a learner's repertoire, this mode of instruction can be improved upon in several ways (Matthews & Hagopian, 2014).

*Behavioral skills training*, or BST, is an intervention package that incorporates instructions, modeling, rehearsal, and feedback to teach new skills (Dib & Sturmey, 2012). These four components allow a learner to hear how a skill is taught, see how it is performed, practice the skill, and receive feedback on his performance.

This method of training has been used to teach a variety of skills to different types of learners across numerous settings. Specifically, BST has been used to effectively teach child safety skills, such as fire safety (Garcia, Dukes, Brady, Scott & Wilson, 2016;

Houvouras & Harvey, 2014), firearm injury prevention (Gatheridge et al., 2004; Hanratty, Miltenberger & Florentino, 2016; Himle, Miltenberger, Flessner & Gatheridge, 2004; Miltenberger, Flessner, Gatheridge, Johnson, Satterlund, & Egemo, 2004; Miltenberger et al. 2004; Miltenberger et al. 2005), pedestrian safety (Harriage, Blair & Miltenberger, 2016), abduction prevention (Johnson et al. 2006), swimming (Jull & Mirenda, 2016), and EpiPen® administration (Whiting, Miller, Hensel, Dixon & Szekely, 2014).

Additionally, researchers have shown that BST can be used to successfully teach caregivers, staff, and clients how to implement various methods of instruction, behavioral techniques, and skills (see Table 15.1).

The four components of BST (instructions, modeling, rehearsal, and feedback) are not implemented in any particular order during training, but are incorporated as needed. For example, instructions on how to perform a skill are often delivered prior to a model, during a model, and during a learner's rehearsal of the skill. Additionally, models demonstrating the skill are often repeated after the learner rehearses the skill, to review again how the skill is to be performed. Finally, feedback may take the form of additional instructions or another model delivered to the learner to help shape the skill being taught.

While the order of the four components of BST is not sequential, helping a learner achieve mastery of a new skill requires implementation of all four. The exclusion of any of these elements may lead to submastery performance, negatively impact maintenance of skill acquisition in the long-term, and result in less generalization of the skill across novel settings (Drifke et al., 2017; Garcia et al., 2016; Houvouras & Harvey, 2014; Kornacki et al., 2013; Rosales et al., 2009). Ultimately, it is up to the trainer to use the four components to adapt to the learner's performance and produce the best outcomes.

# Table 15.1
*Methods of Instruction, Techniques, and Skills Taught Using Behavioral Skills Training*

| Methods of Instruction, Techniques, and Skills Taught Using Behavioral Skills Training | Relevant Citation Examples |
| --- | --- |
| Implementing incidental teaching | Fetherston & Sturmey, 2014; Lerman, Hawkins, Hillman, Shireman & Nissen, 2015; Nigro-Bruzzi & Sturmey, 2010 |
| Implementing discrete trial teaching | Fetherston, Sturmey, 2014; Lerman, Hawkins, Hillman, Shireman & Nissen, 2015; Nosik, Williams, Garrido & Lee, 2013; Sarokoff & Sturmey, 2004 |
| Implementing Natural Language Paradigm protocols | Gianoumis, Seiverling & Sturmey, 2012 |
| Implementing activity schedules | Fetherston & Sturmey, 2014 |
| Implementing prompting | Drifke, Tiger & Wierzba, 2017; Beaulieu & Hanley, 2014 |
| Implementing Picture Exchange Communication System (PECS) | Homlitas & Rosales, 2014; Rosales, Stone & Rehfeldt, 2009 |
| Conducting functional analyses | Ward-Horner & Sturmey, 2012 |
| Writing behavior intervention plans | Hogan, Knez & Kahng, 2015 |
| Food selectivity protocols | Seiverling, Williams, Sturmey & Hart, 2012 |
| Reducing off-task behavior | Palmen & Didden, 2012 |
| Reducing problematic routines | Sawyer, Crosland, Miltenberger & Rone, 2015 |
| Teaching safe guarding practices | Nabeyama & Sturmey, 2010 |
| Teaching social skills compliance | Graudins, Rehfeldt, DeMattei, Baker & Scaglia, 2012; Miles & Wilder, 2009 |
| Teaching conversational skills | Kornacki, Ringdahl, Sjostrom & Nuernberger, 2013; Nuernberger, Ringdahl, Vargo, Crumpecker & Gunnarsson, 2013 |
| Teaching social play | Shireman, Lerman & Hillman, 2016 |

## ▶▶ *Steps to Teach a Skill Using BST*

One of the primary benefits of BST is its versatility in teaching many different types of skills. Any skill that lends itself to instruction, modeling, rehearsal, and feedback can potentially be taught using BST. When implementing BST, the following guidelines must be adhered to:

1. Identify the skill, audience, and goal.
2. Provide the instruction.
3. Demonstrate the model.
4. Provide the opportunity for rehearsal.
5. Shape the skill with feedback.
6. Assess progress and outcomes.

**Identify the skill, audience, and goal.** A skill must be operationally defined before a trainer can use BST to teach it. Operational definitions must be objective, clear, complete, and concise. For example, gun safety may be operationally defined as: in the presence of a firearm without adult supervision, the child should not touch the gun, leave the area, and immediately tell an adult (Miltenberger et al., 2005). For complex behaviors, it may be necessary to perform a task analysis to identify all the steps involved.

As discussed in Chapter 12, a *task analysis* involves breaking down a composite skill or behavior into its component parts. Task analyses are useful because they allow trainers to focus on teaching and developing mastery of individual components of a complex skill. This allows a trainer to work with the learner to develop mastery one step at a time. For example, multiple steps are involved in putting together a car engine. Trainers can develop a task analysis defining each of these steps, and then use BST to teach each component skill to mastery.

Audience information such as age, communication modality, physical ability, and group size also impact how BST is conducted. For example, a training on gun safety developed for a young child with limited communicative skills would look different than a training developed for a group of typically developing adolescents.

BST can be used to teach skills to groups or to individuals. For example, Beaulieu and Hanley (2014) taught teachers how to successfully use BST to teach typically developing schoolchildren compliance and peer mediation. Similarly, Hine (2014) successfully used a treatment package comprised of BST, video modeling, and public display of data to teach seven target skills to a group of child-care workers. When using BST with groups, it is important to ensure that all participants have enough opportunities to practice the skills being taught to ensure generalization across all relevant settings (Himle et al., 2004).

In addition to identifying the target skill and audience to be taught, the trainer must also identify a goal for the training. In other words, the trainer must decide at what point mastery of a given skill is achieved. For example, if the goal of meal preparation training is to increase independence for a resident living in a group home, the training should continue until the resident is able to make several meals independently without assistance. However, if the goal of the program is to increase participation in meal preparations, a mastery criterion may be met after the resident is able to demonstrate the ability to assist with several meals. When determining goals for BST, trainers need to consider how the skill will benefit the learner, as well as the amount of time and resources available to conduct the training.

**Provide the instruction**. In BST, *instruction involves* sharing detailed information on how to perform a skill. The instructional component of BST must be tailored to the audience. Spoken or written instructions may be used when working with an audience capable of speech or reading, but need to match the level of the learner. For example, simple spoken instructions explaining the steps involved in brushing teeth may be appropriate for a preschooler capable of speech. However, this form of instruction would not suffice if the learner was unable to receptively understand language. Under these circumstances, the child would be better served if the trainer adopted another instructional strategy, such as posting pictures outlining the steps involved in brushing teeth.

Before delivering the instruction, the trainer must capture the learner's attention. This may involve looking for nonverbal cues such as eye contact, body positioning, and silence when the instructor is speaking. Establishing attention is made easier when the trainer has been paired with reinforcement and when there is strong motivation to learn the skill being taught. If these conditions are not present, the trainer may need to design reinforcement contingencies around attending and performance during the training. Doing so will allow the trainer to potentially reinforce attending and participation behaviors as well as pair herself with potentially reinforcing stimuli. For example, an outside consultant who is invited to give a mandatory sexual harassment training to uninterested staff may find participation more likely if they allow their attendees to leave early as soon as they demonstrate mastery of the skills being taught.

Instructions must clearly describe each step of the skill being taught and the conditions under which those skills are to be performed. For example, a child being told how to order food at a restaurant would be instructed to read the menu when she sits down and ask for what she wants when the waiter requests her order. Instructions need to be simple and concise for ease of understanding. For example, when explaining the steps involved in driving a car with a standard transmission, the trainer would not make comparisons to the steps involved in driving a car with an automatic transmission, as this could be confusing.

Requiring participation from learners during instruction can help keep the learner engaged and allow the trainer to assess current levels of mastery. For example, after describing the steps involved in changing a tire, a trainer may ask the learner to explain back to him how to use a car jack. Participation can also take place within groups by requiring unison responses from all learners (e.g., asking all trainees to state, at the same time, the first step involved in filling out a time sheet for work).

When using BST, trainers often concurrently deliver instructions when they show a model of the response. For example, a trainer may explain the steps involved in using long division while actively solving a problem. Trainers also may choose to share some initial instructions with the learner before showing the model. For example, the instructor may want to review safety concerns with operating a burner before showing the learner the steps involved in cooking on a stovetop. Likewise, a parent may wish to explain the rules for crossing the street before giving the instructions and modeling the behavior of looking both ways.

A list of the recommended guidelines for providing instructions when using BST can be found in Table 15.2.

## Table 15.2
*Guidelines for the Instructional Component of BST*

| |
|---|
| 1. Present the instruction in a way the learner can understand. |
| 2. Ensure the learner is attending before delivering the instruction. |
| 3. Use clear, concise, simple language when describing the skill. |
| 4. Require active participation from the learner. |
| 5. Determine whether to deliver instructions before the model. |

**Demonstrate the model**. In BST, *modeling* involves the demonstration of a skill to a learner for purposes of imitation. As mentioned, modeling is often combined with instruction. Or, if instruction is delivered prior to the model, it is often repeated concurrently with the model. Trainers need to take several factors into consideration when deciding how to model a skill for a learner, including the following.

1. Can the learner's behavior be controlled by a model? Modeling is only effective as an instructional strategy when a learner has the capacity for generalized imitation. *Generalized imitation* occurs when a learner's behavior is controlled by and has formal similarity to a model's behavior (following its immediate occurrence). When that is not the case, it may be necessary to specifically program for it before using BST (Brown, Peace & Parsons, 2009).

2. Will the model be delivered in vivo or by video? *In vivo modeling* refers to a method of observational learning, wherein a skill is demonstrated live for purposes of imitation by a learner. In contrast, video modeling refers to a method of observational learning, wherein a skill is demonstrated by video for purposes of imitation by a learner.

3. Who will serve as the model? The effectiveness of modeling can be further enhanced when a trainer uses a role model, peer, or, in the case of video self-modeling, the learner, as the model in the video. If a role model is used, choosing somebody with prestige from the learner's perspective might be helpful. For example, having a learner's older brother perform the steps involved in CPR may result in the sibling paying more attention to the model when learning the same skill. If a peer is used, it is important to match as many characteristics between the peer and the learner as possible (e.g., gender, age and race). For example, when teaching a child the steps involved in riding a bike, the ideal model is someone of similar height using the same size bike as the learner.

In *video self-modeling*, the learner observes him or herself performing the skill to be imitated. Creating a video self-model often requires careful editing. For example, the trainer may ask the learner to conduct each step in creating a flower bed individually, and then splice the steps together into a longer video to be used during the training.

In vivo and video modeling methods both offer benefits and limitations when used within BST. One benefit of in vivo training is the ability to demonstrate and make modifications to the model in the moment. For example, a live model can slow down or pause and have the learner walk around to see another angle of the action when showing the proper grip to use when modeling a judo throw. Another benefit is showing the skill being performed in three dimensions, as opposed to two dimensions. This may be an important factor when working with learners who have difficulty matching 2D to 3D objects or actions. For example, an in vivo model may be more appropriate when teaching a person with a severe disability and a weak matching repertoire how to sort their laundry.

Although it offers important benefits, in vivo training does have some limitations. First, vivo modeling only allows the skill to be demonstrated in the current setting with the models that are available. When training some behaviors, this may not be a problem if the skill does not differ significantly across settings. For example, a trainer may not need to show a learner the proper way to swing a baseball bat while standing in front of different plates. However, it may be problematic if there are concerns that the skill may have difficulty generalizing to other settings. For example, if a trainer is teaching a group of students how to exit a building during a fire drill, it might be beneficial to show this skill across multiple settings with different building layouts.

A second limitation is the inability to slow down, pause, or show the action to the learner when demonstrating some behaviors. For example, a trainer may have difficulty demonstrating how a kick flip is performed on a skateboard to an observer.

A third limitation is the extensive time and resources that may be required to demonstrate some skills. For example, showing a learner how to change a car tire requires the tire be removed before every demonstration.

Fortunately, most of these limitations can be addressed using video modeling. First, video modeling can be used to demonstrate a skill across multiple contexts without leaving the training setting. Second, video modeling provides the trainer with an opportunity to pause, slow down, rewind, fast forward, and zoom in on the action for the learner. Finally, although video modeling may be more time consuming initially during production, it can save time later if the video can be replayed for learners.

When video modeling is used, the trainer needs to determine the perspective taken in the video. For some skills, it may be more beneficial to use a third-person perspective so the learner is able to observe all the physical actions the learner is taking. For example, a video model demonstrating the proper way to kick a soccer ball would be more effective using a third-person perspective, as it would help ensure the learner can observe various moves better, such as the proper angle when watching the foot strike the ball.

Other skills may be more easily taught with video modeling by using a first-person perspective. For example, when teaching social interactions using video modeling, a first-person perspective would put the learner in a better position to observe facial cues.

One of the primary benefits of video modeling is the ability to plan for generalization by showing the skill being performed across relevant settings. Prior to recording any video models, the trainer may want to consider developing a generalization map (Drabman, Hammer, & Rosenbaum, 1979) to identify how a mastered skill might generalize across settings and behaviors. Once these areas are identified, footage of the skill being performed across the settings can be taken for use in the training. For example, a trainer may film a model using various anger management strategies across a variety of scenarios and settings.

The number of models shown is dependent on the learner's performance. The trainer must be ready to model the response throughout BST to help the learner achieve mastery of the skill. For example, a learner may benefit from viewing a demonstration of the skill again if they have difficulty when rehearsing the skill.

A list of the recommended guidelines for demonstrating a model when using BST can be found in Table 15.3.

## Table 15.3
*Guidelines for the Modeling Component of BST*

| 1. Determine whether in vivo or video modeling will be used. |
| --- |
| 2. Identify whether a role model, peer, or self will be used as the model. |
| 3. Deliver the instructions concurrently with the model. |
| 4. Decide on the learner's perspective when watching the model. |
| 5. Demonstrate the skill across relevant contexts. |

**Provide the opportunity for rehearsal**. In BST, *rehearsal* involves a learner imitating a modeled skill after receiving instruction. Learners need the opportunity to practice the skill immediately after observing a model. When a learner practices a skill, the trainer is able to assess his or her current level mastery and shape the learner's behavior by offering praise and corrective feedback immediately after the skill is attempted.

When using BST to teach complex skills, it is important that learners rehearse the easiest components first, as this will increase the likelihood that they will contact success early on. For example, when teaching learners how to use holds during a crisis prevention training program, learners practice the easiest holds with the fewest number of steps before the more complicated holds requiring more steps.

It is recommended that rehearsals take place in the context where the skill is expected to occur. For example, if a trainer is attempting to teach an adult with developmental disabilities how to shop, a store might be the best place to practice this skill. When teaching some skills using BST, it may not be feasible or safe to practice the skill in the setting where the response is ultimately expected to occur. Under those circumstances, matching the practice setting as closely as possible to the natural setting helps ensure that the skill generalizes to the appropriate context. For example, it may be unsafe to initially teach a child how to cross the street near a busy intersection. However, a caregiver can build up to practicing in the natural setting by first having his or her child practice this skill in a driveway or a parking lot.

The learner needs to rehearse the skill until a predetermined mastery criterion is reached. The learner's statements about whether he or she knows how to perform the skill, however, cannot be accepted for determination of mastery. Instead, mastery is confirmed by measuring the learner actually performing the skill. There are multiple ways a trainer can measure a skill to determine mastery. Some examples are provided in Table 15.4.

## Table 15.4
*Examples of Measurable Dimensions to Determine Skill Mastery*

| Skill | Measurable Dimension | Example |
|---|---|---|
| Sending emails | Frequency | Counting the number of emails a learner is able to send without making any errors |
| Walking a tightrope | Percentage | Calculating the percentage of times a learner successfully moves between two anchors |
| Skateboarding | Duration | Timing how long a learner is able to stay up on the skateboard while moving |
| Participating in a conversation | Percentage of time | Calculating the percentage of time a learner speaks during a group conversation |
| Avoiding strangers | Latency | Timing how long it takes for a learner to move away from a stranger initiating a conversation |
| Shooting jump shots | Fluency | Counting the rate of jump shots made and missed by a learner during a set period of time |
| Interviewing for a job | Topography | Ticking off the behaviors performed by a learner during a mock job interview using a performance checklist (e.g., making eye contact, leaning forward, speaking clearly, asking follow up questions) |

One of the primary challenges when offering BST to groups of learners is ensuring that all participants have an opportunity to rehearse and receive immediate feedback on the skill being trained. To address this issue, trainers often show a model of the skill to the group and then have the entire group practice the skill at once. While this arrangement provides opportunities for rehearsal, it does not necessarily provide the opportunity for assessment and feedback from the trainer after every practice attempt. This is problematic if a learner is incorrectly practicing a skill repeatedly.

One potential solution is to ask learners to form small groups and to score one another using an objective criterion developed by the trainer. Crucial to this strategy is how objectively the skills are described for the observers. For example, when scoring public speaking performance, a data sheet that describes the target behavior as "spoke with confidence" is less likely to produce reliable scores than a data sheet that uses the description "80% or more of the words spoken were understood."

A list of the recommended guidelines for providing the opportunity for rehearsal when using BST can be found in Table 15.5.

## Table 15.5
*Guidelines for the Rehearsal Component of BST*

| |
|---|
| 1. Allow the learner to practice the skill immediately after the model is demonstrated. |
| 2. Practice easier skills before more difficult skills. |
| 3. Rehearse in settings where the skill is expected to occur. |
| 4. Continue rehearsals until a pre-determined mastery criterion is met. |
| 5. Deliver descriptive feedback and praise immediately after the skill is rehearsed. |

**Shape the skill with feedback.** Feedback involves delivering descriptive contingent feedback to a learner immediately after a skill is rehearsed. Feedback is the most important component of BST and may be delivered using a variety of methods (Ward-Horner, & Sturmey, 2012). Some examples highlighting different forms of feedback are provided in Table 15.6.

# Table 15.6
*Examples of Different Forms of Feedback*

| Feedback Form | Example |
|---|---|
| Vocal | Parent telling her child to dry his hands with a towel after he leaves the bathroom with wet hands |
| Written | Coach drawing arrows on the play board when her team incorrectly runs a play |
| Modeled | Personal trainer demonstrating the appropriate way to pick up a weight after a learner lifts with his back instead of his knees |
| Video | Principal showing a teacher a video of her performance during class and pointing out areas where she could have praised her students |
| Graphic | Friend showing his colleague a graph depicting the number of times she said, "Um," while practicing her class presentation |

Trainers must ensure that the ratio of praise to corrective feedback maintains the learner's interest in rehearsing the skill. If feedback is only corrective, without recognizing gains in performance, the learner may stop rehearsing the skill. Praise or some other form of reinforcement offered after every attempt made by the learner (e.g., praising a learner attempting the backstroke and allowing her a short break after three laps) provides important feedback to the learner.

It is important that any feedback delivered to learners be descriptive. That is, the trainer must clearly specify what the learner did correctly and what he still needs to work on. Generic statements like, "Good job," "Still needs some work," and, "You need to try again," fail to convey meaningful information to the learner that will help him or her improve their performance. For example, a trainer teaching a new rider how to trot with a horse may provide feedback such as, "Great work holding the reins at the right length in front of you—and don't forget to keep your heels down."

Further, it is important to present corrective feedback positively. For example, a trainer providing corrective feedback to a new salesperson after a bungled call may state, "Nice job introducing yourself. For your next call, try asking the customer about her experience with our product more quickly to avoid getting pulled into conversations about her day."

If a learner is struggling to perform a skill after extensive exposure to BST, it is the trainer's responsibility to identify the areas of weakness and work with the learner to improve. If multiple errors are present, it is important to focus on shaping one part of the skill at a time to avoid discouraging the learner. If errors continue to occur, it may be necessary to consider adapting the instruction, modeling, rehearsal and feedback strategies by breaking the skill down to smaller components.

A list of the recommended guidelines for shaping a skill with feedback when using BST can be found in Table 15.7.

## Table 15.7
*Guidelines for the Feedback Component of BST*

| |
|---|
| 1. Deliver feedback immediately after the learner rehearses the skill. |
| 2. Shape the skill by reinforcing improvements and attempts, and gently correcting errors. |
| 3. Use descriptive feedback that provides information on how to improve. |
| 4. If multiple errors occur, correct one component at a time. |
| 5. Adapt the feedback provided if learning is not occurring. |

**Assessing progress and outcomes**. Learners successfully complete BST when they are able to perform the skill at a level specified by the trainer. However, performing a skill in a contrived training setting does not guarantee that the skill will be maintained over time or generalize to a natural setting. One way to confirm that a learner has fully acquired a skill is to perform an in situ assessment by evaluating his ability to perform the skill in his natural environment (e.g., attending a lunch party hosted by a learner using the skills taught to him in a cooking class).

Further training may be required when an in situ assessment shows that a learner has not maintained a mastered skill. *In situ training* involves assessing a learner's ability to perform a skill in her natural environment and intervening immediately with further training if the skill is not performed correctly. If possible, trainers should consider implementing BST with an added in situ training component, as there is evidence to suggest that this component may help learners maintain this skill in their repertoire (Miltenberger et al., 2005).

In situ training may lead to better skill maintenance over time, and may be necessary if a learner is unable to demonstrate mastery of a skill after exposure to BST. For example, Johnson et al. (2006) evaluated BST with and without an in situ training component when teaching schoolchildren abduction prevention skills. The researchers found students exposed to the in situ training component performed better on a three-month follow-up assessment than without.

The benefits of in situ training may be further extended by adding a reinforcement or punishment contingency, depending upon the learner's performance when the skill is assessed in the natural environment. For example, Hanratty et al. (2016) were able to improve children's gun safety performance in the natural environment after adding a reinforcement and timeout punishment contingency during in situ training.

Depending on the skill being taught, trainers may need to enlist confederates when incorporating or evaluating the effects of BST. Confederates may be useful in creating opportunities for the learner to practice their skills during BST. For example, Beaulieu, Hanley and Santiago (2014) asked confederates to provide opportunities for a college student to practice conversational skills. Likewise, confederates may be used to evaluate progress after exposure to a BST program to ensure skills transfer over to the natural environment (e.g., enlisting a confederate to talk to a child at the playground after exposing the child to a stranger danger training program).

## ▶▶ *Summary*

BST is an intervention package that incorporates instructions, modeling, rehearsal, and feedback to teach new skills (Dib & Sturmey, 2012). Trainers interested in incorporating BST to teach a skill are encouraged to review the following steps. First, trainers need to define the skill, identify the audience, and set a goal. Second, the trainer must deliver clear and concise instructions to the learner after attending is established and demonstrated through participation. Third, in vivo or video modeling is recommended to demonstrate the skill across relevant contexts. Fourth, learners need the opportunity to rehearse the skill immediately after the model until a pre-determined mastery criterion is met. Fifth, it is essential to provide descriptive feedback designed to encourage and shape the learner's skill immediately following each practice attempt. Finally, trainers may find that incorporating in situ assessments and in situ training to assess and ensure mastery of the skill in the natural environment increases the effectiveness of the training.

# *References*

Beaulieu, L., Hanley, G. P. & Santiago, J. L. (2014). Improving the conversational skills of a college student with peer-mediated behavioral skills training. *Analysis of Verbal Behavior, 30,* 48-53.

Beaulieu, L., & Hanley, G. P. (2014). Effects of a classwide teacher-implemented program to promote preschooler compliance. *Journal of Applied Behavior Analysis, 47, 594-599.*

Brown, F. J., Peace, N., & Parsons, R. (2009). Teaching children generalized imitation skills: A case report. *Journal of Intellectual Disabilities, 13(1), 9-17.*

Dib, N., & Sturmey, P. (2012). Behavioral skills training and skill learning. In N. M. Seel (Ed.), *Encyclopedia of the sciences of learning* (pp. 437-438). New York, NY: Springer.

Drabman, R. S., Hammer, D., & Rosenbaum, M. S. (1979). Assessing generalization in behavior modification with children: The generalization map. *Behavioral Assessment, 1, 203-219.*

Drifke, M. A., Tiger, J. H., & Wierzba, B. C. (2017). Using behavioral skills training to teach parents to implement three-step prompting: A component analysis and generalization assessment. *Learning and Motivation, 57, 1-14.*

Fetherston, A. M., & Sturmey, P. (2014). The effects of behavioral skills training on instructor and learner behavior across responses and skill sets. *Research in Developmental Disabilities, 35, 541-562.*

Garcia, D., Dukes, C., Bracy, M. P., Scott, J., & Wilson, C. L. (2016). Using modeling and rehearsal to teach fire safety to children with autism. *Journal of Applied Behavior Analysis, 49, 699-704.*

Gatheridge, B. J., Miltenberger, R. G., Huneke, D. F., Satterlund, M. J., Mattern, A. R., Johnson, B. M., & Flessner, C. A. (2004). Comparison of two programs to teach firearm injury prevention skills to 6- and 7-year old children. *Pediatrics,* 114(3), e294-e299.

Gianoumis, S., Seiverling, L., & Sturmey, P. (2012). The effects of behavior skills training on correct teacher implementation of Natural Language Paradigm teaching skills and child behavior. *Behavioral Interventions, 27, 57-74.*

Graudins, M. M., Rehfeldt, R. A., DeMatti, R., Baker, J. C., & Scaglia, F. (2012). Exploring the efficacy of behavioral skills training to teach basic behavior analytic techniques to oral care providers. *Research in Autism Spectrum Disorders*, 6, 978-987.

Hanratty, L. A., Miltenberger, R. G., & Florentino, S. R. (2016). Evaluating the effectiveness of a teaching package utilizing behavioral skills training and in situ training to teach gun safety skills in a preschool classroom. *Journal of Behavioral Education*, 25, 310-323.

Harriage, B., Blair, K. C., & Miltenberger, R. (2016). An evaluation of a parent implemented in situ pedestrian safety skills intervention for individuals with autism. *Journal of Autism and Developmental Disorders*, 46, 2017-2027.

Himle, M. B., Miltenberger, R. G., Flessner, C., & Gatheridge, B. (2004). Teaching safety skills to children to prevent gun play. *Journal of Applied Behavior Analysis*, 37, 1-9.

Hine, K. M. (2014). Effects of behavioral skills training with directed data collection on the acquisition of behavioral practices by workers in a private, not-for-profit child care center. *Journal of Organizational Behavior Management*, 34, 223-232.

Hogan, A., Knez, N., & Kahng, S. (2015). Evaluating the use of behavioral skills training to improve school staffs' implementation of behavior intervention plans. *Journal of Behavioral Education*, 24, 242-254.

Homlitas, C., & Rosales, R. (2014). A further evaluation of behavioral skills training for implementation of the Picture Exchange Communication System. *Journal of Applied Behavior Analysis*, 47, 198-203.

Houvouras, A. J., & Harvey, M. T. (2014). Establishing fire safety skills using behavioral skills training. *Journal of Applied Behavior Analysis*, 47(2), 420-424.

Johnson, B. M., Miltenberger, R. G., Knudson, P., Egemo-Helm, K., Kelso, P., Jostad, C., & Langley, L. (2006). A preliminary evaluation of two behavioral skills training procedures for teaching abduction-prevention skills to schoolchildren. *Journal of Applied Behavior Analysis*, 39, 25-34.

Jull, S., & Mirenda, P. (2016). Effects of a staff training program on community instructors' ability to teach swimming skills to children with autism. *Journal of Positive Behavior Interventions*, 18, 29-40.

Kantor, J. R. (1953). *The logic of modern science.* Bloomington, IN: The Principia Press.

Kornacki, L. T., Ringdahl, J. E., Sjostrom, A., & Nuernberger, J. E. (2013). A component analysis of a behavioral skills training package used to teach conversation skills to young adults with autism spectrum and other developmental disorders. *Research in Autism Spectrum Disorders,* 7, 1370-1376.

Lerman, D. C., Hawkins, L., Hillman, C., Shireman, M., & Nissen, M.A. (2015). Adults with autism spectrum disorder as behavior technicians for young children with autism: Outcomes of a behavioral skills training program. *Journal of Applied Behavior Analysis,* 48(2), 233-256.

Matthews, K., & Hagopian, L. (2014). A comparison of two data analysis training methods for paraprofessional in an educational setting. *Journal of Organizational Behavior Management, 34, 165-178.*

Miles, N. I., & Wilder, D. A. (2009). The effects of behavioral skills training on caregiver implementation of guided compliance. J*ournal of Applied Behavior Analysis, 45*(2), 405-410.

Miltenberger, R. G., Flessner, C., Gatheridge, B., Johnson, B., Satterlund, M., & Egemo, K. (2004). Evaluation of behavioral skills training to prevent gun play in children. *Journal of Applied Behavior Analysis, 37(4), 513-516.*

Miltenberger, R. G., Gatheridge, B. J., Satterlund, M., Egemo-Helm, K. R., Johnson, B. M., Jostad, C., Kelso, P., & Flessner, C. A. (2005). Teaching safety skills to children to prevent gun play: An evaluation of in situ training. JOURNAL OF APPLIED BEHAVIOR ANALYSIS, 38, 395-398.

Nabeyama, B., & Sturmey, P. (2010). Using behavioral skills training to promote safe and correct staff guarding and ambulation distance of students with multiple physical disabilities. *Journal of Applied Behavior Analysis,* 43, 341-345.

Nuernberger, J. E., Ringdahl, J. E., Vargo, K. K., Crumpecker, A. C., & Gunnarsson, K. F. (2013). Using a behavioral skills training package to teach conversation skills to young adults with autism spectrum disorders. *Research in Autism Spectrum Disorders,* 7, 411-417.

Nigro-Bruzzi, D., & Sturmey, P. (2010). The effects of behavioral skills training on mand training by staff and unprompted vocal mands by children. *Journal of Applied Behavior Analysis,* 43, 757-761.

Nosik, M. R., Williams, W. L., Garrido, N., & Lee, S. (2013). Comparison of computer based instruction to behavioral skills training for teaching staff implementation of discrete-trial instruction with an adult with autism. *Research in Developmental Disabilities, 34, 461-468.*

Palmen, A., Didden, R., & Korzilius, H. (2010). Effectiveness of behavioral skills training on staff performance in a job training setting for high-functioning adolescents with autism spectrum disorders. *Research in Autism Spectrum Disorders, 4, 731-740.*

Palmen, A., & Didden, R. (2012). Task engagement in young adults with high-functioning autism spectrum disorders: Generalization effects of behavioral skills training. *Research in Autism Spectrum Disorders, 6, 1377-1388.*

Rosales, R., Stone, K., & Rehfeldt, R. A. (2009). The effects of behavioral skills training on implementation of the Picture Exchange Communication System. *Journal of Applied Behavior Analysis, 3, 541-549.*

Sarokoff, R. A., & Sturmey, P. (2004). The effects of behavioral skills training on staff implementation of discrete-trial teaching. *Journal of Applied Behavior Analysis, 37, 535-538.*

Sawyer, M. R., Crosland, K. A., Miltenberger, R. G., & Rone, A. B. (2015) Using behavioral skills training to promote the generalization of parenting skills to problematic routines, *Child & Family Behavior Therapy, 37, 261-284.*

Seiverling, L., Williams, K., Sturmey, P., & Hart, S. (2012). Effects of behavioral skills training on parental treatment of children's food selectivity. *Journal of Applied Behavior Analysis, 45, 197-203.*

Shireman, M. L., Lerman, D. C., & Hillman, C. B. (2016). Teaching social play skills to adults and children with autism as an approach to building rapport. *Journal of Applied Behavior Analysis, 49, 512-531.*

Ward-Horner, J., & Sturmey, P. (2012). Component analysis of behavior skills training in functional analysis. *Behavioral Interventions, 27, 75-92.*

Whiting, S. W., Miller, J. M., Hensel, A. M., Dixon, M. R., & Szekely, S. (2014). Increasing the accuracy of EpiPen administration with a brief behavioral skills training package in a school for autism. *Journal of Organizational Behavior Management, 34, 265-278.*

# THE SCIENCE OF BEHAVIOR ANALYSIS AS A
# MEANS OF CREATING A BETTER WORLD

*Terrance M. Scott*

Applied behavior analysis (ABA) is both a science and a set of practices associated with that science. Based on a set of principles for predicting how behavior is related to the environments in which it occurs, ABA provides us with both the evidence and the means to change environments for the purpose of promoting behaviors that have led to significant improvements in human health and well-being (Biglan, 2015). While the positive impact of ABA on humanity is undeniable, as a society, we continue to be humbled by inequality, hegemony, and predictable failures—all while available evidence-based solutions are too often eschewed in favor of less logical and disproven strategies.

As a nation – or perhaps even as a world, our societal decisions may seem to operate under the auspice of science, generally relying on research and espousing "evidence-based practice." But upon closer look, many of our key societal decisions are reached with reliance on fad, fallacy, and fiction (Keogh, 2007). When considering the facilitation of a better world and humane treatment of individuals, the skeletons in our closet include such wholly discredited examples as the anti-vaccine movement (van der Linden, Clarke & Maibach, 2017) and spanking (see Taylor, Manganello, Lee, & Rice, 2010). In many respects, the one constant seems to be practice is informed by whatever theory enjoys the popular zeitgeist – despite evidence. Clearly, this process does not follow what would generally be considered a scientific process under the tenets of ABA where evidence leads to change.

As mentioned, the contributions of ABA cover a vast array of human health and behavior. But as a practice, this chapter contends that the contributions of ABA are likely to be most influential in their application to both the structure and practices of public education, the practices in which teachers and other educators engage to produce positive effects on students.

First, education as an institution touches virtually all of the population—providing a tremendous opportunity to affect success. Second, applying ABA principles to teaching creates both the delivery system for positive change and the model for continued practice across the larger society. In this way, effective ABA practices promote both individual success and the perpetuation of effective societal practices.

# ▶▶ *Applied Behavior Analysis and Education*

While education is perhaps the most fertile ground for ABA in terms of making an impact in a quest for a better world, it is also an institution that has a history of ignoring science. In her book, An Elusive Science: *The Troubling History of Education Research*, Lagemann (2000) shares the observations that in the field of education "there is neither a Better Business Bureau nor the equivalent of the Federal Food and Drug Administration. Caveat Emptor is the policy…" (p. 239).

B. F. Skinner described education's aversion to ABA principles as a fear of control that emanated from the 20th-century notion that students learn best when the teacher's influence is minimized. Thus, the child-centered and constructivist movements reinforce a fear that the teacher's control of effective instruction will somehow remove the students' joy of learning (Oldfather & Dahl, 1994). While this approach is often attributed to John Dewey, in reality he rejected a pure child-centered approach, believing that the learning environment must be engaging for students — but at the direction of the teacher (Dewey, 1904).

While it seems more logical that effective instruction and fostering of student success would more readily promote a love of learning (e.g., Tarver & Jung, 1995; Wehby, Falk, Barton-Arwood, Lane, & Cooley, 2003), this is not the prevailing conceptual model under which education operates (Taylor, Pearson, Clark, & Walpole, 2000). In essence, we have created an educational system that, if not unconcerned with facts, has greatly confused what it means to have evidence and identify high-probability practices.

What would schooling look like if instruction more accurately reflected the principles of effective behavior change that are both incorporated in a practice of ABA and reinforced by its science?

Current educational systems and practices leave much to be desired for many of our students. One particularly egregious failure is the overwhelmingly disproportionate number of students from nondominant cultures (i.e., racial/ethnic minorities and students with disabilities) who fail in school, drop out, and end up being involved with the correctional and social service systems (Lane, Carter, Pierson, & Glaeser, 2006; Sum, Khatiwada, McLaughlin, & Palma, 2009; Wagner, Kutash, Duchnowski, Epstein, & Sumi, 2005). Clearly, current educational practices have been ineffective in changing these outcomes and, thus, have failed to live up to education's promise of promoting social justice and equality. But social justice, as an outcome of effective education, can be achieved only when we are able to distinguish between fact and fiction, or between actions that do and do not offer a high-probability of achieving desirable outcomes.

Some of the criticism leveled at ABA and the scientific method in education is founded on the premise that human beings are inherently biased and that the direction of research is often as much bound by status, politics, and financial incentive as by fact (e.g., Heshusius, 1994; Rorty, 1991). As stated succinctly and directly by Broad and Wade (1982), "In the acquisition of new knowledge, scientists are not guided by logic and objectivity alone, but also by such nonrational factors as rhetoric, propaganda, and personal prejudice" (p. 9).

While a degree of bias cannot be avoided, this criticism seems to be leveled not solely on the scientific method but also the sloppy, illogical, and self-serving manner with which it has been applied. But in an illogical twist, the solution offered by the critics of ABA has been to adopt a qualitative methodology that disregards this as a concern. The post-modern movement from which this logic is derived can is a direct precursor to our contemporary disregard for objective truth—and the rise of "alternative facts." Clearly, the best chance of advancing success and equality in society lies in attention to methodology rather than epistemology. Attention and adherence to the principles of ABA will do more to contribute to a better world than reconceptualizing the way in which we conceive of truth.

Inherent in much of the critical rhetoric surrounding ABA as the driver of practice is a notion of fairness and equity. For example, a simple ERIC search for "teacher assessment instruments" yields over 100 instruments focused on such ill-defined student outcomes as *young adult ethos, self-esteem, freedom, democratic values, ego orientation, democracy, critical thinking,* and *social justice.* Each conjures an intuitive feel for the reasoning of its inferred importance, but with little direction for measuring how each might result in specific interventions. While it would be both difficult and uncomfortable to argue against the importance of such emotionally laden concepts as democratic values or social justice, the argument is not with the social validity, it is with the construct validity. That is, what are the outcomes by which we judge the quality or effect of ABA, and how can ABA account for constructs such as social justice?

## ▶▶ *Social Justice and ABA*

According to Sensoy and DiAngelo (2009), social justice is a way of seeing and acting — actively addressing and recognizing inequality. There is much to unpack here, but the focus of social justice seems to be on a sort of societal self-reflection and processing of inequity as a means of change, but without measures of objective outcomes. While analysis of problems and causes fits well within an ABA framework, a focus on measureable outcomes is also essential. In short, there must be an outcome by which we judge the selected means (intervention). In line with an ABA perspective of social validity, any means—no matter how positive and agreeable—must produce a socially desirable outcome. A focus on social justice that fosters discussion and reflection but produces no measurable positive outcomes cannot be considered to be socially valid.

Effective instructional practices, functional communication training, antecedent manipulations, and frequent performance feedback toward a goal are all components of ABA technology that are known to maximize the probability of success (Hattie, 2009; Johnston, Foxx, Jacobson, Green, & Mulick, 2006). As such, these components provide a means for achieving social justice. Of course, one might argue that the end cannot justify the means, but the means cannot be more important than the end either.

The struggle for equality across all beings must be more important as an outcome than the means for getting there. In this essential struggle for ABA as a means of producing better outcomes, there are inherent theoretical, societal, and structural impediments that must be effectively addressed and overcome.

## ▶▶ *Inherent Roadblocks for Behavior Analysis in Education*

This section identifies issues inhibiting the scientific logic and rigor of ABA. While the issues presented are not exhaustive, they represent an assessment of current shortcomings of educational research in light of ABA and the scientific method.

**Teachers as agents of change.** Biesta (2007) voiced the concern that "evidence-based education seems to limit severely the opportunities for educational practitioners to make such judgments in a way that is sensitive to and relevant for their own contextualized settings" (p. 56). This view seems to imply that the teacher is important, but reflects a concern that identification of best practice somehow lessens the teacher's ability to make professional judgments.

But these are empirical questions, and, as one might expect, students who fail have a negative view of both their teacher and school in general (Cornelius-White, 2007). These negative views result in increasingly negative interactions that often manifest in escalating behaviors on the part of both the teacher and student (Colvin & Scott, 2015). Students perceived as problematic end up receiving less and poorer teacher instruction (Stichter et al., 2009; Sutherland, Lewis-Palmer, Stichter, & Morgan, 2008), and are likely to be the recipients of more negative teacher comments, regardless of behavior (Hirn & Scott, 2014).

The purpose of ABA in education is neither to develop a cookbook nor to create dogmatic prescriptions for intervention. Rather, it is to identify those practices that offer the highest probability of success in a given context (see Sackett, 1996) and to further identify the best means by which qualified professionals identify and apply those strategies. Active teacher participation is a foundation of ABA and has been repeatedly identified as a high-probability practice for promoting student engagement and achievement (Hattie, 2009).

It is clear that ABA has provided a well-established science for managing classrooms and instruction in a manner that effectively maximizes the probability of student success (Simonsen, Fairbanks, Briesch, Myers, & Sugai, 2008). Alarmingly, the literature just as clearly shows that, on average, teachers are not well trained in effective classroom and behavior management strategies (Coyne, Kameenui, & Simmons, 2001; Oliver & Reschly, 2010). When teachers do not know what to do, they tend to resort to punitive consequences and exclusion (Banks & Zionts, 2009), even though there is no evidence that such responses are associated with a positive change in behavior (Gable & VanAcker, 2000). Moreover, these failures are significant predictors of future student failure in both the academic and social realms (Sprague et al., 2001).

At the heart of this argument is the manner in which we prepare teachers in our teacher training institutions (i.e., colleges and universities). As a field, ABA must continue to make a case for social justice: What science supports as providing the highest probability of success is the best chance we have of removing inequity, hegemony, and failure.

**The nature of evidence: Public vs. private truths**. ABA is founded on the value of every human being's right to hold personal views and to act on these views as they see fit—so long as it does not harm others' right to the same. But there must be clear delineation between what we hold to be true personally and what science publicly shows us to be true. Everybody is free to believe that effective instruction is harmful and to make choices for their own education and that of their children. However, when evidence clearly and overwhelmingly demonstrates the preferential outcomes associated with instruction tied to the principles of ABA, this must be the foundation for how we train teachers and other professionals. Because we know the cost of failure on the outcomes of our students, to do otherwise would be considered at best irresponsible, and at worst, abusive.

In a sense, education research has come to focus on what might more accurately be defined as documenting rather than evaluating practice. There is a distinct and critical difference *between documentation and evaluation* of practices: qualitative documentation infers that an intervention is associated with perceived outcomes, whereas empirical evaluation, as emphasized in ABA, determines whether the evidence is sufficient to believe that the observed outcomes are truly the result of intervention. Standards for establishing functional relations through single-subject research designs provide teachers with practical methods for evaluating the effects of an intervention, helping to ensure that students are not subject to meaningless—or even counterproductive—intervention.

Part of the problem with much of the less empirical evidence is associated with poorly defined variables. Recall young adult ethos, self-esteem, freedom, democratic values, and ego orientation that are used as dependent variables (outcomes) across popular educational assessments. When outcomes are vague, it is difficult to measure the effects.

In an 1877 issue of the journal *Popular Science Monthly*, Charles Peirce discussed the nature of research as engaging science to find out what we don't know. He observed, "Where hope is unchecked by any experience, it is likely that our optimism is extravagant" (p. 3). Hypothesizing connections between instruction and ill-defined constructs may be acceptable as the beginning of a line of inquiry. However, in many cases, educational inquiry has stopped at this level, with continued optimistic espousals of how to reform practice despite an absence of evidence from research (e.g., Adams, Bell, & Griffin, 1997; Ayers, Hunt, & Quinn, 1998).

**Research questions and evidence: Logic vs. convenience**. Except for the social sciences, we do not live in a world driven by theory over science. Bridge engineers, pilots, and physicians do not base their profession on qualitative judgments of effect—and for good reason. The costs of failure are alarmingly and immediately obvious when an engineer decides that smaller supports look and feel better on a bridge, despite the fact that they are mathematically insufficient to support load. Society requires these professionals to adhere to a professional standard based on a science that dictates the best probability for success. But in general education, qualitative research is the norm—allowing perceptions of reality to be the de facto arbiter of truth.

From an ABA perspective, research questions are focused on the effects of an intervention with an individual or small group of students. This limits generalizability but bolsters validity, by focusing the methods to a very particular question, which can be definitively answered. As a field, behavior analysts must speak out to ensure that educational research strives to focus on answering important questions rather than answering the questions that are comfortable or that fit a preferred research methodology. That is, we must commit to allowing our questions to drive our methodology, rather than the converse. That is, the value of any study must be judged first on the importance of the question for advancing our knowledge with regard to (a) the probability of increasing operationally defined outcomes, and then by (b) the degree to which the study was able to provide a trustworthy answer to that question.

What level of trust in any particular claim of truth warrants our efforts, our money, and our belief in outcomes that affect the future of our children? Trust in research is enhanced to the degree that we believe there are no plausible alternative explanations for the observed effects (i.e., internal validity) (Fraenkle & Wallen, 2009; Shadish, Cook, & Campbell, 2002). As Stephen J. Gould so succinctly stated, "The primary desideratum in all experiments is reduction of confusing variables" (1995, p. 11).

Specific ABA evaluation procedures and techniques protect against threats to internal validity. For example, the ABA protocol for evaluating intervention recognizes that observed effects may be attributable to a number of potential variables, and those variables are then controlled for through the selection of the appropriate single-subject design and associated procedures to increase internal validity. Similarly, repeated testing, history, maturation, regression to the mean, experimenter bias, and a host of other threats to our trust in evidence require specific techniques so that we may trust that the observed effects do not have plausible alternative explanations. This all begins with a clear definition of what constitutes sufficient evidence to warrant trust.

## *The Role of Behavior Analysis*

Imagine ABA represented by a spider's web, where the center represents the highest level of student success. All around the web are the individual students who populate our schools. Each thread and cross thread represent both an educational practice and a probability for the student's success in moving closer to the center of the web (success).

Given that an individual student has his own skills, deficits, histories, and so on, we must ask: Which threads need to be avoided and which represent the best route to reach success? In order to answer this question, we first need to define success; next, we need to define each of the potential educational practices. We then need to determine the relative probability of success for each thread in the web, given a variety of different content, ages, skill levels, and a myriad other relevant variations found in the natural world.

This web analogy is a metaphor for ABA. When we know the starting and ending points, we can use information about the student to select from among our evidence-based practices to maximize the probability of success. Clearly, this is an enormous undertaking that is often expensive, time-consuming, and inexact, in that the results represent probabilities for success that likely will never be near 100%. But it is hard to imagine that this is any more difficult than sequencing the human genome—an effort being shared across research sites and supported by the government.

At the heart of this process is the integrity with which ABA and its research are conducted, and adherence to the scientific method. Clear definitions of procedures, outcomes, and criteria must be developed in advance of any study, and the focus directed on answering questions regarding relationships and probability. Ideally, specific research questions dictate that specific research design be used—not the skills of the researcher. This requires the use of double-blind procedures, avoidance of conflicts of interest, and replication of all findings, both within and across investigators, a part of the larger research plan.

## ▶▶ *Personal Commitments to ABA*

As stated, the goal is not to create a cookbook approach to education, in which teachers look up a student's demographics and abilities and apply a stipulated intervention. Rather, identification of the relative probabilities for success under a variety of contexts and circumstances would provide the professional with guidelines for considering a course of intervention. These guidelines would be no different than what a mason uses in determining the best way to lay mortar or what a nurse does in assessing the best course of action for a patient. While there are likely no universal absolutes, some approaches provide better probabilities for success than others, and science is our best hope for establishing these.

In pursuing these goals for ABA as a means of making a better world through education, there are five specific behaviors that can help to move ABA forward in this context. These goals are summarized in Table 16.1.

## Table 16.1
*The Keys to ABA*

| |
|---|
| 1 .Commit to science and data. |
| 2. View social justice as an empirical outcome and a personal responsibility. |
| 3. Defend principle over practice. |
| 4. Invest in probability and view mistakes as opportunities to make corrections. |
| 5. Speak out for truth and those who cannot speak for themselves. |

1. **Commit to science and data**. The scientific and data-based foci of ABA provide the best opportunity for identifying facts and truth. We must both advocate for and adhere to this commitment to allow empirical evidence to be the arbiter of success. As humans, it is all too easy to allow our personal convictions and preferences to influence our perceptions of reality. To combat these issues of implicit confirmation bias, ABA dictates that we set measurable goals for behavior change, measure outcomes in a formative manner, and make decisions based on observed performance in comparison to predetermined and socially valid outcomes. These are commitments that can be made as personal convictions as well as standards that we advocate for the field at large.

2. **View social justice as an empirical outcome and a personal responsibility.** Regardless of the means, we must measure the value of an intervention by its impact on socially valid outcomes. An ABA perspective of social justice must be defined by the outcomes for individuals and must evaluate interventions by the degree to which those outcomes are achieved. It is ironic that much of what passes for social justice practice is appreciated more for its adherence to theoretical tenets than to actual student outcomes. We can view ABA as a means to social justice—but the proof is in the difference it makes for our students. Because the environment is the vehicle for our intervention, when intervention fails to produce meaningful change, we cannot blame the environment; we must instead renew a focus on our responsibility for acting to change it in a manner that is more likely to produce the desired change.

3. **Defend principle over practice.** We must not get caught up in arguments over practice. For example, there is no one best way to conduct a functional (behavior) assessment (FA). Rather, there are principles of operant behaviors: They occur predictably in the presence of some specific stimuli and serve a purpose for the student (maintained by consequences). What type of assessment we use to assess for this connection between the environment and behavior is dictated by a variety of circumstances, including the nature, frequency, and severity of behavior. So long as the assessment provides valid information that leads to an effective function-based intervention, it is potentially useful. Further, at some point, someone may develop a novel way of developing an antecedent-behavior-consequence (ABC) for analysis of function. Being wed to any particular method increases the likelihood that we ignore the advance of science. We must select the methods from based simply on which ones provide the best probability of success for an individual case.

4. **Invest in probability and view failures as opportunities to make corrections.** Because social science methodologies and practices do not share the same degree of certitude as the hard sciences (e.g., engineering and medicine), we have few sure things in our bag of tricks. However, some things do work better than others, and we must invest in probability. There is no logic in abandoning an evidence-based practice because it is not a certainty. The logic is to select the intervention that provides the greatest probability for success based on the knowledge we have of a given student and environment. But because there are no certainties, there will be failed interventions. From an ABA perspective,

our intervention failures must be seen as additional information regarding the complexities of a given case, giving rise to an amended intervention that takes into account information gleaned from the failure. For example, an FA leading to a failed intervention simply serves as the foundation for a more focused and intensive FA, repeated until success is observed. This brings us back to considerations of principle over practice. Failures are *not* evidence of flaws within ABA; they *are* evidence of fixable flaws in our practices.

5. **Speak out for truth and for those who cannot speak for themselves.** Social validity as a key tenet of ABA ensures that we strive to provide interventions that are widely seen as beneficial for the student. But we are also responsible for promoting and advocating for the truth, justice, and those who cannot speak for themselves. If we truly believe that adherence to the principles of ABA in education is in the best interest of our students, we might consider it a responsibility to speak out in support of science, evidence, and the promotion of socially valid outcomes. A belief in ABA creates a responsibility to speak out, just as a belief that abuse is wrong entails a responsibility to speak out against abusive treatment.

## ▶▶ *Summary*

Applied behavior analysis provides the scientific framework and a set of high-probability practices that can improve the lives of all people, with special attention to those from disadvantaged backgrounds, those with histories of failure, and those with disabilities.

ABA is no panacea — it is not the sole remedy for the ills of contemporary society. But the tenets of ABA do have enormous implications for public policy, in education and elsewhere. The fate of our world, for better or worse, lies in our collective ability to advocate for the principles of science and a set of practices that provide us with the best possible chances of achieving successful outcomes.

# *References*

Adams, M., Bell, L. A., & Griffin, P. (1997). *Teaching for diversity and social justice: A sourcebook.* New York, NY: Routledge.

Ayers, W., Hunt, J.A., & Quinn, T. (1998). *Teaching for social justice: A democracy and education reader.* New York: New Press.

Banks, T., & Zionts, P. (2009). Teaching a cognitive behavioral strategy to manage emotions. *Intervention in School & Clinic,* 44(5), 307-313.

Biesta, G. (2007). Why "What Works" won't work: Evidence-based practice and the democratic deficit in educational research. *Educational Theory,* 57(1), 1-22.

Biglan, A. (2015, February 27). *Behavioral science may prove to be our most important science.* [web log post] Retrieved from http://www.huffingtonpost.com/anthony-biglan/perhaps-behavioral-science-may-prove-to-be-our-most-important-science_b_6764296.html

Colvin, G., & Scott, T. M. (2015). *Managing the cycle of acting out behavior* (2$^{nd}$ ed.). New York, NY: Corwin Press.

Cornelius-White, J. (2007). Learner-centered teacher-student relationships are effective: A meta-analysis. *Review of Educational Research,* 77(1), 113-143.

Coyne, M. D., Kame'enui, E. J., & Simmons, D. C. (2001). Prevention and intervention in beginning reading: *Two complex systems. Leaning Disabilities Research & Practice,* 16, 62-73.

Dewey, J. (1904). The relation of theory to practice in education. In C. A. McMurry (Ed.), *The Third Yearbook of the National Society for the Scientific Study of Education.* Part I (pp. 9-30). Chicago, IL: The University of Chicago Press. https://archive.org/details/r00elationoftheorynatirich

Fraenkle, J. R., & Wallen, N. E. (2009). *How to design and evaluate research in education* (7th ed.). New York, NY: McGraw Hill.

Gable, R. A., & Van Acker, R. (2000). The challenge to make schools safe: Preparing education personnel to curb student aggression and violence. *The Teacher Educator,* 35(3), 1-18.

Goddard, A. (1997). The role of individualized education plans/programmes in special education: A critique. *Support for Learning*, 12(4), 170-174.

Gould, S. J. (1995). Curveball. In S. Fraser (Ed.), *The bell curve wars* (pp 11-22). New York, NY: Basic Books.

Hattie, J. A. C. (2009). *Visible learning: A synthesis of over 800 meta-analyses relating to achievement.* New York, NY: Routledge Press.

Heshusius, L. (1994). Freeing ourselves from objectivity: Managing subjectivity or turning toward a participatory mode of consciousness? *Educational Researcher*, 23(3), 15-22.

Hirn, R. G., & Scott, T. M. (2014). Descriptive analysis of teacher instructional practices and student engagement among adolescents with and without challenging behavior. *Education and Treatment of Children*, 36(4), 585-607.

Johnston, J. M., Foxx, R. M., Jacobson, J. W., Green, G., & Mulick, J. A. (2006). Positive behavior support and applied behavior analysis. *Behavior Analyst*, 29(1), 51.

Keogh, B. K. (2007). Celebrating PL 94-142: The education of all handicapped children act of 1975. *Issues in Teacher Education*, 16(2), 65-69.

Lagemann, E. C. (2000). *An elusive science.* Chicago, IL: University of Chicago Press.

Lane, K., Carter, W., Pierson, M., & Glaeser, B. (2006). Academic, social, and behavioral characteristics of high school students with emotional disturbances or learning disabilities. *Journal of Emotional & Behavioral Disorders*, 14(2), 108-117.

Oldfather, P., & Dahl, K. (1994). Toward a social constructivist reconceptualization of intrinsic motivation for literacy learning. *Journal of Literacy Research*, 26(2), 139-158.

Oliver, R. M., & Reschly, D. J. (2010). Special education teacher preparation in classroom Management: Implications for students with emotional and behavioral disorders. *Behavioral Disorders*, 35(3), 188-199.

Peirce, C. S. (1877). The fixation of belief. *Popular Science Monthly*, 12, 1-15. Reprinted online at Peirce.org, http://www.pierce.org/writings/p107/html.

Rorty, R. (1991). *Objectivity, relativism, and truth: Philosophical papers Vol. 1.* Cambridge, England: Cambridge University Press.

Sackett, D. (1996). Evidence-based medicine - What it is and what it isn't. *BMJ, 312,* 71-72. http://www.bmj.com/cgi/content/full/312/7023/71.

Sensoy, Ö., & Diangelo, R. (2009). Developing social justice literacy an open letter to our faculty colleagues. *Phi Delta Kappan,* 90(5), 345-352.

Shadish, W., Cook, T., & Campbell, D. (2002). *Experimental and quasi-experimental designs for generalized causal inference.* Boston, MA: Houghton Mifflin.

Simonsen, B., Fairbanks, S., Briesch, A., Myers, D., & Sugai, G. (2008). Evidence-based practices in classroom management: Considerations for research to practice. *Education and Treatment of Children,* 31(3), 351-380.

Sprague, J., Walker, H., Stieber, S., Simonsen, B., Nishioka, V., & Wagner, L. (2001). Exploring the relationship between school discipline referrals and delinquency. *Psychology in the Schools,* 38(2), 197-206.

Stichter, J. P., Lewis, T. J., Whittaker, T. A., Richter, M., Johnson, N. W., & Trussell, R. P. (2009).

 Assessing teacher use of opportunities to respond and effective classroom management strategies: Comparisons among high- and low-risk elementary schools. *Journal of Positive Behavior Interventions,* 11, 68-81.

Sum, A., Khatiwada, I., McLaughlin, J., & Palma, S. (2009). *The consequences of dropping out of high school. Boston,* MA: Northeastern University, Center for Labor Market Studies.

Sutherland, K. S., Lewis-Palmer, T., Stichter, J., & Morgan, P. L. (2008). Examining the influence of teacher behavior and classroom context on the behavioral and academic outcomes for students with emotional or behavioral disorders. *Journal of Special Education,* 41(4), 223-233.

Tarver, S. C., & Jung, J. S. (1995). A comparison of mathematics achievement and mathematics attitudes of first and second graders instructed with either a discovery-learning mathematics curriculum or a Direct Instruction curriculum. *Effective School Practices,* 14, 49-57.

Taylor, B. M., Pearson, P. D., Clark, K., & Walpole, S. (2000). Effective schools and accomplished teachers: Lessons about primary-grade reading instruction in low-income schools. *The Elementary School Journal*, 121-165.

Taylor, C. A., Manganello, J. A., Lee, S. J., & Rice, J. C. (2010). Mothers' spanking of 3-year-old children and subsequent risk of children's aggressive behavior. *Pediatrics, 125*, 1057-1065.

van der Linden, S. L., Clarke, C. E., & Maibach, E. W. (2017). Erratum to: Highlighting consensus among medical scientists increases public support for vaccines: evidence from a randomized experiment. *BMC Public Health*, 17(1), 284.

Wagner, M., Kutash, K., Duchnowski, A. J., Epstein, M. H., & Sumi, W. C. (2005). The children and youth we serve: A national picture of the characteristics of students with emotional disturbances receiving special education. *Journal of Emotional and Behavioral Disorders, 13*(2), 79-96.

Wehby, J. J., Falk, K. B., Barton-Arwood, S., Lane, K. L., & Cooley, C. (2003). The impact of comprehensive reading instruction on the academic and social behavior of students with emotional and behavioral disorders. *Journal of Emotional and Behavioral Disorders*, 11(4), 225-238.

# CODA – APPLIED BEHAVIOR
## ANALYSIS FOR EVERYONE

*Robert C. Pennington*

Behavior analysis served for me as a light in the dark. As a young special education teacher, I often struggled. Each day brought new challenges to which I was unprepared to face. I collected interventions and strategies from professional development trainings, other teachers, and related service professionals and then unsystematically hurled them towards my students hoping they would work. Sometimes, an intervention would stick but often times I was called to reach back into my quiver and sling another arrow. This process was exhausting, but more importantly resulted in inefficient and sometimes ineffective programming for my students.

My world changed with the introduction of applied behavior analysis . It offered explanations for my student's behavior and provided me a critical lens through which I could evaluate my selection and implementation of procedures. My practice improved and I became more confident in my capacity to serve others. I became increasingly optimistic.

Interestingly, behavior analysis crept into other facets of my life. I began to acknowledge the role of people's past experiences on their behavior and sought to understand those whose behavior appeared unconventional given a set of circumstances or expectations. I also viewed my own behavior differently and learned to change my environment to produce growth. Overall, behavior analysis was teaching me compassion and to more effectively navigate a contingency-laden world.

I am forever grateful to my mentors in behavior analysis and it is to them I offer this book. They gifted powerful lessons, not from a pulpit, but through gentle demonstration, guidance, and feedback. It is my hope, that the words in this text also might connect with those struggling to improve their own lives and/or the lives of others and maybe for some, illuminate spaces dark to understanding.

It is important to note that this book is not a call for the reader to cast away their own approaches or viewpoints, but instead to consider those places where behavior analysis might be helpful. For example, a speech/language pathologist might consider using differential reinforcement procedures to support clients' engagement during therapy sessions or an occupational therapist might use functional (behavior) assessment  to determine whether a behavior is truly maintained by sensory feedback. Further, parents, teachers, and members of law enforcement might certainly benefit from understanding that misbehavior  problem behavior is related to context and that it is amenable to intervention and support. The understanding and application of a few of these basic behavioral principles and procedures and can have a powerful and lasting impact.

We also must acknowledge that behavior analysis has its limitations and as a result, behavioral analytic practitioners must work in concert with other professionals. Behavior analysts can and have learned a great deal from educators, related service providers, doctors, parents, and consumers. In my own experience, I have benefited greatly greatly from working alongside other professionals from different fields and have learned to respect their valuable contributions. These interactions have provided me an opportunity to apply behavioral principles in new contexts and in some cases rethink the applications of those principles. Additionally, these interactions have helped me to dispel myths related to behavior analysis and more importantly to increase access to it.

In sum, behavior analysis encompasses a powerful body of knowledge and procedures for use in improving lives. The talented and genuine authors assembled to produce this text, have drawn from their personal experiences and research to present to the uninitiated reader some of the field's most important principles and practices. I hope their narratives evoked several "aha" moments as you read, and that you found yourself thirsty for more (or a motivating operation in effect).

# GLOSSARY

**0-second delay.** Initial training trials used in the time delay response prompting strategy in which the stimulus and controlling prompt are delivered simultaneously.

**Abolishing operation.** A type of motivating operation that weakens the value of a reinforcing stimulus.

**Analytic.** A characteristic of ABA in which practitioners focus on a clear demonstration of the relation between particular aspects of the environment and changes in behavior.

**Applied.** A characteristic of ABA in which practitioners address changes in behavior that are important to the individual whose behavior is targeted for change.

**Applied behavior analysis.** A branch of behavior analysis in which procedures derived from behavioral principles are systematically applied to improve socially significant outcomes.

**Anecdotal recording.** Informal writing or notes collected on a target behavior.

**Aversive stimuli.** Environmental changes that function as a punisher for a behavior.

**Baseline.** A session or condition in which an intervention is not in effect.

**Behavior.** Things that people do.

**Behavior Analyst Certification Board.** A credentialing body for behavior analysts.

**Behavior change.** When a target behavior increases or decreases in level (amount of behavior that occurs), trend (direction over time), or variability (changes from day to day).

**Behavioral.** A characteristic of ABA in which practitioners focus on observable changes in behavior rather than on what is said about a behavior.

**Behavioral contrast.** A phenomenon that takes place when behavior is punished or reinforced in one context and later decreases or increases in another context.

**Behavioral skills training.** An intervention package that incorporates instructions, modeling, rehearsal, and feedback to teach new skills.

**Bias.** Conscious or unconscious belief that data will change across conditions; this can impact the accuracy of data collection, especially when occurrences are ambiguous.

**Choice.** The means to express a preference.

**Circular reasoning.** A type of reasoning where the claim is supported by ultimately restating the claim.

**Conceptually systematic.** A characteristic of ABA in which practitioners use only procedures derived from and conceptually linked to established principles of behavior analysis.

**Concurrent schedules of reinforcement.** Two or more schedules of reinforcement operate independently for two or more behaviors.

**Conditioned stimulus.** A previously neutral stimulus that through pairing with an unconditioned or another conditioned stimulus elicits a conditioned response.

**Conditioned response.** A respondent behavior elicited by a conditioned stimulus.

**Constant time delay.** A response prompting procedure that involves simultaneous presentation of the stimulus and the controlling prompt in initial training trials followed by fading of the controlling prompt by inserting a constant amount of time prior delivering the controlling prompt.

**Continuous reinforcement.** A schedule of reinforcement in which each correct response is reinforced.

**Control variables.** Procedures that are designed to remain the same in both baseline and intervention conditions.

**Control.** Ensuring that a specific variable does not confound study results.

**Controlling prompt.** A prompt that when delivered by the instructor consistently results in a correct response by the learner.

**Count.** The number of occurrences of a behavior.

**Covariation.** A phenomenon that occurs when intervention is applied to one individual, behavior, or context and effects generalize to another individual, behavior, or context for which intervention is not occurring.

**Data paths.** On a line graph, connects consecutive data points within the same phase or condition and allows for the evaluation of the level, trend, and variability.

**Data points.** On a line graph, plotted values that represent the amount of the target behavior or dependent variable at a specified point in time.

**Delay trials.** Trials used in the time delay response prompting strategy that follow an initial set of 0-second delay trials and involve inserting an amount of time between the stimulus and deliver of the controlling prompt.

**Demonstrations of effect.** Occurrences of behavior change that occur when and only when conditions change. Generally, three demonstrations of effect are needed in a single case study.

**Dependent variable.** The behavior targeted for intervention.

**Determinism.** All events, including human behavior, are determined by causes external to will.

**Differential reinforcement of alternative behaviors (DRA).** A procedure in which behaviors trained to replace a targeted problem behavior are reinforced.

**Differential reinforcement of high rates of behavior (DRH).** A procedure in which higher rates of a target behavior access reinforcement and access to reinforcement is gradually made more difficult by increasing the number of times the individual must engage in the target behavior.

**Differential reinforcement of high rates.** A schedule of reinforcement in which reinforcement is contingent on the number of responses exceeding a preset, gradually increasing criterion.

**Differential reinforcement of incompatible behaviors (DRI).** A procedure in which behaviors that cannot occur at the same time as a targeted problem behavior are reinforced.

**Differential reinforcement of low rates of behavior (DRL).** A procedure in which lower rates of a target behavior access reinforcement rather than every instance of the target behavior.

**Differential reinforcement of other behaviors (DRO).** A procedure in which the absence of problem behavior or the presence of any and all other behaviors besides problem behavior are reinforced.

**Differential reinforcement.** The principle by which stimulus control is established in which a behavior is reinforced when a stimulus is present, but the behavior is not reinforced when the stimulus is absent.

**Direct verbal prompt.** A verbal statement provided by the instructor that provides specific direction to the learner on how to perform the target behavior.

**Discriminative stimulus.** A stimulus that when present signals the learner that reinforcement is going to occur.

**Drift.** Gradually decreasing accuracy in data collection over time.

**Duration recording.** Collecting and reporting data on the length of occurrence of a behavior.

**Duration.** The period of time that elapses from the beginning to the end of a behavior.

**Ecologically relevant.** The extent to which an assessment reliably emulates the situations and interactions typically experienced by the individual. For example, a functional analysis test condition is considered ecologically relevant when it includes demands that the individual is typically asked to complete, as well as the same consequences that he or she typically experiences following problem behavior.

**Effective.** A characteristic of ABA in which practitioners are expected to seek improvements that have "practical value."

**Empiricism.** All knowledge is derived from the objective observation of phenomena.

**Establishing operation.** One type of motivating operation that strengthens the value of a reinforcing stimulus.

**Event recording.** A data collection method for capturing the number of times a behavior occurs.

**Exclusionary time out.** The loss of opportunity to access reinforcement contingent on the target behavior occurring.

**Experimentation.** Causal relations are derived from the comparison of some objective measure of a phenomenon under at least two different conditions.

**Experimental control.** Determination that the intervention caused behavior change, rather than other likely variables.

**Explanatory fiction.** An explanation in which the cause and effect are the same things.

**Extinction burst.** An initial, temporary increase in responding after an extinction procedure is started.

**Extinction.** Withholding reinforcement for a previously reinforced behavior.

**Eye gaze.** A selection procedure wherein a choice is indicated by the stimulus the student looks at.

**Fading.** Removal of prompts.

**Faulty stimulus control**. When a behavior is evoked by irrelevant antecedent stimuli.

**Feedback.** Delivering descriptive contingent praise or correction to improve future performance to a learner immediately after a skill is rehearsed.

**Fidelity.** The extent to which procedures are implemented as planned.

**Figure captions.** Short explanations or descriptions of the content displayed in an accompanying figure.

**Fixed ratio.** A schedule of reinforcement in which emitting a specific number of responses leads to reinforcement. In other words, the response ratio remains constant.

**Fixed interval scallop.** A pattern of responding observed in fixed interval schedules in which responding accelerates near the end of the interval.

**Fixed interval.** A schedule of reinforcement in which reinforcement is available after a set amount of time has elapsed. The first correct response that occurs after that set amount of time has elapsed will be reinforced.

**Fixed.** A schedule of reinforcement in which the response ratio or the interval requirement remain fixed.

**Free operant assessment.** A preference assessment in which an array of items are presented to a student, and the student is given a period of time (e.g., 5 min) to engage with (or not) any of the items made available. The student's engagement with the items is observed.

**Frequency (rate).** The number of occurrences of behavior during a set amount of time.
Full physical prompt. The instructor uses physical guidance to completely assist the learner in performing the behavior.

**Functional analysis (FA).** The direct observation of problem behavior under two or more distinct conditions in which environmental events are systematically manipulated to detect their influence on problem behavior.

**Functional (behavior) assessment.** The process of gathering information about the types of problem behavior that regularly occur, the situations in which problem behavior is reported to occur and not occur, and the events and interactions that tend to occur after the problem behavior. The sometimes iterative process first yields hypotheses about the reinforcing function of an individual's problem behavior via interviews and observations, then evaluates the veracity of the hypotheses through analysis, and culminates in a reinforcement-based treatment designed from the results of the process.

**Functional communication response (FCR).** The response that an individual is taught as a replacement for his or her problem behavior. It is considered functional because it serves the same function as problem behavior (i.e., produces the same reinforcers as problem behavior). These responses are individualized for the learner based on the function of their problem behavior and existing language system; responses reliably recognized by those with whom the individual typically communicates are favored, and these can be a spoken word or phrase, sign, gesture, card touch, or selection of an icon on a voice-output device.

**Functional communication training (FCT).** An intervention for addressing problem behavior that relies on prompting and differentially reinforcing a more desirable alternative behavior with the reinforcers shown to maintain problem behavior. FCT, therefore, necessitates the conduct of a functional assessment process to identify the reinforcers maintaining problem behavior.

**Functional contingencies.** The relationship among a behavior and its antecedents (i.e., conditions present before the behavior) and consequences (i.e., environmental changes following the behavior).

**Functional mediators.** A variety of techniques used to prompt/cue a behavior's occurrence in settings beyond initial training conditions.

**Functional relation.** The causal relation between behavior and some event in which a change in the event reliably produces a change in the behavior. With regard to problem behavior, the event is usually a reinforcement contingency suspected of influencing problem behavior. A functional relation between problem behavior and some reinforcement contingency means that problem behavior occurs when that contingency is in place, and does not occur in its absence. A functional relation between problem behavior and environmental events can only be demonstrated in a functional analysis.

**Functional relation.** When all likely plausible confounding variables are controlled for, and behavior change consistently occurs when and only when intervention is introduced or removed.

**Functionally equivalent.** The property describing two different behaviors that when emitted results in access to the same reinforcer.

**Generality.** See generalization.

**Generalization.** A broad term referencing the extension of behavior change across four critical domains (i.e., settings, behaviors, people, and time; see stimulus generalization, response generalization, generalization across people, and maintenance).

**Generalization across people.** Behavior change observed among individuals not directly involved in initial training.

**Generalization across settings.** Behavior change observed in settings not directly targeted in initial training (often used interchangeably with stimulus generalization).

**Generalized imitation:** occurs when a learner's behavior is controlled by, and has formal similarity to, a modeled behavior in novel occurrences without explicit training.

**Gestural prompts.** Nonverbal behaviors provided by the instructor to assist a learner in completing the target behavior.

**History.** An unplanned incident that results in temporary or permanent behavior change during the course of baseline or intervention conditions.

**Horizontal axis.** Also referred to as the abscissa or x-axis; part of a Cartesian coordinate system that displays a unit of time on a line graph (e.g., minutes, days, weeks, sessions, classes).

**In situ assessment:** assessing a learner's ability to perform a skill in their natural environment.

**In situ training.** Assessing a learner's ability to perform a skill in their natural environment and intervening immediately with further training if the skill is not performed correctly.

**In vivo modeling.** A method of observational learning wherein a skill is demonstrated live for purposes of imitation by a learner.

**Independent variable.** Procedures intended to change behavior (i.e., the intervention).

**Indirect verbal prompt.** A verbal statement provided by the instructor that provides direction to the learner on how to perform the target behavior but does not state the exact behavior the student is to perform.

**Instruction.** Providing a verbal description of how to perform a skill.

**Intermittent reinforcement.** A schedule of reinforcement in which some but not all correct responses are followed by a reinforcer.

**Interresponse time**. Calculated to determine the duration of time that lapses in between each instance of problem behavior.

**Interval schedule.** An intermittent schedule of reinforcement that is reliant upon time. A specific amount of time must pass before a correct response will be followed by a reinforcer.

**Interview-informed synthesized contingency analysis (IISCA).** A type of functional analysis (FA) that alternates a single test and a single control condition, both comprehensively informed by an open-ended interview with relevant caregivers. All of the co-occurring environmental events reported by caregivers to evoke and maintain co-occurring types of problem behavior are combined into a single reinforcement contingency in the test condition; these same reinforcers are all provided continuously and noncontingently during the control condition.

**Intrusiveness.** The extent to which the prompt impinges or intrudes upon the student's body.

**Latency.** The time between when a behavior is requested and when the behavior begins.

**Level.** The extent to which data are relatively high, medium, or low as they appear on a line graph.

**Limited hold.** Used with interval schedules of reinforcement, this procedure restricts the amount of time a reinforcer is available.

**Line graph.** In ABA, the most common way to display data points representing quantifiable values plotted across time and conditions.

**Magnitude.** The strength or force of a behavior.

**Maintenance.** Continued correct responding following complete or partial removal of intervention components.

**Maturation.** Change in behaviors that occur over time without intervention.

**Mixed prompts.** The instructor uses a combination of prompts to assist the learner in performing the behavior.

**Model prompt.** The instructor demonstrates the exact behavior the learner is expected to perform.

**Modeling.** The demonstration of a skill to a learner for purposes of imitation.

**Momentary time sampling.** Collecting and reporting data on a behavior at a preset interval of time (usually a longer period of time than whole or partial interval recording); behavior is noted only if it occurs during that "snapshot" in time.

**Most-to-least prompting.** A response prompting strategy in which the instructor identifies a series of prompts and then fades those prompts by delivering them to the learner in a sequence from the prompt that provides the most assistance to the prompt that provides the least assistance to the learner.

**Motivating operation.** Antecedent changes or conditions that alter the effectiveness of a stimulus as a reinforcer and thus the frequency of a behavior previously reinforced by that stimulus.

**Multiple schedules.** A procedure that is used to thin or reduce the schedule of reinforcement by informing the individual when reinforcement is available and unavailable.

**Multiple stimulus without replacement assessment.** A systematic preference assessment in which an array of stimuli is presented. After the student makes a choice, that item is not replaced in the array. The student continues to make choices until all items in the array have been selected.

**Multitreatment interference.** When two interventions are being tested, and one of the interventions has an impact on the other, making it more or less effective.

**Natural S$^D$.** The stimulus that occurs naturally in the environment that signals the learner to perform the behavior.

**Negative reinforcement.** The contingent and immediate removal of a stimulus following a behavior, that results in it occurring more often, for longer periods of time, or with more intensity in the future.

**Negative punishment (Type 2 punishment).** The removal of a stimulus immediately after a behavior occurs, resulting in a decrease or weakening of the behavior in the future.

**Non-reversible behaviors.** Behaviors that are likely to be impacted by learning history such as academic skills and self-help behaviors; these behaviors are likely to maintain even when intervention is removed.

**Neutral stimulus.** Stimulus that does not elicit a respondent behavior.

**Operant behavior.** Behavior that occurs because of its history of consequences.

**Operational definition.** A clear, accurate, measurable, and concise description of behavior.

**Overgeneralization.** Behavior change extended across inappropriate or problematic settings, behaviors, people and/or amounts of time.

**Paired stimulus assessment.** A systematic preference assessment in which two stimuli are paired, and the student makes a choice between the two items. Each item is paired with every other item in the assessment.

**Parsimony.** Considering simple explanations prior to more complex and abstract ones.

**Partial interval recording.** Collecting and reporting data on the frequency of a behavior that occurs at any point during a preset interval of time.

**Partial physical prompts.** The instructor uses physical guidance to partially assist the learner in performing the behavior.

**Permanent product recording.** Collecting data on a student's product (e.g., worksheet, project)

**Phase change labels.** On a line graph, short pieces of text used to briefly describe the environmental changes contacted by the target behavior or dependent variable.

**Phase change lines:** solid or dashed vertical lines extending from the horizontal axis to a height that matches the top of the vertical axis that is used to indicate a change in condition on a line graph.

**Philosophic doubt.** Continuous questioning of what is considered fact.

**Physical prompts.** The instructor physically touches the learner to manipulate them to perform the behavior.

**PLA-Check (Planned Activity Check).** At a set interval, an observer notes the number of students who engaged in a target behavior.

**Positive practice overcorrection.** An individual is required to engage in an appropriate behavior for a set number of times contingent on an emission of problem behavior.

**Positive punishment (Type 1 punishment).** The presentation of a stimulus immediately after a behavior occurs, resulting in a decrease or weakening of the behavior in the future.

**Positive reinforcement.** Following the contingent presentation of a specific stimulus, an individual emits a behavior that is immediately followed by some favorable consequence that results in the individual emitting that behavior again in the future.

**Postreinforcement pause.** A brief pause in responding that is sometimes observed after reinforcement in fixed-ratio and fixed interval schedules.

**Preference assessment.** A systematic assessment conducted to identify a person's preferences.

**Preference.** The liking of one thing over another at a specific moment in time.

**Prompt hierarchy.** A series of prompts the instructor identifies that are then used in a sequence to fade the assistance provided until the learner responds to the target stimulus.

**Prompt.** Assistance given to learners that helps them perform a behavior correctly.

**Punishment.** A stimulus change (e.g. presentation of an unpleasant stimulus, removal of a reinforcing stimulus) occurring immediately after a behavior that weakens the future occurrence of behavior.

**Rate of reinforcement.** A measurement of reinforcement over time.

**Ratio requirement**. The number of correct responses required for reinforcement.

**Ratio run.** A return to rapid responding following a postreinforcement pause in a fixed ratio schedule of reinforcement.

**Ratio schedule of reinforcement.** A schedule of reinforcement in which a specific number (fixed ratio) or an average number (variable ratio) of correct responses must be emitted before one response will be followed by a reinforcer.

**Ratio strain.** This occurs when the ratio requirement is suddenly increased in a fixed ratio schedule and there is a weakening or cessation of the responding.

**Registered behavioral technician.** An assistant or paraprofessional that practices on direct supervision of a behavior analyst.

**Rehearsal.** A learner imitates a modeled skill after receiving instruction.

**Reinforcer Assessment of Individuals with Severe Disabilities (RAISD).** A survey tool that can help respondents identify potentially reinforcing stimuli across various sensory modalities.

**Reinforcer.** A stimulus provided or removed as a consequence that will increase the future probability of a behavior.

**Reliability.** Dependability of data; usually assessed by measuring whether two observers agree on the occurrence or non-occurrence of target behaviors (interobserver agreement).

**Response cost.** A form of negative punishment where the removal of a reinforcer contingent on the occurrence of the target behavior.

**Respondent behavior.** A part of a reflex that is elicited by an antecedent stimulus.

**Respondent extinction**. The repeated presentation of a conditioned stimulus (in the absence of the unconditioned stimulus) that results in a gradual decrease in the respondent behavior.

**Response generalization.** Behavior change observed involving response forms (i.e., topographies of behavior) not directly targeted in initial training conditions.

**Response prompts.** Actions that an instructor provides to a learner that increases the likelihood the learner will respond correctly in the presence of the $S^D$.

**Response rate.** The ratio of targeted responses to an interval of time.

**Restitutional overcorrection.** An individual is required to return a disrupted environment to a state even better than what it was behavior the problem occurred contingent on an emission of problem behavior.

**Reversible behaviors.** Behaviors that are likely to change based on current contexts rather than learning history, such as problem behaviors and social behaviors.

**Ribbon timeout.** A form of exclusionary timeout where an individual is given a ribbon or a tangible item to signal that reinforcement is available and when the ribbon or tangible item this serves as a timeout from positive reinforcement.

**S-delta.** A stimulus that when present signals the learner that reinforcement will not occur.

**Sampling.** The opportunity to engage with each stimulus to be presented in the preference assessment.

**Schedule thinning.** A process of making reinforcement available less often or contingent upon a greater number of correct responses.

**Seclusionary timeout.** An individual is removed from an environment where any stimulation and social interaction are available.

**Selection.** The choice the student makes.

**Single stimulus assessment.** A systematic preference assessment in which one stimulus is presented at a time, and a student's engagement with each item is measured.

**Spontaneous recovery.** The reappearance of a response that has undergone extinction.

**Stability.** The extent to which data follow a steady and consistent path (in terms of level) as they appear on a line graph.

**Stimulus control.** A behavior consistently and reliably occurs when a stimulus is present and does not occur when that stimulus is absent.

**Stimulus generalization.** Behavior change observed in the presence of untrained/novel stimuli.

**Stimulus prompts.** Prompts that are added to the stimulus that increase the likelihood the learner will respond correctly.

**Target stimulus.** The terminal stimulus to which the instructor wants the learner to respond without prompting.

**Task analysis.** Breaking down a composite skill or behavior into component parts to identify the discriminative stimulus and response for each step within a behavior chain.

**Task direction.** A direction given by the instructor that tells the student to perform the behavior.

**Technological.** Characteristics of ABA in which practitioners describe all procedures with such detail that they can be implemented by others with limited training in behavior analysis.

**Thinning.** Gradually increasing the amount of responses required in order to access reinforcement based on successful sessions of low levels or no problem behavior and independent appropriate responding.

**Time-lagged.** A class of single case research designs in which intervention is applied sequentially to multiple individuals, behaviors or contexts.

**Time out from positive reinforcement.** A form of negative punishment that occurs when access to stimuli that have a history of reinforcing behavior are temporarily made unavailable.

**Topography.** The physical form of a behavior or what the behavior looks like.

**Train diversely.** A generalization promotion strategy emphasizing the use of a variety of instructional materials, response examples, and functional contingencies during initial training to reduce overly restricted stimulus control.

**Transfer of stimulus control.** Shen the behavior that occurred when prompts were given begins to occur when the target or natural SD is presented without the need for prompts.

**Trend.** An increasing or decreasing data path on a line graph.

**Unconditioned stimulus.** Stimulus that elicits a respondent behavior without prior conditioning Variability. The extent to which data do not follow a steady and consistent (in terms of level) as they appear on a line graph.

**Variable interval schedule of reinforcement.** A reinforcement schedule in which reinforcement is available for the first correct responses that occurs of an interval of varying length has elapsed. For example, in a VR 3 schedule a reinforcement will be available for the first correct response after an average of 3-minutes have elapsed.

**Variable ratio.** A schedule of reinforcement in which reinforcement is provided after an average number of responses.

**Variable schedule.** A schedule of reinforcement in which the interval requirement or ratio requirement varies. The reinforcement is provided after an average amount of time or an average number of responses.

**Verbal model prompt.** The instructor demonstrates the exact verbal behavior the learner is expected to perform.

**Vertical axis.** Also called the ordinate or y-axis. Part of a Cartesian coordinate system that displays a quantifiable dimension (e.g., frequency, rate, latency, duration, force, percentage) of the dependent variable on a line graph.

**Video model prompt.** A video that shows the exact behavior the learner is expected to perform.

**Video modeling.** A method of observational learning wherein a skill is demonstrated by video for purposes of imitation by a learner.

**Video self-modeling.** A method wherein the learner observes themselves performing the skill to be imitated.

**Visual analysis.** The act of inspecting graphed data to determine whether behavior change occurred and whether a functional relation exists.

**Whole interval recording.** Collecting and reporting data on the frequency of a behavior that occurs for the entirety of a preset interval of time.

CPSIA information can be obtained
at www.ICGtesting.com
Printed in the USA
LVHW021100051119
636386LV00007B/75